JOHN BRYDEN

Deadly Allies

Canada's Secret War
1937–1947

D0874832

An M&S Paperback from
McClelland & Stewart Inc.
The Canadian Publishers

An M&S Paperback friom McClelland & Stewart Inc.

First printing October 1990
Cloth edition printed 1989

Canadian Cataloguing in Publication Data

Bryden, John, 1943–
Deadly allies : Canada's secret war, 1937–1947

An M&S paperback.
Includes bibliographical references.
ISBN 0-7710-1726-X

1. Chemical warfare – Research – Canada.
2. Biological warfare – Research – Canada.
3. World War, 1939–1945 – Chemical warfare.
4. World War, 1939–1945 – Biological warfare.
5. World War, 1939–1945 – Canada. I. Title.

UG447.B78 1990   358′.34′0971   C90-093961–3

Cover design by Martha Staigys
Cover illustration by Cliff Kearns

Printed and bound in Canada

McClelland & Stewart Inc.
The Canadian Publishers
481 University Avenue
Toronto, Ontario
M5G 2E9

Contents

"Great is Truth
and Mighty in All Things"

PREFACE

When the first edition of this book came out in November 1989, the Cold War seemed finally to be ending. The Berlin Wall was being torn down. Dictatorial regimes in Eastern Europe were tottering. The Soviet Union was plainly stating that it was no longer interested in an arms race that has persisted for the last 43 years.

A book that reveals Canada's pioneering role in the development of chemical and biological warfare weapons seems suddenly out of place. But is it? Perhaps by peeling away the secrets of the past it can contribute to the peace that now seems to loom ahead.

Grosse Ile is a charming island in the St. Lawrence River downstream from Quebec City. From the 1840s onward it was a quarantine station for the thousands of impoverished immigrants, mostly Irish, who came to Canada seeking new lives in a new land. Nearly twelve thousand of them lie buried where the long grass slopes down to a pretty cove called Cholera Bay. It is slated to become a national park.

Government scientists are currently preparing to probe the island for anthrax, a deadly type of bacteria which was the key component of the most important germ weapons developed during the Second World War. Grosse Ile is where Canada mass-produced this lethal agent for use in bombs by Britain and the United States. It was the first such germ warfare station among the Western nations.

Until this book appeared, Grosse Ile's dark secret had been so closely guarded that the details had been forgotten. Most of the records pertaining to Canada's wartime research in chemical and biological warfare were believed to have been destroyed. They weren't. In 1941–42 the Department of National Defence took direct control of chemical and bacteriological warfare research and kept comprehensive records. Every memo, every invoice, every report of a meeting was collected in appropriate files and eventually put on microfilm. The reels were then deposited in the National Archives and forgotten.

Until fairly recently, those nineteen reels could have been had for the asking. No one asked; Canada is not the kind of country people associate with weapons research. In the 1971 lead-up to the United Nations Biological Weapons Convention, the Stockholm International Peace Research Institute's comprehensive world-wide survey of chemical and biological warfare made scant mention of Canada. "Little information has been published about the scale of the Canadian wartime BW effort," the SIPRI authors noted. They found the same for chemical warfare. Canada was cast as a comparative innocent during the disarmament talks of the day.

The reels of mircrofilm tell a different story, which has been difficult to obtain. Eight years ago Canada's Access to Information Act came into force. The act is badly misnamed. It is actually a Secrecy Act, for it provides that no government document, no matter how old, shall be released to the public for the first time without being reviewed for its sensitivity. When in doubt, a National Archives reviewer consults the government department concerned.

My request to see the chemical warfare microfilms evidently caused much consternation. When the departments of National Defence and External Affairs were consulted they declared them to be, sight unseen, "very sensitive" and archives staff spoke of them as a "nightmare" problem. Nevertheless, a former Defence Department person under contract to the Archives undertook to review the films and sever those documents his experience told him he should. He and a successor selectively blanked out 160 of approximately 800 files, including most that dealt with formal meetings on chemical or biological warfare topics.

What remained were mainly files dealing with administrative humdrum – transfers of staff, purchase of supplies, equipment specifications and so forth. However, on the second to last reel, someone had gathered documents from various files and put them under separate headings to tell specific stories. Thus a fairly complete record of the anthrax factory at Grosse Ile was in file 4354-33-13-2 even though some documents came from elsewhere, including from files that had been withheld.

In the open material there were also documents which only referred to biological or chemical agents and experiments by their wartime code letters. Once it was determined what these code letters meant from references elsewhere, they could be "read."

Finally, due to wartime clerical inefficiency, some documents were occasionally misfiled altogether. These have been vital in filling gaps in the story, although thousands of items had to be scanned to find them. Furthermore, while the microfilm copies of the minutes of the Chemical Warfare Inter-Service Board were generally withheld by the Defence reviewers, copies were found in a collection from the National Research Council, the government-sponsored science agency. It had had a representative at the meetings.

The National Research Council records are the happy other side to the research story. For the first two years of the war, it was the NRC that was mainly responsible for work on chemical and biological warfare. It, too, kept comprehensive records and saved them systematically. When they were turned over to the National Archives they were complete in almost all essential details. There appears to have been no attempt to withhold documents for fear of adverse public reaction, embarrassment, or the unfortunate light they might cast on people or institutions.

It was actually possible for this researcher to read the early bacteriological warfare files exactly as they had been collected, organized and read by the people about whom one was writing. Professor E.G.D. Murray, for instance, commented several times on the contents of specific Top Secret documents that he kept in his safe. These files were available in 1988 to be read just as he saw them in 1941 and 1942. Their value in describing the beginnings of biological warfare research has been inestimable.

Although the NRC collection was also vetted before release under the Access to Information Act, the appropriate authorities at the National Research Council made it clear that they were not going to obstruct access. Those few documents that subsequently were withheld were not important.

This description of research is not to show how clever the author is. It is intended to demonstrate how a fairly detailed story of Canada's wartime chemical and biological warfare program can be told even though thousands of relevant documents were unavailable. Many of these were formally requested by file title under the Access to Information Act on October 28, 1988. Nineteen months later nothing had been released.

A key reason for all this official unease is the fact that the closest co-operation existed during the war between Canada, the United States and Britain on chemical and biological warfare matters. If anything, however, secrecy in the other countries has been even more stringent than in Canada. Many of the relevant files, particularly in Britain, remain firmly closed but the Canadian files reveal much of what they contain. To tell the story of Canada is to tell it also of Britain and the United States.

I have used secondary sources sparingly. I have tried to refer to them only when statements were attributed to personal experience, interviews, or primary material. Similarly, the endnotes for each chapter describe sources of information as well as the origin of quotations. I have tried to back everything up from existing documents of the period, or from the recollections of the scientists who were involved. I have tried to write dispassionately rather than judgmentally. The reader can form his own conclusions.

In the interests of the future, I believe it truly matters that this particular record be set very straight, for the United States and Britain as well as Canada. If we all are to survive into the twenty-first century, and beyond, then we need to understand our past, and who and what and why we are. That applies to all people, all nations, past and future adversaries.

John Bryden
Lynden, Ontario
June 6, 1990

C·H·A·P·T·E·R
O·N·E

ABC Beginnings

The wind blew chill off the grey water of Bedford Basin, Halifax. Major Donald Dewar pulled his greatcoat tighter as he walked beside the train, thirty-eight box-cars on the tracks beside the water. At each, he stopped at the open doors and peered in at the steel drums in their wooden cradles. He sniffed carefully. As an experienced chemical warfare officer, he had long ago learned to be led by the nose. It was still the best detector of poison gas.

It was early February 1946. This was the last train of five. The 45-gallon drums contained liquid mustard gas, a substance that seared the skin on contact, that clotted the lungs and burned the eyes to blindness. It was American-made Levinstein mustard, code-name HS. This shipment brought the total up to 10,982 drums – approximately 2,800 tons. Dewar's assignment as safety officer was to oversee its burial at sea.

The gas had given Dewar indescribable trouble. It had been acquired in 1942 following Japan's entry into the war and had been stored in a field near Cornwall, Ontario, next to Canada's own mustard gas plant. It was worth about $2 million. Useless now. Some of the drums bulged dangerously and it was only a matter of time before seams would split or rust would bore through the metal. It had been decided to get rid of it – secretly.[1]

Unfortunately, just as the first train was pulling out of Cornwall in January, a local newspaper, the *Standard Free-Holder*, broke the story. It blew like a blizzard along the route of the train,

11

through Montreal and on to Halifax. The government tried to dampen the alarm by having Dewar record a radio broadcast that described the safety measures that had been taken, but the military authorities ordered it cancelled. The less said, they hoped, the better.

"The good citizens of Halifax were sure they were going to wake up one morning and find themselves dead," Dewar remembered many years later. "The stevedores threatened a strike and all the rest of it. I was tearing my hair."[2]

The mustard gas was loaded aboard a war surplus Landing Ship (Tank) and the idea was to tow it out and sink it in deep water off Sable Island. Special sea cocks had been installed and holes bored into the upper deck so that it would go down readily. Because these holes posed a danger to the workmen during loading, temporary covers were put on them. On February 17 the tug *Foundation Franklin* attached a hawser and pulled LST 209 away from its berth and headed out to sea.

In a bid to deflect public concern, the local press was invited to witness the sinking. A newsreel cameraman and a reporter and photographer from the Halifax *Chronicle* joined Dewar aboard the old army supply ship, the *General Drury*. As they moved out of harbour, the minesweeper *Middlesex* took up station as escort. The operation was running with perfect military precision.

The nightmare began the following day. The little convoy was hit by a massive winter gale; grey waves hurled themselves against the prancing ships and soon the journalists aboard the *General Drury* were violently seasick. On the tug there was near-panic. The vessel was attached to a hulk many times larger in size and weight which wrenched and yanked at the end of its tether. A bright Aldis light flashed across the heaving waves. Would the *Middlesex* permit the tug to slip its tow?

The *Middlesex* agreed. The heavy seas prevented sending over the scuttling party so the minesweeper moved in with depth charges. Crack! No effect. Crack! Another fountain of foam and spray. Crack! LST 209 rolled away drunkenly, unperturbed, unaffected. The minesweeper drew off to rethink its strategy.

Later in the afternoon the seas moderated. After great manoeuvring, the *Middlesex* managed to put its scuttling party aboard. The men opened the sea cocks and quickly abandoned ship. Too quickly. They had forgotten to open the after sea cocks and, worse yet, they did not realize the covers were still on the holes that had been bored in the deck. If air could not escape, water could not enter. As twilight turned to night it gradually dawned on the captain of the *Middlesex* that the wallowing hulk with its 2,800 tons of deadly cargo was not going to sink.

B.P. Young, RCN, captain of the *Middlesex*, probably acquired more grey hair that night than at any time during the war. He was responsible for the ultimate in hazards to navigation: an unmanned, uncontrolled vessel filled to the gunwales with poison gas loose on the high seas – at night – in the middle of a storm. The *Middlesex* chased after LST 209 like a ferret, trying to hold it in its searchlight. Once, for forty heart-stopping minutes, it was lost. Then found again.

With dawn, the *Middlesex* came alongside and pumped 400 rounds from its Oerlikon gun into the vessel. LST 209 sank by the stern at 40°50′N 60°12′W in 1,350 fathoms.[3]

Dewar was lucky. The newspapermen aboard the *General Drury* were too preoccupied by their stomachs to appreciate the drama that was going on around them. Besides, two days earlier the Igor Gouzenko defection story had broken and the newspapers were full of tales of Soviet espionage in Canada and the arrests of those named as spies by the Russian embassy clerk. Even the Halifax *Chronicle* gave only token play to the sinking of LST 209.

"I was perhaps the only person in town that was glad that spy thing broke," Dewar recalled. "Everyone got talking about Gouzenko."

Canada's chemical and biological warfare program began in 1937 when its military leaders decided to undertake secret research into the defensive and offensive aspects of chemical warfare, apparently without consultation with either the government or Parliament.[4]

Britain, Canada and the United States had all been signatories of the 1925 Geneva Protocol outlawing the use of chemical and bacteriological weapons, although it was not ratified in the United States until the early 1970s. Both the United States and Britain had continued desultory study of the gas weapons of the previous war, particularly those which the Germans had used to such good effect.[5] But in Canada there had been no similar research. The accepted wisdom was that Canada could rely on British technology in the event of another war.

The Department of National Defence file on chemical warfare covering the period from 1922 to 1939 is still closed to the public, so one can only speculate on why Canada's military leaders decided to go it alone on developing gas weapons. It was probably because fascist Italy resorted to gas in its war in Abyssinia. Frustrated by the bravery and military prowess of the supposedly backward Ethiopians, in the spring of 1936 the Italians sought to break the spirit of their adversaries by mustard attacks on civilians. The subsequent newspaper reports made lurid reading. The following is from an interview with an Abyssinian general reported in the *Toronto Star Weekly*:

> "Daily, deliberately and systematically hundreds of tons mustard gas were sprayed over hundreds of square miles of the country, like the foam from a waterfall. Our people called it the 'dew of death.' Peasants would be working in their fields, women would be gossiping in the villages, children would be playing in the sun – all scores and scores of miles from the battlefront. They would hear airplanes and run for cover. They would feel a moisture in the air. Then they would be coughing and choking, and their skins would be burning with ferocious heat that water wouldn't cool, and they would be going blind and screaming to God."[6]

The Abyssinian's description was made through a translator, giving the reporter ample scope for colourful prose. But such descriptions, typical in Britain as well as Canada, spread a deep sense of alarm. Another *Star Weekly* article summed up world reaction when it accused Italian dictator Benito Mussolini of breaking the "sacred pledge" of the Geneva Protocol: "From this point on in international politics gas looms as the terrifying probability if and when another war comes – a war which will not be fought half out, as the other one was, but to the finish."[7]

The message was clear to Britain and her allies. Should war come again to Europe, dictators like Mussolini and Germany's Adolf Hitler might not scruple to use gas. The press in Britain soon teemed with articles on the probable effects of a gas attack on cities, and with how-to advice on home shelters and personal protection. In September the British government announced it was going to manufacture gas masks for the entire civilian population – fifty million people.[8]

The English-speaking world was different fifty years ago in a way which is often forgotten. The horrors of the First World War and its slaughter of millions of young men had scarred the survivors and their children. It was hoped that it had been a "war to end all wars," and in Britain, the Commonwealth and the United States pacifism and disarmament was the policy of government for two decades. It was the exact opposite to the constant military preparedness that has characterized the politics of the nuclear age. Regardless of the various peace movements of the 1960s and 1970s, people since the Second World War have generally accepted the idea that national safety requires keeping up in military technology.

That attitude owes as much to Nazi Germany's near victory as it does to the rivalry engendered by the Cold War. The Germans startled the world with Blitzkrieg and dive-bombers, with tanks and tactics superior to anything their enemies possessed. They nearly conquered Europe. It convinced the generation that won the war that they could not afford to let military science languish as it had in the 1920s and early 1930s. Britain's technological response to the threat posed by Germany and Italy had been almost too late. An adequate fighter aircraft and radar became available only just in time to meet the German bombers that swarmed over the English Channel in 1940. They were beaten back by the slenderest of margins.

The First World War had taught a different lesson. It had shown that modern warfare was a frightful instrument of political ambition. The best solution was to do away with it. At Oxford University in 1933 students voted that they "would in no circumstances fight for King and country." The resolution was a general reflection of the public rejection of war and with it, military research. Almost nothing was done further to develop the airplane or tank, decisive military innovations of 1914-18, and with the exception of Britain's Winston Churchill, most politicians fell into step with public sentiment. Not until Nazi Germany began testing her new aircraft in the Spanish Civil War in the 1930s did British scientists and engineers finally set to work, often without encouragement from government. Italy's use of gas in Abyssinia, however, no one could ignore.

Poison gas in 1930s conjured up the same kind of image of death and destruction that hydrogen bombs do in the nuclear age. It was considered to be the ultimate modern weapon, capable of killing soldiers or civilians en masse, indiscriminately. Its widespread use in the First World War probably did more than any other single weapon, including the airplane and the machine gun, to convince military leaders in all countries that personal courage in combat was no longer decisive, and that modern battles were to be won by whichever side had the superior technology. Germany, France and Britain squandered millions of lives in front of the machine guns of the Western Front without substantially changing their nineteenth-century tactics. Only when gas was used by the Germans in 1915 did war finally modernize.

The Germans launched the first gas attack at Ypres on August 22, 1915, at a portion of the line held by French colonial and Canadian troops. The ensuing battle is a much-told story in Canadian military history. The French broke but the Canadians held on despite the terror of a white cloud that seared the lungs and made breathing agony. According to one widely distributed Canadian history of the war, the men were intrigued by the white cloud that flowed along the ground toward them, until it poured into their trenches:

> Then passive curiosity turned to active torment – a burning sensation in the head, red-hot needles in the lungs, the throat seized as by a strangler. Many fell and died on the spot. The others, gasping, stumbling, with faces contorted, hands wildly gesticulating, and uttering hoarse cries of pain, fled madly through the villages and farms and through Ypres itself, carrying panic to the remnants of the population and filling the roads with fugitives of both sexes and all ages.[9]

What is most significant about that passage, taken from one of a plethora of similar popular histories that came out during and immediately after the war, is that it, and others just like it, would be familiar in 1937 to almost everyone who was in a position to make decisions about Canada's military preparedness. Tales of gas attacks made for lurid descriptions and there were a great many popular histories with similar passages in France, Britain, Germany and the United States.

The Canadians survived the attack and won genuine immortality. The Germans had not expected their novel weapon to be so effective and failed to exploit the breach in the line. Reserves were rushed to the aid of the Canadians and a major disaster narrowly averted. It had been a near thing, and the Allied generals were never to be caught by surprise like that again, rushing into production crude gas masks and poison gases of their own.

A distinguished German chemist, Fritz Haber, was the inspiration behind this first gas attack. He had already saved his country from premature defeat by developing a method of synthesizing ammonia which was essential to making explosives. The German General Staff had expected a quick war and when its troops bogged down in the trenches of France and Flanders, they realized they did not have the raw material to make sufficient ammunition for a long-term struggle. The key ingredient was saltpetre (sodium nitrate) which was mined in Chile, but the British naval blockade severed this source. Haber's new process saved the day because it enabled Germany to make synthetic ammonia in unlimited quantities. He was awarded the Nobel Prize for his discovery in 1919.[10]

Haber was next involved in trying to develop chemical irritants that might drive enemy soldiers from entrenched positions and hit upon the idea of using chlorine gas because it was available in large quantities from the German chemical industry, and easily transported in cylinders. What he unleashed instead was a chemical arms race which saw the French launch an attack of their own in early 1916 with shells filled with a new gas called phosgene. It was designed not just to drive men from their trenches, but to kill. Haber responded with diphosgene, chloropicrin and, the most effective of all, dichlorodiethyl sulphide – soon to be known as mustard gas.

Mustard gas had been discovered in 1886 and was known for its remarkable blistering effect on the skin. A liquid rather than a gas at normal air temperatures, when splashed on the ground it vaporizes slowly. Vapour and liquid have the same effect, except that the former immediately attacks the eyes with blinding effect; inhaled, it can severely damage the lungs. Haber predicted that it would be a year before the Allies would be able to build up stocks to counter-attack with the gas, but Germany would lose the war when they did.[11] The German General Staff took the chance and introduced it in July 1917, also on British troops near Ypres, with devastating effect, the majority of casualties being blinded. The Allies could not respond until June 1918, when the war had less than five months to run.

Gas, in the end, did not turn out to be decisive in the First World War. Neither Germany nor the Allies were able to rise to the technological challenges of the new weapon. Nevertheless, it caused immeasurable suffering. There was something especially terrible about men blinded by mustard gas or covered in blisters, even if the injuries were usually temporary and actual deaths relatively few. The other gases created their own atmospheres of horror, never better described than in lines from Wilfred Owen's famous poem, "Dulce et Decorum Est":

> Gas! Gas! Quick, boys! An ecstasy of fumbling,
> Fitting the clumsy helmets just in time;
> But someone still was yelling out and stumbling
> And flound'ring like a man in fire or lime. . . .
> Dim, through the misty panes and thick green light,
> As under a green sea, I saw him drowning.
>
> In all my dreams, before my helpless sight,
> He plunges at me, guttering, choking, drowning.
>
> If in some smothering dreams you too could pace
> Behind the wagon that we flung him in
> And watch the white eyes writhing in his face,
> His hanging face, like a devil's sick with sin;
> If you could hear, at every jolt, the blood
> Come gargling from the froth-corrupted lungs,
> Obscene as cancer, bitter as the cud
> Of vile, incurable sores on innocent tongues –
> My friend, you would not tell with such high zest
> To children ardent for some desperate glory,
> The old Lie: Dulce et decorum est
> Pro Patria mori.

Those lines, very well known in their day, were probably much on the minds of the many who worried as they watched Nazi Germany arm for war.

General Andrew McNaughton was one Canadian who had little doubt that war was on its way. A career soldier and a graduate of McGill University in physics and engineering, he had fought at Ypres and had seen the gas attack with his own eyes. After distinguished wartime service in the artillery, McNaughton had risen to Chief of the General Staff in the Depression years. When Canada's Conservative government faced a general election in 1935, the then prime minister, R.B. Bennett, dismissed McNaughton from his military post and appointed him president of the fledgling National Research Council of Canada. The move was political rather than insightful because McNaughton had been the author of a program that employed the jobless in labour camps run by the military. This had earned both him and the government severe criticism from all sides.[12]

The National Research Council had been established in 1916 as an advisory body to promote scientific and industrial research. Such was the primitive state of science in Canada, in both industry and the universities, that it was decided that the NRC should operate labs of its own, and in 1932 research and administrative headquarters were established in a brand-new building at 100 Sussex Street in Ottawa. Built in the depths of the Depression when material and labour were cheap, the building was erected on a magnificent cliff-side site overlooking the Ottawa River and lavishly appointed, with limestone facing outside and marble within. Georgian in style, it is architecturally one of the most pleasing of the city's public buildings and the last place one would expect to find working laboratories.

There was nothing quite like the National Research Council in Britain or the United States. Both countries had well-established research facilities at their universities and in industries. Consequently, the parallel U.S. National Research Council was strictly an advisory body which did no research of its own. In Britain research tended to be spread among the major universities and fragmented, competitive and poorly co-ordinated. Canada's NRC was a bold attempt to make up for the science deficiencies of Canada's industries and institutions by research directly funded by government.

Then, as now, Canada was a great, empty land of forest and prairie thinly inhabited by people who were perceived by the British to be sort of American and by the Americans to be sort of British. To the world it was a nation of farmers, loggers and miners, a perception most Canadians would not then have disagreed with. It was cold, "British" and remote. It was best known for the red-coated Mounties who galloped through works of fiction always getting their man. Its splendid quasi-Gothic Parliament Building on a limestone bluff above the Ottawa River still overlooked rafts of logs cut from the neighbouring wilderness. It had some industry – steel, chemical, manufacturing – but nothing to compare with Britain and the United States.

When McNaughton took up his appointment in 1935 at the NRC – it is always referred to by the letters – he found the quality of science in most of the labs fell far short of the quality of the building. Much of the work had little application to industry and little permanent value. There was considerable unease among some of the scientists when the general arrived because they feared a soldier would aim research toward military applications. They were right. McNaughton laid down the law. The scientists on staff were not there to indulge themselves in academic fantasies, but to do research which would benefit the country. He introduced the army style of keeping records, with secret files and a central registry.[13] There were grumblings at first, but soon valuable work was being done in electronics, aerial mapping and ballistics. The chemistry division, however, remained weak.

In the early 1930s a young Canadian chemist named E. A. (Alison) Flood studying at Brown University in the United States watched a newsreel of Mussolini reviewing his troops in a lavish display that had echos of Imperial Rome, with the dictator playing the new Caesar. "I was a pacifist like most young people were – most of the young scientists," he recalled. "But I thought, 'Shoot, sure as guns there's going to be a war before long.'"[14] Though opportunities for graduate chemists were more plentiful in the United States, Flood sent applications everywhere in Canada hoping he could get a job in his native land. Only the NRC replied, and he promptly accepted.

Flood is a key figure in the beginning of Canada's chemical warfare program, but he was a shy man and awkward when it came to expressing his ideas, especially on paper. He left no written record, not even memos, but a brief taped interview was done with him in 1976. During it, he described how McNaughton decided that the army must have a scientific adviser because he was convinced that war was coming and he had learned that Britain would not be able to supply gas masks for Canada. While being paid by the NRC Flood was secretly assigned to work under the Master General of the Ordnance, the army official responsible for weapon procurement. His first job in 1937 was to go over to Britain and learn everything he could about poison gas.

"I was interviewed (before leaving) by the Navy technical research people, and the Army and Air Force," Flood remembered. "All the right people. I remember Crerar, who later became General [H.D.G.] Crerar, was then Director of Staff Duties as a full colonel. He said, 'Don't forget, the best defence is offence and if you don't come back with knowledge on how to make offensive chemical weapons, I won't think you've done a proper job.'"[15]

Ironically, at approximately the same time as Flood was in Britain touring the gas warfare proving station at Porton Down in the south of England and "learning how to make mustard gas on a large scale," Canada's prime minister, William Lyon Mackenzie King was in Berlin having a personal chat with Hitler: "My sizing up of the man as I sat and talked with him was that he is really one who truly loves his fellow-men and his country. . . ."[16] King was a pompous 62-year-old bachelor with a mother-complex and a penchant for discussing affairs of state with ghosts at private seances. He had also managed to stay in power for ten of the previous sixteen years and was to remain for another eleven. His was a mystic mission to make Hitler see the merits of peace; but the fact that he was impressed by the German dictator did not mean that he failed to see the danger in the man. He warned Hitler that he could expect the Commonwealth to stand by Britain if war came. Under King's veneer of naive simplicity there was often a man of hard practicality. That same year he hiked Canada's defence spending sharply.[17]

It is not known whether the prime minister or his cabinet were aware of the army's move to learn how to wage gas warfare, although it seems unlikely. When Flood returned from Britain the army could only provide $1,000 for an ambitious program that included gas mask assembly, poison gas production and gas weapons research. McNaughton helped out by providing Flood with space rent-free in a nearby disused lumber mill owned by the NRC, and there, with two assistants, he began work on the charcoal-filled containers for gas masks. He was also warned that on no account were members of Parliament to find out what was going on.[18]

McNaughton was not the only senior person at the NRC worried about war. That year Sir Frederick Banting, the Nobel prize-winning discoverer of insulin, was named to the NRC's board of governors and on September 11, 1937, the two men had a conversation which McNaughton thought sufficiently important to put on record:

"Had conversation with Banting re. possibilities of BW and he referred to instances of cholera-infected sugar during World War I and that Italy had recalled its expert on tropical diseases. Banting spoke of 'worst danger' – the possibility that virus diseases could be distributed on dust. I agreed to look up certain papers on BW and he agreed to prepare a general memo on the subject with the idea it be transmitted to Defence Department and to British authorities to put 'all on their guard.'"[19]

It would have been interesting to know, considering subsequent events, which of the two men actually brought up the subject of bacteriological warfare. It may have been McNaughton, who certainly was behind the concern about gas warfare, although Banting would have been prompt to react favourably. Both men had served on the Western Front during the First World War and had no illusions about the decisiveness of new technology in battle. Banting had been a medical officer with first-hand knowledge of the suffering, while McNaughton had been a senior officer in the artillery.

The concept of bacteriological warfare was genuinely novel. Although the 1925 Geneva Protocol had banned it as well as gas, it had not been used systematically in the First World War and whether it would be used in the next was a relatively new subject of debate in the press of the day.[20] Nobody knew much about it. Medical science had had enough to do in the First World War just to handle gangrene and the other infections that threatened the lives of wounded soldiers, without contemplating how germs could be deliberately spread. Yet gas warfare had demonstrated that chemical agents could be used with deadly effect. Why not biological agents?

McNaughton culled his files and sent Banting everything he could find on the subject. It was not much. A few days later Banting replied with a seven-page memo in which he pointed out that the airplane had enormously increased the danger of chemical weapons and the same applied to the spreading of bacteria. Open water reservoirs could be the target of diseases like typhoid, cholera and dysentery which could be grown in large quantities in laboratories. Projectiles could be poisoned with the germs of tetanus, rabies or gangrene, or possibly with the toxins of snake venom or botulinus bacteria (food poisoning). Psittacosis (parrot fever) could be made into "dust bombs," and anthrax and foot and mouth disease used against domestic animals. "There's no doubt that Germany, Italy or Japan would use certain of the above . . . in the eventuality of war," he concluded.[21]

Banting's view was far from universally held. Shortly after his memo someone, probably McNaughton, sent him a clipping from The Times of London in which the Cambridge biochemist J.B.S. Haldane was reported as being doubtful that bacteria could be used with significant effect in a new war. In Haldane's view, it would take at least forty years before an effective germ weapon would be developed and scientists were better occupied trying to develop novel means of defence against "old methods of warfare." With the benefit of hindsight, it is worth noting another of Haldane's predictions from the same article: "He did not think it possible to get explosives enormously more efficient than they were now. Nor was there any prospect within the next few centuries of blowing up the world with the bombs releasing artificial radio-activity of which Mr. [H.G.] Wells had written."[22] How wrong he was.

The Times was the establishment newspaper of Britain and the opinions expressed in it tended to be influential in that country's corridors of power. Haldane's view was widely shared, but McNaughton and Banting, as well as the Germans and Italians, did not agree. In December McNaughton sent Banting a document that he had had especially translated. It was a German reprint of an Italian analysis of the use of "microbes" in war. The author thought a number of diseases had real potential – plague, glanders, anthrax, typhoid, dysentery and cholera – and speculated they might be effectively spread by airplane or saboteurs. Much more work, he wrote, had to be done in the laboratory before one could be sure of the effectiveness of germ weapons.[23] To Banting and McNaughton, this article was a sure indication of the direction of German and Italian thinking.

The two men now became fast friends and partners in trying to get Canada ready for war. They could hardly have been more different. Banting, 48, was gregarious, demanding, awkward, paunchy, insecure and liked a good stiff whisky from time to time. McNaughton, 50, was lean, strait-laced, health-conscious, almost morbidly serious, and convinced he was going to go down in history. He saved every scrap of paper that crossed his desk so that future biographers would not want for detail.

Banting, however, had already made history. As a young, newly graduated medical doctor in 1922 he had latched onto the idea that diabetes, a widespread wasting disease that killed remorselessly, was caused by the failure of the pancreas to produce a substance that enabled the body to convert blood sugar into energy. Its victims, and there were thousands every year, literally starved to death. He persuaded a senior professor at the University of Toronto to give him facilities to try extracting this substance from the healthy pancreases of dogs. With the help of a young undergraduate named Charles Best, he succeeded in proving there was such an extract, earning bitterness, controversy, fame and Canada's first Nobel Prize in that order.

Banting's great sin in the discovery of insulin was that he was a nobody, an ordinary small-town physician with no research credentials. When it became apparent that he and Best had made some kind of breakthrough, despite amateurish methods, there was a deliberate attempt to shut him out of his own discovery. He was denied the opportunity to run trials with the new substance on patients dying of diabetes at Toronto General Hopital and a skilled, young biochemist named J.B. Collip was brought in to purify the extract. Banting fought back and by sheer luck, because Collip temporarily failed in his assignment, he and Best actually got the credit that was due them.[24]

Controversy still surrounds the discovery of insulin that is peculiarly Canadian. It was argued at the time among scientists and academics, and still is, that Banting did not deserve the primary credit because he only had the idea that led to the discovery and without the technical help of the senior researchers at the university, he and Best would never have achieved the extract. This is exactly like saying that Sir Alexander Fleming should not be credited for penicillin because others perfected the techniques of extraction and production. Fortunately, the public doesn't split such hairs and perceived that without a Fleming there would be no penicillin, and without a Banting no insulin.[25]

The experience permanently coloured Banting's attitude to science and to people. There were those who had ideas and those who never did, and so either blocked or stole them. At the peak of his fame and head of his own lab, Banting scrupulously avoided putting his name on the publications of others in his department, unless he had been in on the actual research. As for having ideas, he considered this the quality most to be sought and fostered in researchers. When new ideas of his own faltered, he pushed others to develop theirs.[26] Those who knew and liked him thought this was humility; it was actually the philosphical attitude of a man who believed that discovery was handmaiden to originality.

There was little that Banting or McNaughton could do to further develop the idea of germ warfare. Bacteriology was not Banting's field, and his lab was not set up for that kind of research. Instead, at McNaughton's insistence, he took charge of an NRC committee on aviation research and led a determined assault on the physical problems associated with high-altitude, high-speed flight: decompression, cold, oxygen starvation and the blackouts caused by acceleration. Within a few years, Banting's team of aviation researchers would lead the world in this line of inquiry.

On August 23, 1939, much to the chagrin of many people world-wide who saw Russia's communist experiment as an enlightened alternative to capitalism and fascism, Joseph Stalin signed a pact with Hitler. On September 1 Germany invaded Poland without warning. Shortly afterwards, Britain and France honoured their treaty obligations and declared war, followed about a week later by Canada.[27] Before the end of the month, Poland had been overrun and Germany and Russia had divided the spoils.

With the declaration of war McNaughton immediately wrote the presidents of all the Canadian universities and asked them to discourage graduate students in science programs from joining up. They were to be told they were of more value in the lab than in uniform. In the First World War the Allied science effort had been crippled because many of its educated young men were killed in the trenches. McNaughton did not want to see that happen again.

McNaughton did not stay at the NRC long enough to mobilize it for the war he had so long foreseen. As Canada's most highly regarded soldier, he was almost immediately put in charge of the first levy of Canadian troops to go overseas, despite the Liberal prime minister's misgivings about his links with the former Conservative government. When King asked whom he recommended as his successor as president of the NRC, McNaughton promptly said, "Jack Mackenzie."

"But he's another Conservative!" King is said to have exclaimed.

"Does that really matter?" McNaughton asked.

"No, it does not," King replied.[28]

If ever there was a man of ideas along the lines Banting admired, C.J. Mackenzie was that man. Mackenzie was a graduate of Dalhousie University in Nova Scotia where he had studied engineering under C.D. Howe – now a minister in King's government – and had set out in 1909 for western Canada to seek his fortune. He found it in a wide variety of entrepreneurial engineering projects which led to his establishing a fine engineering department at the University of Saskatchewan. He liked to drink, smoke, had a sharp sense of humour and, most of all, was an excellent judge of character. During the First World War he had won the Military Cross.

Two Conservatives in key wartime positions must have been a little too much for King. McNaughton was to retain the title of president of the National Research Council and Mackenzie would only be acting president. That way if King was displeased with McNaughton in his army role, he could bump him back to the NRC without fuss and Mackenzie would simply disappear. It was a typical King ploy of the sort that made him Canada's longest serving prime minister, and the least-loved.[29]

If Mackenzie was bothered by the arrangement, which went on for four years, he never showed it. He plunged into his new role with his usual zest, touring the labs in the NRC building and trying to figure out how he was going to organize the expansion that was bound to come. Already scientists at the universities were asking how they could help. The question was, what projects to assign them? Flood's visit to Porton was the only significant liaison Canada had had with Britain's scientific community in recent years. There would be no point in duplicating work that Britain was already doing.

Mackenzie had scarcely settled into his new job when he was visited by Otto Maass, head of chemistry at McGill, a member of the NRC's governing council and chairman of the Canadian Institute of Chemistry. McNaughton had warned him about

Maass. American-born of German parentage but raised in Mont-real, Maass was keen to get chemical warfare research under way, and fast. He had already toured the country, visiting labs in universities and industry to assess their chemical and, significantly, biological research capabilities. Since then, he had been pestering McNaughton relentlessly. Mackenzie's prompt answer was to give him the task of getting chemical warfare research outside the NRC started wherever he could and Maass went to work with a will.[30]

Maass was one of the most prominent Canadian chemists of the day and a study in contradictions. He was connected by family to well-known German scientists and as a boy made many visits to relatives in Germany. Yet he showed a deadly hatred of the Nazis and was an outspoken advocate of chemical warfare. It puzzled his colleagues. One theory was that he was embarrassed by Germany's actions in the First World War; another was that the early death of his father somehow made him anti-German in his attitudes. There is one interesting clue, however, that his contemporaries seemed to have overlooked.[31]

When the First World War broke out, Maass was in Berlin studying under the German chemist, Professor Hermann Walther Nernst. Maass realized he risked internment and one day slipped away from the lab and made his way across Germany to Switzerland, posing as someone suffering from tuberculosis to account for not being in the army. When in danger of being questioned too closely, he put red dye in his mouth so that he appeared to cough up blood. He managed to get back to Canada safely.[32]

Professor Nernst was one of the most famous German scientists, and graduate students from around the world eagerly sought to work in his department, the Physikalische Chemisches Institut of the University of Berlin. It was to Nernst that the German army turned in the first few months of the First World War for help in improving the effectiveness of high explosive shells by adding chemicals. Consequently, it was Nernst who directed the first systematic chemical warfare experiments, chiefly with tear gas and irritant compounds, until his work was surpassed by the enthusiastic Fritz Haber.[33] Maass had first-hand knowledge of German chemists and reason to fear their abilities.

Otto Maass stories are legion. At 49, he was an imposing figure as head of chemistry at McGill. He was always smartly dressed, had piercing blue eyes, and a gruff, no-nonsense manner behind an ever-present cigar. He was also a man of vigour and fun. One of his prewar students remembered how the roof of the chemistry lab overlooked Royal Victoria College, the women's residence across the street.

"There was one girl who used to go up on the roof in a bathing suit at exam time," Dr. Tom King recalled. "She was rather . . . she had large hips and she'd go up on sunny days and take a book and lie on the roof on her stomach. And one of the fellows said, 'I'm going to get her. I've got a nice, powerful B-B gun and I'm going to bring it to school.'"

A few days later a group of the graduate students sneaked up onto the roof of the lab and hid behind a rooftop structure built to house elevator machinery. "We waited there until she presented a good target and this boy ups with the gun and – whit! – nails her. Well, Jesus, she went up in the air . . .!"

The students raced downstairs and hid the gun. The next day, Maass came into the lab and reported that the head of the women's residence had complained, saying that the girl had been sure the shot had come from the chemistry building. The young men couldn't resist Maass's determined questioning and confessed, insisting that they were all responsible and all should take the consequences, not just the person who fired the shot.

> Maass said: "Get me the gun!" So we presented the gun to him and he said, "That's the gun, eh? Where did you do it?"
>
> "Up on the roof."
>
> "Show me." And we took him up on the roof and showed him – "There she is now!"
>
> "Where did you stand?" And we showed him. "She really does present a good target . . ." and, boom!, he shot her and boom!, he shot her again and she fled downstairs. In a few minutes the phone rang in his office and he answered it.
>
> "I can assure you, Mrs. Stewart, I know for certain none of my students is responsible for shooting that girl."[34]

That kind of behaviour on the part of a senior professor endeared Maass to his students, and as Canada's wartime chemical warfare research expanded, he filled the key posts with his former students. None would dream of refusing him.

❖   ❖   ❖

For months after the fall of Poland, nothing much happened in Europe. The British were content to leave the French and Germans glaring at one another across their frontier. It was a reprieve for Hitler. After the war it was revealed that Germany was ill-equipped in the fall of 1939 to resist a determined attack by the British and the powerful French army. Instead, with nightmare visions of bombing attacks on Paris and London, the two allies decided not to provoke Germany and waited for Hitler's next move. It seemed never to come.

"We all thought that there might be epidemics due to bacteriological warfare and the migration of large numbers of people to less sanitary districts," Sir Edward Mellanby, head of Britain's Medical Research Council, wrote Banting. "As you well know all these ideas up to the present have proved false. ... At the present time many of our workers are carrying on with their normal work and waiting for a special war problem to present itself."[35]

The Canadians were also waiting for special war problems to present themselves, and it gave Mackenzie the opportunity to get to know Maass and Banting. His first meeting with Banting was particularly memorable.

> We found ourselves alone in the Château Laurier [hotel]. And I had never known him before. I knew his reputation. He didn't know me I suppose at all, only by name. But we talked a minute and he finally looked at me over his glasses and he said, "Do you ever take a drink?"
>
> And I said, "Yes, I take a drink."
>
> He said, "Can you drink rye whisky?"
>
> And I said, "Yes."
>
> He said, "I have a bottle up in my room and I think it would be a good idea to have a drink before we go down to dinner." So we did.
>
> We became very intimate friends and this evolved into very interesting experiences. We would sit down in the Grill, in the Chateau, and Banting would take the waiter's pad and he would draw people's portraits – not portraits but, you know, sketches. And people would come up to Banting. All sorts, quietly. It might be a waitress. It might be a Mounted Police. It might be somebody else to speak to Banting. A life had been saved, you see.

And it was very impressive, but there wasn't anything flamboyant at all. It was just somebody would come up and whisper something. "I'm glad to see you," or so forth. But there was no spilling over. There wasn't any melodrama to it at all. It was very – an awful lot of people came up. . . . We used to have meetings and dinner together. So I got to know Banting extremely well as a man. I was very fond of Banting. He was a great man. One of the most modest men I have ever met in my life.[36]

At the British Medical Council's suggestion, it was decided to send someone over to Britain to see first hand what the British were doing in wartime medicine, and how Canadians could help. Banting was the obvious choice, particularly because Mackenzie thought his reputation would open doors in many other areas and enable him to bring back a broad picture of the British research effort.[37] He was accompanied by Israel Rabinowitch, a Montreal doctor who had expressed interest in the physiological effects of poison gas. His job was to see what progress was being made in chemical warfare research.

The crossing was fearful. Banting had expected the ship to be in a convoy surrounded by destroyers to protect it from submarines. Instead, they were alone on a dark and hostile sea.

One looks about the cabin & checks the various things he must wear for warmth. I pick up my boots and loosen the laces so I can get into them in a hurry. I look to trousers, coat, overcoat and all, before I go to bed. I know well where everything in the cabin is. I could do it in a minute & in the dark. I have it fixed in my memory – socks, pants, boots, shirt, coat, overcoat. In the pockets I have the urgent things I need. I know where all these things are. Rab in the next room is ready too. He cannot swim but I have promised to tow him if he needs propulsion & he says "Let's talk to each other" if anything happens, and "Keep on talking to each other."[38]

Nothing happened. The two men arrived in England on November 25 and, after some initial red tape, began their tour of Britain's defence establishments.

Porton Down was opened in early 1916 in open countryside on the southern edge of Salisbury Plain. It was set up in direct response to the German gas attacks of the First World War and its mandate was to develop both offensive and defensive techniques of chemical warfare. This it did, and in the interwar years maintained a modest program of research which was not forbidden under the Geneva Protocol.[39] More restrictive was the general spirit of pacificism and disarmament, so that while some work was done on existing gases and weapons, there were no new discoveries or significant advances. By 1939 Britain's choice of chemical weapons was essentially the same as that of 1918.[40]

Archival records pertaining to Porton during the Second World War are still secret in Britain, but Banting and Rabinowitch left detailed descriptions of their visits. Neither knew much about chemical warfare, so they were readily impressed, but in fact Porton was anything but the sophisticated weapons research establishment that it is sometimes painted to be. In comparison to the kind of effort to be put forward in the United States and Canada within a few years, Porton on a wartime footing in 1940 was not elaborate. It consisted of a scatter of mostly one-storey buildings which housed the ten main departments and a total of 56 scientists, 52 technicians and about 300 support staff, including military personnel. This was about the same station strength as in 1922.[41]

Banting spent two days at Porton although Rabinowitch stayed on for a month. They found the entire British chemical warfare effort, except for actual gas production, concentrated in the one spot. The scientists studied the various toxic compounds, designed defensive equipment like gas masks and protective clothing, designed weapons, tested the effects of gas on animals and human volunteers, and undertook limited field trials with artillery and a few aircraft. Both Canadians felt that the British were covering all the bases and there was not much for Canada to do.

There was one obvious deficiency, however. The British were particularly keen on the possibilities of spraying mustard gas from aircraft but the space available for field trials was only about 9,600 yards by 4,000, the Porton "cricket pitch." A recent aerial experiment had been discontinued because the gas had drifted beyond the Porton perimeter, leading to complaints from neighbouring villages. Rabinowitch suggested Canada's "open spaces" could be made available for such tests. Porton's superintendent of experiments, E. Ll. Davies, welcomed the idea and Rabinowitch pressed for it in a flurry of memos sent back to Canada's National Research Council.[42]

Porton's main preoccupation in the preceding six months, both Banting and Rabinowitch learned, was the development of defence against arsenical compounds. The British intelligence service had apparently learned that the Germans had found that these compounds could be scattered on the ground in solid form and would react with moisture in the air to produce a gas called arsine.[42] Porton killed 1,600 animals in studying this gas and when the reports of the two Canadians reached Canada, Maass and Flood undertook urgent experiments to devise methods of defence. Later the gas turned out not to be practical, was easily neutralized chemically, and probably was never seriously considered by the Germans in the first place.

While Banting continued his tour of the various centres of aviation and medical research, in early January Rabinowitch visited the mustard gas plant at Sutton Oak in Lancashire. Here he found a facility capable of producing "blister" gas in quantity and of three main types: the basic and somewhat unstable dichlorodiethylsulphide (code-named H) and diluted with carbon tetrachloride (code-named HS); the more toxic, longer-lasting bis(2-chloroethylthioethyl)ether (code-named HT), and 2-chlorovinyldichloroarsine known as Lewisite. The last caused searing burns immediately on contact; with true mustard like the first two gases, the burns took eight hours to form. Sutton Oak was able to produce 20 tons of HS, 50 tons of HT and a half ton of Lewisite each week. The main thrust of Britain's chemical warfare effort was on mustard gas.[44]

It should be noted that these chemicals were all extraordinarily vicious. The smallest drop would raise a severe blister as though the skin had been burned. Though handling procedures were stringent, there was a steady procession of injuries at the Sutton Oak plant. Out of 450 employees in 1939, there were forty-seven mustard burns, two caused by Lewisite, and seven eye injuries.[45] In a letter back to the National Research Council, Rabinowitch observed that Canada might have some trouble with Workmen's Compensation when it started manufacturing poison gas on its own.

Rabinowitch wrote about 20,000 words describing his thorough tour of Britain's chemical warfare establishment. The state of the art that he found can be summarized as follows:

1. Almost the entire effort was concentrated on the war gases that had been developed in the First World War;

2. mustard gas was regarded as the most feasible gas weapon, best distributed by spraying from aircraft;

3. gas bombs and shells were essentially the same as those used in the First World War, although some work was underway to develop a mustard gas mine which sprayed its victim when stepped on;

4. the practice of using soldier volunteers to determine the effectiveness of mustard gas in causing injuries was well established;

5. the British were anxious to do full field trials with their gas weapons but were sharply limited by the lack of suitable unpopulated areas.[46]

Rabinowitch stayed on in Britain, becoming chemical warfare adviser to General McNaughton who had arrived to mother-hen the training of the Canadian troops that had been sent over. He also became the general's personal physician and the object of considerable resentment because of the influence he appeared to wield. He was eventually sent back to Canada and dropped from sight, at least as far as chemical warfare was concerned.

Banting also stayed on for a number of months, but for entirely different reasons. He had left questions of gas warfare to Rabinowitch, and took little further interest after his visit to Porton. His main attention was on aviation medical research, and he found his own team ahead of the British. Other medical committees and discussions also took up a lot of his time but whenever opportunity presented itself, he asked questions about what was going on in bacterial warfare research.

He was not short of prominent British scientists to talk to – Mellanby, Sir Henry Dale, Sir Joseph Barcroft – but the response was always the same. Germany was not expected to resort to such reprehensible tactics. His Majesty's Government had also rejected them. The deliberate spreading of foot and mouth disease of cattle by Germany was a possibility, but not likely. The existing organization of emergency medical services was adequate for all eventualities. Research into such questions was not officially sanctioned and therefore not done.

Banting continued to be insistent in his questioning. Word began to get around that the discoverer of insulin was meddling in areas he knew nothing about.[47]

C·H·A·P·T·E·R
T·W·O

Banting's Crusade

"It is a war of scientist against scientist," Banting told his diary. "This war above all in history will be one in which the application of science to warfare will give one side or the other the advantage."[1]

Banting had been keeping a daily diary for years. As he once explained to Mackenzie, he started it shortly after going down to Yale in late 1921 with University of Toronto professor J.J.R. Macleod to present some of the early results of his work on diabetes to the American Physiological Society. Banting read his paper and, as he told Mackenzie, "There was no reaction and Macleod, who hadn't done anything, got up and made a speech and everybody got up and cheered and claimed Macleod had discovered insulin." Banting vowed then and there that he would learn to write and "ever since that night I have written for an hour or two, every day."[2]

Banting told Mackenzie of another incident that also had a major effect on him: "I was embarrassed when I went over for my Nobel Prize. I was entertained at Oxford and we returned to the Common Room and the conversation was brilliant and light. And I was ignorant as a peasant. I didn't know what they were talking about. I had no knowledge. I had no culture. And I determined to correct this. . . . " He told Mackenzie that from then on, he read everything he could lay his hands on. But the sting of the incident appears never to have gone away.[3]

On this day, December 22, 1939, the entry in Banting's diary is lengthy. He had seen General McNaughton and had complained to him that on his tour of Porton and in his talks with various British scientists, he had found no evidence that anyone in Britain took the threat of bacterial warfare seriously. There was no research being done, leaving the country wide open to this kind of attack by Germany. All other research seemed shallow and futile if this supreme threat was overlooked.

McNaughton was sympathetic. Write a memo, he advised, and fully outline your fears and recommendations. Send it to the National Research Council with a copy to Canadian Military Headquarters. In due course it would be passed up through channels to him and he would try to get the British Army interested. If he was successful, the idea could then be pitched to the Canadian government.

It was still a phoney war. After three months there had been no significant fighting. The French Army remained facing Germany holed up like badgers in the steel and concrete dungeons of their impregnable Maginot Line. The British Army dallied on the Belgian border ready to leap forward when the Germans repeated their First World War invasion of Flanders. The Royal Navy was busy rounding up the flotsam and jetsam of enemy shipping, while the Royal Air Force sprinkled anti-Nazi leaflets over Berlin. It was all very gentlemanly. So far.

Banting plunged into the writing of his memo, labouring on it through Christmas and into the new year. He remained convinced that sooner or later Germany would begin fighting total war, one in which there would be no holds barred. The British had been caught napping when the Germans launched the first gas attacks in the last war and now they were prepared with gas masks for the entire population. Yet they were again ignoring a new possibility. Banting feared bacterial warfare would catch them napping again.

On Christmas Eve Banting had tea at the home of Sir Edward Mellanby, head of Britain's Medical Research Council. The Canadian was not reassured. "Sir Edward does not think that the Germans will use bacteria, except for foot and mouth disease of cattle," Banting wrote. Even if they did, Mellanby doubted it would be a serious threat. Moreover, he said the council would never undertake the kind of research Banting proposed.[4]

This attitude scandalized Banting. He felt it was a betrayal of trust by Britain's medical profession, which had a sacred duty to warn the country's political and military leaders of the potential dangers of germs being deliberately spread. Yet he felt he had to win over these "stodgy British bacteriologists" if he was going to get any support for research back in Canada. At this point in history Canadians generally deferred to Britain's leadership in science and politics.

"As far as I can find out," Banting wrote in his diary, "it is just as much against the law to use poison gas in warfare as it is to use bacteria. Yet these British spend enormous sums on gas warfare research. . . . And yet they sleep securely oblivious to the greater dangers of Bacterial warfare."[5]

Banting put in his nineteen-page memo in early January, addressing it as McNaughton suggested, with an extra copy to the Royal Army Medical Corps. It is a historic document, in a strange, ironic way. Nobel laureate, saver of hundreds of thousands of lives through the discovery of insulin, Banting had written what turns out to be the blueprint for bacteriological warfare research for the next two decades. Even within four years, before the war was over, his ideas for infected bullets and shells, the rearing of disease-carrying insects and the aerial spraying of deadly bacteria became weapons of reality. The dangers he wrote of from secret agents, infected propaganda pamphlets, and contaminated water supplies were echoed in the American, Canadian and British appreciations of the years to come. He raised spectres of invisible death that haunt us yet.

Banting also showed considerable prescience in enunciating a principle of modern warfare which we take for granted now, but was still widely ignored or regarded with skepticism in early 1940.

In the past, war was confined for the most part to men in uniform, but with the increased mechanization of armies and the introduction of air forces, there is an increased dependence on the home country, and eight to ten people working at home are now required to keep one man in the fighting line. This state of affairs alters the complexion of war. It really amounts to one nation fighting another nation. This being so, it is just as effective to kill or disable ten unarmed workers at home as to put a soldier out of action, and if this can be done with less risk, then it would be advantageous to employ any mode of warfare to accomplish this.[6]

Within a few years the British and the Americans were to put this principle to the test – somewhat unsuccessfully – with the saturation bombing of German and Japanese cities. After the war it became the very cornerstone of nuclear preparedness, which assumes civilians are going to be the primary targets in an atomic war.

The British authorities, however, did not want to listen. The copy of his memo sent to the medical corps got Banting an interview with Sir Maurice Hankey, the career Whitehall mandarin who had been responsible for advising the government on the subject of bacteriological warfare since 1934. "The good Lord set forth all that had been done and evidently wanted a little praise. . . . I tried to make only one point – the necessity for immediate research into Bacterial warfare." Lord Hankey accepted a copy of Banting's memo, complimented him on being the first "scientist of standing" to come forward with definite proposals, and promised to raise the matter in committee.[7]

The memo was already dead in the water. In its preamble Banting ridiculed the shortcomings of a Medical Research Council report prepared shortly after the outbreak of war (October 24) and entitled: "Some Notes On Defense Against Bacteriological Warfare." He spoke of the "failure" of its authors to recognize that security of the country rested on their advice, and chided them for the shallowness of their deliberations and their sole recommendation that the public laboratory service be extended. He pointed out they failed even to mention the need for research.[8]

Such criticisms Banting would have thought temperate, and for him they were. Nevertheless, though he may not have realized it, it was Hankey and Mellanby that he was accusing of dereliction of duty. The former was chairman of the newly established Bacteriological Warfare Committee of the War Cabinet and it would have been he who assigned the Medical Research Council – chaired by Mellanby – the task of preparing the report. Banting, in blissful ignorance, was savaging both men, and one a peer at that.[9] It is not surprising that there was mostly silence from Hankey in the weeks that followed.

The only bit of encouragement Banting got was from the urbane Lord Victor Rothschild, a multi-millionaire and Cambridge graduate attached to military intelligence. Banting appreciated that he was in favour of bacterial warfare research, but bridled under the younger man's condescension. He also recorded in his diary that Rothschild "seems to be familiar with all the ideology of Communism."

Banting hung around until the end of the month and then he headed home, later describing Hankey in his diary as "a superb example of the servile, all-important complacent superior ass that runs British government." Back in Ottawa, he poured out his heart to Mackenzie at the NRC. "He gave me this whole series of things that were bothering him, from chemical and bacterial warfare," Mackenzie recalled. "I went over them and said, 'Well, listen. This is worth doing, this won't work, and so forth.' And when we got through, he said, 'Thank you very much. I can get to sleep now.'"[10]

It is important to see Banting's fears in the context of the year 1940. Antibiotics had only just been discovered and were hardly known, much less in use. Many diseases whose cures are taken for granted in the late twentieth century were deadly or debilitating in Banting's day. Yet science had advanced to the point where it was recognized that many micro-organisms could be cultivated and preserved through freezing or drying. Systematic bacterial warfare was inconceivable in the First World War; with the full development of the long-range, high-altitude bomber twenty years later it suddenly became entirely practical. The parallel, in another twenty years, was the combination of nuclear bomb and intercontinental ballistic missile.—

Banting had found a powerful ally in Mackenzie. For all that the acting president of the NRC was diplomat and administrator, he was still the engineer with a firm grip on the practical applications of science. By January 1940 he had the NRC scientists working on twenty-six war projects, twelve of them in chemistry, plus another twenty chemical projects at the universities. The latter were the result of the energy of Otto Maass who, as Mackenzie's special assistant, had taken responsibility for all chemical warfare work and by March had thirty-six projects under way both within the NRC and in labs across the country. The real hang-up, however, was lack of cash.[11]

Canada's Mackenzie King government was also fighting a phoney war. So far, there had been no great mobilization of forces, either material or financial. Soldiers had been sent overseas, it is true, and a plan had been drafted to train Commonwealth pilots in Canada, but otherwise the effort had been so meagre that in January the Ontario Legislature had voted forty-four to ten to condemn the federal government's handling of the war. There was no extra money for the NRC and none likely for some time to come.

Banting returned to Toronto and immersed himself in administering the aviation research projects and studies of poison gas. University of Toronto chemist George F Wright, under prodding from Maass, was already brewing various toxic compounds and Banting's medical researchers did many of the animal tests. They also sought methods of treating mustard gas burns, producing a training film for soldiers entitled "Gas Gets in Your Eyes" that graphically showed the effects of the gas on rabbits. Banting even joined in the research, volunteering to be a guinea pig and allowing a small patch of mustard to be painted on his leg followed by an ice pack. It developed into a festering, painful wound.[12]

In May Germany invaded France. Hitler ignored the formula of the previous war and struck between Belgium and the Maginot Line, his tanks slicing across northern France behind the British and trapping them against the coast. The French government reeled, its army in tatters from the co-ordinated pounding of aircraft and tanks. The Germans were demonstrating once again that they were the masters of war, and of technology.

The events in Europe were shocking to any who had served in the First World War. The French Army was supposed to be the most powerful in the world, and here was Hitler chopping it to pieces. Canadians like Banting listened to the radio and heard the crump of shell-fire and a new sound, the scream of dive-bombers. Every day the news got incredibly worse. By May 19 the Germans had driven a deep wedge into France and Banting was already considering the implications if they gained control of the Channel coast:

> I cannot bring myself to the belief that Germany contemplates an invasion of England and, this being the case, I am all the more convinced that there will be the attempt of bacterial warfare along the lines on which I have already written. . . . I think that McNaughton agrees with me that the most serious situation that faces our dear, old England is that of Bacterial warfare. The sad part is we have not the means to

retaliate. England suffers from a plithora [sic] of senile Brains that live in the late victorian period.[13]

A little more than a week later it was clear to the world that catastrophe was overtaking France. German tanks reached the Channel south of Dunkirk, trapping both French and British armies now tumbling back out of Belgium. To Banting it appeared that "the Brute Force of the German is rampant and threatening the destruction of Civilization. It is all too horrible for words."

He considered approaching cabinet ministers directly for support on bacterial warfare, but despaired of getting a hearing. He had too low an opinion of those in power, and of the prime minister in particular. "Our government is led by a senile fossil of a vintage that would do credit to whisky," he wrote. "I feel like giving up my life to the hangman in order to rid Canada of the sonombalent [sic] Mr. King." Finally, on June 24, after the British Army had fled back across the Channel and France had surrendered, he wrote to Mackenzie at the NRC and suggested that together they bring the matter before the new Minister of Defence, Colonel J.L. Ralston.

It was a bleak week in Ottawa, that last of June 1940. The inconceivable had happened. France had been crushed in forty days. England stood alone with a new prime minister, Winston Churchill, on the radio rasping defiance: "We shall fight in France, we shall fight in the seas and oceans, we shall fight. . . ." Maass ruefully told Banting that the British had just finished exchanging chemical warfare information with the French when the Germans struck, so now all their secrets were in enemy hands. It was all very depressing.[14]

Then help came from a remarkable quarter. In the course of his chairmanship of the aviation medical research committee, Banting had occasion to visit James Duncan, then Deputy Minister of National Defence for Air. Duncan was an ambitious former vice-president of Massey Harris, the international farm implement conglomerate, and was one of those businessmen brought into government to help in the war effort. He listened with fascination as Banting unfolded a woeful tale of NRC research stymied for lack of funds and offered to help. He knew some wealthy Canadians who might be willing to make some patriotic donations.[15]

One of those he approached was John David Eaton, head of the T. Eaton Co. department store chain. Sir Edward Beatty, president of the Canadian Pacific Railway, was also sympathetic to the idea. On the strength of their interest, Duncan phoned Mackenzie "out of the blue" and asked him to prepare a report on how the NRC would use donations to the tune of several hundreds of thousands of dollars. By a stroke of luck, the timing of the call was perfect.

Mackenzie had been spoiling for the NRC to get seriously into war research but it was not just money that had been holding him back. The British up to then had been extremely tight-lipped about their major lines of research and Mackenzie didn't want his scientists ploughing ground already furrowed. Then Mackenzie received an unexpected visit from A.V. Hill, science adviser to the British ambassador in Washington, who had arrived in Ottawa, unasked and unannounced, to organize medical research in the dominion.

Mackenzie was astounded. He told Hill that Canada already had an excellent program of medical research and did not need the British to run it. Moreover, there were plenty of scientists in a variety of disciplines, both at the research council and at the universities, just waiting to find out where best to concentrate their efforts. It was Hill's turn to be astounded, and embarrassed. A senior member of Britain's scientific establishment, he said he had not realized that Canadian science was fully organized. It was a classic example, and by no means the last during the war, of British ignorance when it came to their largest Commonwealth ally.[16]

Hill immediately phoned Washington and called off the team of scientists and administrators he had organized for Canada. Instead, he said he would arrange for a science liaison officer to come over from Britain and cut Canada in on British research as soon as possible. Duncan's call came just as this was happening. On July 6 Mackenzie drew up an NRC shopping list with price tags that was presented at a meeting with Beatty and Eaton in early July. Within a month he was able to expand this to include work Britain wanted done as well.[17]

Mackenzie got his money. Eaton and Beatty pledged $250,000 each, a colossal sum in 1940, with Sam Bronfman, the head of the Canadian distillery giant, Seagrams, following with a similar amount soon after. Eventually, with the addition of mainly corporate donations, the fund grew to over $1.3 million and for the next year and a half provided the start-up money for just about every war research project then undertaken in Canada.

The group formed to administer the money was called the War Technical and Scientific Development Committee. Mackenzie, Maass and Banting represented the NRC, and there were six appointees from the major government departments, Defence, Supply, External Affairs and so on, plus three one-year non-voting members representing the private benefactors. Because they had contributed the most, these were John Eaton, Sam Bronfman and R. E. Stavert on behalf of Beatty.[18]

As a war committee it was unique. And amazing. It placed three civilians, Eaton, Bronfman and Stavert, at the focus of the Allies' most closely guarded secrets. They had to take the oath of secrecy and the oath of allegiance and only four copies of the minutes of meetings were made. Mackenzie even had momentary misgivings, warning Beatty and presumably Eaton and Bronfman after the fact that certain projects he had described were highly secret and they were not to breathe a word of them to anyone. These were RDF, the early code letters for radar; Asdic, the acoustic detection of submarines; Uranium 235 as a possible super-explosive; and bacteriological warfare.[19] These became the four biggest scientific secrets of the Allies.

Eaton, for one, certainly took Mackenzie at his word. Though he attended just about every meeting of the WTSDC over the next four years, coming up to Ottawa from Toronto, he appears never to have told a soul about it, not even after the war. His son, John Craig Eaton, knew nothing of the donation nor of the wartime activities of his father until contacted by the writer of this book. Mackenzie's confidence was not misplaced.

The fund was a boon. It arbitrarily thrust Canadian war research forward, with the government paying back the money spent as soon as a project proved its worth. And none of the donors profited from it, even in terms of public recognition. It was, in Mackenzie's words, "a pure outburst of patriotism," brought on by the German victories. Nevertheless, the irony remains that it was corporate Canada, not the government or the military, that firmly placed Canadian scientists on a research path that led to pioneering work on poison gas, germ warfare, code-breaking and Canada's first nuclear reactor.

Right from the start, however, the non-scientific members of the committee had little say in how the money was spent. Basically, Mackenzie would come to a meeting with a list of projects he thought should be supported, and by how much. Sometimes Maass or Banting would also speak. It all would have been decided by the trio before the meeting, later usually to be rubber-stamped. It was an excellent arrangement, for it gave the three scientists almost total control over war research, enabling them to explore long shots and hunches.

One such long shot was work on germ warfare. Mackenzie's initial outline of research requirements, which went to Beatty and Eaton, says: "Some scientists feel we should be prepared [for BW] both offensively and defensively as we know Germany is. Others think that the weapon is so dangerously two-edged that no nation would initiate it. Sir Frederick Banting is very much of the opinion that we should at least do some elementary preliminary experimentation. . . . " Mackenzie asked for $50,000.[20]

Things started to move for Banting, and it was Mackenzie doing the moving. Three days later he arranged for them to meet Ralston, and they persuaded the defence minister to agree to a program of bacteriological warfare experiments financed by the money from the wealthy Canadians. Ralston raised the matter later that same day, July 9, at a meeting of the Cabinet War Committee, describing Banting's group as a voluntary committee set up to study "the spread of infectious diseases from aeroplanes and shells." Banting had misjudged Mackenzie King and his ministers. They endorsed the idea.[21]

The way was now clear. Germ warfare research had been approved by government and Mackenzie had found a source of money. Banting swung into action. Over the next few weeks he held a series of meetings with the scientists from the Banting Institute, the Connaught Laboratories and the University of Toronto. They discussed what germ would be most appropriate for warfare, settling on psittacosis, otherwise known as parrot fever. It was decided that Dr. James Craigie of the Connaught would be in charge of the investigation.[22]

Nearly fifty years later the buff brick and limestone building on College Street in Toronto seems an unlikely birthplace for germ warfare research in North America. The Banting Institute has a rather drab, factory-like appearance inconsistent with the glass and stainless steel picture of a secret-weapon laboratorary painted by three decades of James Bond-like novels and movies. But it served the purpose.

In 1940 the Banting and Best Department of Medical Research occupied the top floor and specialized primarily in physiological research, the study of living organisms. Since the beginning of the war, at Banting's urging, Drs. Dudley Irwin and Colin Lucas had been studying the effects of toxic compounds on live animals, testing mustard gas in the eyes of rabbits and the new poison gases developed by the university's chemistry department on mice. Wilbur Franks, as part of Banting's aviation medicine team, was working on the concept of a pressure suit for pilots to prevent blacking out during rapid acceleration. The experimental animals were quartered on the roof.

The building also contained pathology labs, a very large autopsy theatre, library, offices, and on the second floor, the University of Toronto's department of bacteriology, headed by Dr. Philip Greey, remembered by his students for his dapper dress and quick wit. A tunnel ran under College Street to link the building with the Toronto General Hospital.

The Connaught Labs are a little harder to define. Established in 1914 to do research into preventative medicine and produce vaccines, it had offices in the university's School of Hygiene building and research and production facilities out at "The Farm," 140 acres of land and buildings on the city's outskirts where it kept its live-animal requirements. Dr. Robert Defries was the acting director and Drs. Donald Fraser, Ronald Hare and James Craigie were the principal researchers. This was to be the nucleus of Banting's bacteriological warfare team and he appears to have had no trouble getting them all on side for his scheme, with the temporary exception of Craigie. Banting wrote on July 18:

> Saw Craigie in PM. He is a curious sort of duck. I think he has a mind for minute detail and a capacity for knowledge that surpasses his capacity for original research. . . . But he is a most valuable man if one can utilize his superiority complex to make the son of a Biliol work. He has the idea, shared with other members of Connaught, that Psitcosis [sic] is the only thing worth working on. I think he still thinks of virus and bacteria in terms of platinum loops instead of tons. . . .[23]

Bacterial research was not Banting's area of expertise. As with almost every other project he got involved in, Banting was the catalyst who got the most out of the expertise of others. Franks did the original work that led to the first practical pressure suit; Banting got on his temperamental back and kept him at it. It was the same with the pioneering high-altitude research which also was being done under his aviation medicine committee, and with a host of other projects in which he had no official rôle. One finds jottings in his diaries of suggestions to others that range from the composition of mustard gas ointments to the design of bullet-proof vests. His great strength, which Mackenzie particularly admired, was his ability to mobilize the talents of others.[24]

And so it was with germ warfare research. Banting needed Craigie because he was recognized as the Connaught's expert on certain diseases. He needed Greey because he had the necessary bacteriological knowledge and the lab facilities in the same building as the men who could do the live-animal assessments. If anyone hesitated about germ warfare research on ethical grounds, Banting didn't mention it in his diary. He believed absolutely in the threat of bacterial warfare and, when gripped by any idea, he could be passionately persuasive.

Back in Ottawa at the NRC, things were also happening for Mackenzie. In mid-August a high-powered British delegation led by the distinguished scientist Sir Henry Tizard stopped by on its way to Washington. With the Germans in sight of Dover, frightened Britain now wanted to exchange her technological secrets with the United States in an effort to woo her into the war. The most valuable offering was something called the cavity magnetron, a device which vastly improved the image resolution of radar. Two years later, when aircraft began using it, it tipped the balance of the Battle of the Atlantic in favour of the Allies because it enabled pilots to see targets as small as the coning towers of submarines, day or night. The hunters became the hunted.

Banting was invited to lunch with Mackenzie and Tizard and it is easy to guess at least one thing they talked about. When Banting returned to Toronto a few days later, he went straight to the library and got out a book on Madame Curie's discovery of radium, one of the first known radioactive elements. In the week that followed he devoured everything he could find about radio-activity, uranium, isotopes and the theory of nuclear fission, complaining in his diary about the unnecessary complexity of some of the scientific papers. The cover of his notebook is crowded with scribbles as he struggled to grasp concepts totally alien to his training and background.

Within a week of being introduced to the subject, Banting was building castles in the air out of the concept of radioactivity, striking incredibly near to the bone with his ideas at a time when nuclear science was truly in its infancy.

> I have had a quiet day. For some time I toyed in my mind with the idea . . . of alpha, beta and gamma radiations in relation to carcinogenic response. . . . The cancer cell may be the result of minute traces of misplaced energy emanating from radioactive organic elements in its constituency. . . . [25]

Had he lived a little longer, Banting would have had the dubious satisfaction of seeing the cancer-causing consequences of radiation become recognized as the principal peril of nuclear energy, whether used for peace or war.

Even though Tizard intended discussing uranium research with the Americans, little so far had been done in Britain because it was considered a remote bet as a possible weapon for this war. Fission – the splitting of a uranium atom and consequent enormous release of energy – had only been discovered just before the war and the problems of practical application were mostly unknown and enormous. Nevertheless, the concept fired Banting's imagination and he urged Mackenzie to back experiments with uranium by the NRC's George Laurence, who already had some experience with radium. Mackenzie responded by sending Laurence to the United States to look at what was being done there. It was the first step toward Canada becoming the second country in the world to acquire nuclear power. [26]

The incident was typical of Banting. As a member of the NRC's review committee, he was entitled to a polite interest in all of its projects. Since the outbreak of war that interest was always passionate. Whether it was research on wooden aircraft, chemical warfare, radio or anti-aircraft devices, Banting always had opinions, and even when these were ill-informed, they served to prod people forward. He tapped a fundamental characteristic of human nature. People like to talk about themselves, and what they're doing. Banting was always interested.

Research into bacterial warfare, however, remained uppermost in his thoughts. It was even more important than the aviation medical research he was supervising, because it was the area in which he thought science would be most decisive in the war against Germany. He had seen the potential of chemical warfare, but that was already well served by the enthusiasm of Otto Maass. Theoretically, the techniques of bacterial warfare were complementary and it was here that Banting decided to focus his energy.

Throughout early September he held various meetings with the scientists at the Banting Institute and the Connaught Labs. It was pointed out to him that it was one thing to decide on a suitable war germ, but quite another to successfully get it to the enemy. Craigie, Hare, Irwin, Lucas and Greey all offered suggestions on how to dry and revive infectious bacteria, and what should serve as a carrier. Sawdust took the lead over powdered carbon, starch or sand, and within the week Banting was back in Ottawa asking for an airplane for an experiment in aerial dispersal.[27]

Banting's formal request for a grant for bacterial warfare research went before the War Technical and Scientific Development Committee on September 20. Mackenzie made the presentation and along with various grants for projects in chemistry, medicine and physics, the committee granted $1,500 for studies on the chemical destruction of field crops and $25,000 "for medical researches in co-operation with chemical warfare field studies."[28]

There is a little chicanery here. Banting did not fill in the formal application form until two weeks after the money was approved. Because it was not going to be seen by the committee, he was probably more specific than he might otherwise have been:

> For some weeks experiments have been in progress on bacterial warfare. These have been done by Drs. Greey, Irwin and Lucas in the Department of Medical Research University of Toronto and by Dr. Craigie of the Connaught. These experiments have now (Oct. 8, 1940) reached the point where field work must be carried out on the means of distribution from the air. When this information is obtained, further laboratory experiments on drying, preservation and production as well as selection must be carried out.[29]

In mankind's long history of war this is a milestone document marking the beginning of a whole new category of modern weapons.

Banting, however, was not the only person in Ottawa thinking of bacterial or biological warfare. The grant for the chemical destruction of crops sprang from work on toxic plant hormones done by the NRC's biology group with the enthusiastic support of Maass. Other proposals, also involving Maass, dealt with deliberately poisoning Germany's North Sea fishing grounds and sprinkling German fields with selenium compounds so that the food grown would be covertly toxic. These ideas soon proved impractical.[30]

In the age of hydrogen bombs and ICBMs it might seem odd that scientists once felt it important that credit be fairly shared among the pioneers of biological warfare. But the early 1940s was still a time of scientific innocence. Mass destruction was only theoretical and the natural environment seemed immutable. In 1942, when a fully developed bacteriological warfare program was being presented to the Canadian government, one of the members of the new germ warfare committee felt a little too much credit was being given to Banting in the report. Charles Mitchell, a Department of Agriculture pathologist with the Animal Disease Research Institute, wrote a "corrective" letter for the record:

Several years before the outbreak of the War, in common with many persons, I [Mitchell] became interested in the possibilities of bacteriological warfare and carefully went over, one by one, the infectious diseases in animals and man. From what could be learned from the literature, together with the historical records of great epidemics of the past, the diseases whose etiological agents might be directly or indirectly sown with the hope that they might afterwards spread and for which means of control are at present rather unsatisfactory appeared to be rinderpest and foot and mouth disease of cattle; plague, typhus and cholera of man.

During the course of a private conversation with the Prime Minister in 1940, the possibility of the use of the above agents was discussed. Mr. King stated that so long as the enemy refrained from using such weapons, more especially on the human population, it was very unlikely we would resort to their use. However, it did seem necessary that the matter be kept in mind both as to its defensive and offensive possibilities. He was greatly interested in the question of rinderpest and the possibility of destroying food supplies.

He suggested that I should approach the Minister of National Defence and discuss the matter. Having no connection with this Department, I hesitated to pursue his suggestion. This was ended, however, when a few days later Colonel Ralston, following the suggestion of the Prime Minister, called by telephone and asked me to report to General Crerar, Chief of Staff, with whom he was arranging an interview. The matter was discussed with this Officer who stated that Sir Frederick Banting had conducted some preliminary experiments on bacterial warfare. He also stated that it would appear to him that such a matter should come before Sir Frederick Banting, who was acting in a dual capacity, having a connection with the National Research Council and with the Department of National Defence.[31]

Mitchell goes on to tell of meeting Banting (on October 3) and proposing that they ask the government to obtain an island "in the West Indies" where research could be safely done, especially on rinderpest which might be used against Germany with good effect. Banting doubted they could get an island but liked Mitchell's ideas and talked to him subsequently about other animal diseases.

Unknown to Mitchell, the prime minister had been introduced to the concept of germ warfare months earlier when Ralston proposed Banting's voluntary group at the July 6 meeting of the Cabinet War Committee. It is interesting to see how completely and actively Mackenzie King subsequently supported it, both in terms of defensive measures and as a possible weapon. Banting had underestimated King's ability to respond to a novel idea. He was not even put off by the prospect of spreading disease to humans, and it is significant that word of Banting's early experiments had reached the ear of the Chief of Staff. Thanks to the prime minister he despised, Banting's idea was no loose cannon on Canada's wartime ship of state. Germ warfare research was national policy.

It is not any wonder, then, that Banting had no trouble obtaining a suitably equipped airplane to do dispersal experiments over Balsam Lake in cottage country northeast of Toronto. The idea was to sprinkle a stream of sawdust from various altitudes to determine how far such particles would spread should they be the carriers of infectious bacteria. Balsam Lake was chosen because Colin Lucas had a cottage there.

The experiment was pretty elementary. The plane made low passes over the lake and Banting, Lucas, Greey and Irwin measured the size of the particle plume on the surface from boats and with the help of a theodolite on shore. Some grades of sawdust worked better than others and that was about all that was demonstrated. Nevertheless, Banting (who obviously had never heard of crop dusting) concluded on the first day that the trial was a brilliant success and the way was open to a practical germ warfare weapon. The following day he flew back with the airplane to Ottawa to report to Colonel Ralston.[32]

It is just this kind of impetuosity that has muddied assessments of Banting as a scientist. The Balsam Lake exercise proved little more than that gravity works. Yet there was Banting, that night in Ralston's office, telling the Minister of Defence that they "were beyond the purely experimental stage – it was a matter of production." Nonsense. Banting's infected sawdust idea eventually was made into a weapon, but it took a team of scientists three years to perfect it. He had no conception of the problems involved.

Ralston puffed on his pipe as he listened. Banting talked of the need to build a pilot plant to mass-produce bacteria in sufficient quantity to retaliate one-hundred-fold if the Germans used bacterial warfare. Would the Canadian government back such a plan? Ralston promised a decision soon.

That night, well after midnight, Banting scribbled in his diary about killing "3 or 4 million young huns – without mercy – without feeling" and watching the Germans "wriggle & stew in their own juice – even as they with cruel and evil eye would see us of inferior heritage and stock wriggle." There is much more in the same vein and one suspects Banting had had a few late-night whiskies to dull his excitement. "Those Huns at home, those huns of Hitler – It is our job to kill them."

Banting was desperately tired. For the past year he had been constantly going back and forth to Ottawa by train. He hardly saw Henrietta, his 28-year-old second wife, whom he had romanced and married just two years earlier. He was sometimes too tired for sex. He could not sleep. He could not get his mind off the war. He was cranky and irritable at home and impatient with subordinates at the lab. He drank often, usually very late at night while writing in his diary. He felt sorry for himself. He had the classic symptoms of a man labouring under extreme stress.[33]

Mackenzie, probably Banting's only real confidant, was exactly the opposite. He had a zest for the war. He made it into a bit of a game. As the Tizard mission left Ottawa for Washington bearing its secrets, Mackenzie invited himself along. He had no official status, and no permission from either the Canadian or British governments. Yet there he was, right in the thick of the historic exchange of secrets that did much to make the United States an ally of Britain more than a year before it actually entered the war.

Mackenzie revelled in the encounter with the elite of U.S. science, and marvelled at some of the projects the British suggested the three countries work on. One that most fascinated him was something called the proximity fuse, a device which later proved to be almost as devastating a success as radar.

The concept is simple. Guns aimed at small moving targets such as airplanes have almost no chance of doing damage unless they score a direct hit, or are timed to explode at the precise instant they are passing nearby. The trouble is a gunner has to calculate the position of a moving target in three dimensions, so an immense quantity of shells were being expended for every aircraft downed. Anti-aircraft damage to the German bombers then ranging over Britain tended to be more psychological than real.

If one could put a tiny radio or photo-electric cell in the nose of a shell, which would enable it to detect its nearpoint to target and then explode, the efficiency of anti-aircraft fire would be vastly improved. The devices would also be useful for bombs, making it possible to have them explode at a precise distance above the ground regardless of topography. This became another highly secret project financed by the War Technical and Scientific Development Committee, with work soon beginning on it at Toronto under Drs. E.F. Burton and Arnold Pitt.

The thing that most impressed Mackenzie, though, was the film presentation the British made to the Americans. It showed radar in operation, from the blips on the cathode ray (TV) screen as German aircraft rose from their bases in Europe to the gunsight footage of British fighters as they shot them down. "This was what brought the Americans in on radar," Mackenzie later recalled. "They didn't know anything about this. Don't forget, it can be lab stuff but there's a very big difference [from that] to spotting a plane that's leaving Germany, or Belgium, or Holland and coming to London and shooting it down."[34]

The film was all the more impressive because as the Americans sat watching it the Battle of Britain was raging to a climax with the U.S. ambassador in London, Joseph Kennedy, cabling a steady series of secret messages saying that Britain was doomed. The film suggested this assessment might be premature.

The British presentation also included question and answer sessions from air, army and navy representatives who had been in actual combat. They described bombing the *Scharnhorst*, fighting in the encirclement at Dunkirk and the sinking of the French fleet at Oran. "These people were straight out of battle and you could see the blood all over them," Mackenzie remembered. "This was very impressive." Roosevelt's top military and science advisers were sold.[35]

What worked in the United States should work in Canada. While most of the scientists in the British mission headed home, Mackenzie persuaded the military types to come back to Ottawa with their film. He arranged a dinner in the R.B. Bennett suite in the Chateau Laurier and invited the most important members of the War Cabinet: Ralston (Defence), C.G. Power (Air), J.L. Ilsley (Finance) and C.D. Howe (Supply). Banting was also invited. All were tremendously impressed by what they saw and heard. Mackenzie bragged in later years that after this one meeting he could get anything he wanted from the government for the rest of the war.[36]

Banting continued to fret for word from Ralston. It finally came on November 19 when Duncan, the Deputy Minister for Air, phoned to say "the green light is on!" This was the go-ahead for the actual production of war bacteria; Banting immediately met with Greey, Irwin and Lucas and they decided Horace Speakman, head of the Ontario Research Foundation, should be asked to join the team. He came over that afternoon and pledged his support after Banting, with some drama, told him: "Give me a mill or a plant where I can produce a hundred tons of virulent organisms with safety to the workmen, economy and speed."[37]

For the next week, meeting followed meeting in rapid succession. The group was to be called the M-1000 Committee. Greey was to be in charge of research. Speakman suggested sugar instead of sawdust as a carrier because it would dissolve without trace. The pilot plant could be in the Banting Institute. Maybe they should get into crop diseases. Perhaps they should contact other experts in Canada for their opinions on what would be the best germ warfare agents? Greey was given that task.[38]

Enter Professor E.G.D. Murray of McGill and Professor Guilford Reed of Queen's University in Kingston. Both were prominent Canadian bacteriologists and Reed, in particular, had a considerable reputation for the study of anaerobic bacteria, the organisms that thrive in the absence of oxygen and cause food poisoning and gangrene. They had been keen to help out right from the beginning of the war, but so far had only served on an NRC committee on wound infections. Both welcomed Greey's overture.[39]

Banting himself talked to Charles Mitchell, the Department of Agriculture pathologist. Mitchell already had been testing how well hog's blood (as a germ medium) sticks to sawdust and introduced Banting to his boss at the Animal Diseases Institute, E.A. Watson. He also was interested, and said he would clear the institution's co-operation with the Deputy Minister of Agriculture. Banting solicited suggestions on spreading plant pathogens like wheat rust from the NRC's biology department and received a promise from Defries, now head of the Connaught, that Hare would do "influenza work."

The influenza reference is interesting. A virus, it is easily grown in large quantities in the laboratory and can be stored for a long time. Not usually fatal in itself, it gives rise to complications like pneumonia which made it a disease to be feared before the general availability of antibiotics. Millions died in the great influenza epidemic of the First World War. As late as 1985, because of the ease with which new strains are developed, it was considered a prime agent of biological warfare. Banting and Defries apparently had in mind the danger of it being deliberately introduced in military camps.[40]

By late autumn Banting was sagging under the pressures he himself had created. His wife was the unfortunate victim of his increasing abrasiveness, and their marriage began to be marked by petty quarrels. Typical was a spat that erupted from Henrietta's objection to Banting's rudeness to the milkman. She slammed out of the house and he retreated to his study in a heavy sulk. Later she came back and went up to bed, noisily blowing her nose and fussing to attract his attention. She wanted to make amends. Banting stubbornly stayed downstairs to sleep on the couch. While there, he wrote:

> I am all upset. I hate life. Hate everything. Hate her. I hate the things I am trying most to do. I lose spirit in spite of myself. I wish I could be sent overseas and never return. . . . I have until now been wrapped up with wife and sweetheart but by this night it is all plain to me that I mean nothing or little so why should I delay. . . . Get me overseas to expose myself – medals or death . . . death in Country's service.[41]

Within three months of writing this, Banting had indeed died in the service of his country. The significance of the passage, and others like it, is that after his death Lady Banting had custody of all his diaries for many months and read through them. She could not have missed the bitter references to their quarrels. It is testimony to her strength of character – and her love for Banting – that she resisted the temptation quietly to destroy those few pages that must have made her heart especially ache.

The next morning she served him coffee in bed. She mothered him a little and he felt much better. That night's diary entry reveals what is troubling him. "Constantly I worry I have made wrong decisions that involve other people. Shock, blood work, chemical warfare, the multiple problems of the Council, the lab and the University – aviation medicine. . . . " Banting was trying to do it all.

That afternoon, December 11, Banting had received written observations on germ warfare from the scientists he and Greey had approached to be members of their M-1000 Committee. In the light of subsequent events, the thoughts of each are instructive. Professor Murray's were the most lengthy, eleven foolscap pages in his tiny, cramped hand. He began by observing that the concept of bacterial warfare was not new, and cited short stories of de Maupassant and claims that the Germans in Africa deliberately polluted wells with feces and dead animals during the last war as they retreated across the Kalahari Desert. Then he gave his imagination free rein.

He listed at length possible animal and human diseases, with suggestions on how they could be distributed. He particularly favoured using insects – lice in slum areas, fleas and rats in city dumps, mosquitoes and ticks – as well as break-apart containers dropped from aircraft or contaminated letters sent through the mail. He envisaged enemy agents disguised as kitchen staff injecting infection in the food of restaurants and hotels.

Dr. Reed's memo was somewhat shorter but much more carefully reasoned. He proposed that the bacterial agents chosen for attack should either be totally unknown by the opposition, or particularly well known. In the latter case the aim would be to use several simultaneously so that the enemy doctors would be confused by conflicting symptoms. He recited some of the practical difficulties of preservation and delivery, and concluded that research on defensive measures against possible war bacteria should be pursued at once.[42]

The memos reflect the complementary characters of the two men. Murray tended to focus on possibilities, Reed on probabilities. They had the potential of being a strong team and both stressed that the key to bacterial warfare defence was research on methods of attack. This was precisely what Banting wanted to hear and the week before Christmas the two men came to Toronto to brainstorm in Banting's Rosedale home.

Over the holidays, Banting had a chance to unwind. He spent a couple of days touring the air force facilities at Trenton, prodding the pilots into giving him roller-coaster plane rides while he peppered them with questions on flying problems. In the officers' mess at night he revelled in the jokes and story-telling. The relaxed magic was abruptly interrupted when he returned to Toronto and to a letter from the U.S. Public Health Service requesting information from him on the Canadian bacterial warfare committee. Banting nearly had a conniption. The M-1000 Committee was supposed to be super-secret. How did they find out about it? He wrote back that he could not discuss the matter by letter. They could talk about it on his next visit to the United States.[43]

In January Duncan announced he was resigning as Deputy Minister for Air to assume the now-vacant position of president of Massey-Harris. In his diary, Banting was scathing in his opinion of Duncan's decision. Duncan was genuinely talented and had done such a fine job setting up the Commonwealth Air Training Plan that the prime minister had offered him a position in his cabinet, proposing to provide him with a safe seat to run in. Duncan turned him down.

Banting owed a lot to the deputy minister. Not only had he been instrumental in getting the Eaton and Bronfman money for his research, but several times he had greased Banting's access to Ralston on bacterial warfare. Now Banting was disgusted with him. He was giving up a chance to serve his country for a position that merely offered wealth and power. It was a poor bargain, in Banting's opinion, and Duncan must have known him well enough to sense his disappointment. He made a point of seeing him and pleading poverty as the reason he was leaving, plus the fact he wasn't being given a free hand. Banting thawed, but just a little.[44]

For all his human frailties, and they were many, Banting had the capacity for making people want him to think well of them. Demanding of himself and others, but notoriously modest and self-effacing, Banting had tremendous influence. In the NRC files there is much amusing correspondence from groups and individuals courting Banting's attention, much of it on matters as mundane as poison ivy at Camp Borden. Mackenzie noted that Banting was a "very great influence, not only in medical aviation but through the Research Council, and as a man. Throughout the country, it was a quiet support, but it was very intense, and vigorous, and personal support. And a great help to me."[45]

There were cocktails on Duncan's last day and Banting turned up. There he got chatting with an air commodore responsible for ferrying bombers across the Atlantic from Newfoundland to England. Banting asked if he could hitch a lift. No problem. Banting had been pestering Mackenzie for weeks about going over to Britain to check on scientific developments, and now he had got his way. Space on a plane became available in February.[46]

In the ensuing weeks, rather than being happy, Banting fretted. He had no real excuse for going over. He wanted to do so for the same kind of reason that prompted him to rejoin the army, to put on a uniform. He didn't want to be a scientist safe at home. He dreamed of being in the front line, serving the troops as he did in the previous war. "When I get there, if I ever do, I feel I will not want to come back. I will not want to leave. My heart is there where Democracy with all its faults stands where brave men defend the Empire."

There is much reflection on death in his diary at this time. His mood became so sombre that it worried Sadie Gairns, his secretary of sixteen years. He had never been like this before a trip. She suspected he had a premonition.[47] She would have been frightened by his diary entry the day he said goodbye to her, and to his 11-year-old son.

> I also told him of the danger but it was one's duty. He became quite serious and in a funny way said words to the effect that I could live as long in cold water as any person. And I promised I would do my best to give good account of myself. He wanted me to bring him back a bomb fragment.
>
> When the conversation was finished, he did not seem to want to leave. When he was ready (and) he was going down the stairs, he called back, "Goodbye, dad." He took a long time to get his coat on and his final farewell was, "See you later."

Banting had a day's stopover in Montreal before heading east, and took the opportunity to visit with his old insulin discovery rival, James Collip. They talked for two and a half hours and when it was time to go, Collip drove Banting to the station. As he got out of the car, a gust of February cold reminded Banting that he had no gloves.

"Here. Take mine." Collip stripped his own from his hands and gave them to Banting.[48]

As his train hammered through the frozen night, Banting stared out the window long and hard at the blackness beyond his own reflection. He wrote:

> Time please fly
> Be fast in speeding past
> For tomorrow holds fate
> Life, experience, or doom
> risk is high
> but duty must be done
> Life & honor or blackout
> where all ceases;
> Whatever comes
> I can take it.

C·H·A·P·T·E·R
T·H·R·E·E

Z, You're Dead!

Had the Germans been able to decipher the secret messages exchanged between Canada's military headquarters in London and Ottawa, they would surely have been puzzled by the following:

March 12, 1941

Canmilitary to Defensor

One hundred bullfrogs urgently required at physiological dept. of Chemical Defence Research Experimental Station, Porton. Not obtainable in England. Understand they can be supplied by National Research Council or by extra mural laboratories at McGill, Toronto, etc. To ensure arrival in England alive they should be sent clipper. Request early advice on arrangements.[1]

The Canadian authorities were mildly amazed, particularly by the assumption that bullfrogs, much less ordinary frogs, were common as rats in Canadian laboratories. But war was war and you asked no questions. An urgent search was begun for bullfrogs.

In a little-known breach of the U.S. Neutrality Act which forbade the Americans from supplying war materials to belligerents, 144 bullfrogs were purchased in the United States for $150 and rushed to the NRC in Ottawa. There they waited while the military authorities argued about how to send them so they would arrive alive:

"We received a message in cypher re. bullfrogs, suggesting we send them by clipper but afraid that possible delay between Lisbon and U.K. might cause frogs to die en route. . . ." And further, "It is of utmost importance that we obtain early decision on these bullfrogs. They have been received at the National Research Council and we have already had a few casualties." Eventually, they were successfully dispatched to Britain by air direct from Newfoundland.[2]

The frogs were wanted by Porton for mustard gas experiments, someone there thinking they would be particularly suitable because they are naturally hairless.[3] It was a bit of foolish whimsy but the British certainly could not fault the alacrity with which the Canadians tried to help when it came to chemical warfare research. They might make good junior partners and, with the overrunning of France by Germany in 1940, the British perceived a real role for Canada. Porton only had seven thousand acres on the edge of the Salisbury plain for open-air tests with chemical weapons and had previously arranged with the French to do its large-scale trials at their chemical warfare proving ground in Algeria. That plan collapsed when France was knocked out of the war. Might Canada be an appropriate alternative?

In October 1940 the superintendent of experiments at Porton arrived in Ottawa with an unusual request. Would it be possible, E. Ll. Davies asked, to find in Canada a space about fifty miles long by fifty wide where both countries could do chemical warfare experiments? He put the question first to Otto Maass, who immediately steered him to Mackenzie. There had been talk around the NRC that summer about setting up an experimental station in the bush north of Lake Huron, but to Mackenzie the West was where you found the kind of space the British were talking about. He arranged that same afternoon for a survey of possible sites and in the week that followed the three men, plus Alison Flood, now Major Flood, worked out what would be required in terms of equipment and staff.[4]

The arrival of Davies was a godsend to Maass. Here, at last, was a chance for Canada to get cracking on chemical warfare. The British now really needed the Canadians. There would be no more talk of using Canadian talent for fill-in positions at Porton. While they awaited the results of the site survey, Maass took Davies on a tour of the labs where chemical warfare work was under way. It included a visit to Toronto where Davies looked at Wright's efforts to find new poison gases, and to the Banting Institute to see animal experiments on the effects of mustard gas and other toxic products. Davies was effusive in his praise, saying that the British "had no idea of the quality or quantity of work done here."[5] The two men then headed off to the United States to look at what the Americans were doing at Edgewood Arsenal, the army proving grounds in Maryland.

At Edgewood, Davies and Maass were not impressed. Because the United States had not yet entered the war, the Americans treated their visitors with the deference of amateurs to professionals, giving demonstration firings of their gas mortars and laying out their new flame-throwers, gas masks and smoke generators for inspection. Davies was critical of what he considered the primitive state of mustard gas spraying techniques. American aircraft could not hit ground targets above 4,000 feet, and as they used pure mustard without thickeners, the droplets were too small by the time they reached the ground to do any harm. Davies bragged that at Porton they were able accurately to dose an area a mile in diameter from 15,000 feet.[6]

The Americans were not without some novel ideas of their own, however. They had done tests on spraying a mixture of mustard and solvent from nozzles in the back of bombers, with the idea of dissolving the plastic windows of pursuing fighters and gassing the pilots. They had also developed a solution of liquid mustard that could be sprayed on dirt roads so that drivers of enemy trucks would be blinded by the dust of their own vehicles. Nevertheless, the American effort was still small enough to be treated with condescension and Maass invited his hosts to send representatives to look at the work being done in Canada. The visit to Edgewood was a gratifying experience for the Canadian and British egos.[7]

It was a strange time, that fall of 1940. With Hitler in control of most of Europe, things looked pretty bleak for the British, but promising for chemical warfare. Gas was one of the few effective weapons left to Britain should the Germans launch an invasion across the Channel. The British Expeditionary Force had left most of its guns and equipment on the beaches of France at Dunkirk.

Overriding some modest army reluctance to use gas in defiance of the 1925 Geneva Protocol, Churchill ordered the army and air force to be prepared to use gas, particularly mustard, should the Germans land on England's south coast. An appropriate array of bombers were fitted with spray tanks and put on standby. Churchill also ordered that production of chemical weapons be stepped up with utmost urgency.[8] Fortunately, the chief of the German Air Force, Hermann Goering, assured Hitler that Britain could be brought to her knees through air power only. That fall British fighters and German bombers battled it out in the skies over southern England while the invasion barges waited at their berths along the coast of France.

It was just as well. Despite all the prewar concern about chemical warfare, the stockpile of weapons was pitifully small. An angry Churchill discovered that he had only about 450 tons of mustard gas on hand, and maybe 50 tons of phosgene. This might last three days. Then the Germans would have had licence to retaliate freely, with stocks of gas estimated at four times British reserves.[9] It was in this context that Davies returned to Britain with the assurance that the Canadians would co-operate in every way they could.

Davies and a few selected personnel from Porton returned to Canada early in the new year and by March were on a train drumming across Canada to Medicine Hat, Alberta. A short distance from town they found a meagre shamble of buildings called Suffield and from there they could survey their vast, new promised land. Miles and miles of frozen prairie and rolling hills stretched before them, interrupted by the occasional speck of a barn. The Canadians had set aside a thousand square miles of semi-arid grassland in an area known as the Palliser Triangle. Here the farms were marginal and the land dry. Rabbits and wild horses fared better than agriculture, as did the geese and ducks in their tens of thousands that flooded down to the shallow sloughs and ponds during the fall and spring migrations. It was an outdoorsman's paradise.

Work started immediately. Ironically, for an establishment whose primary task was experimenting with poison gas, it was found that directly underneath the site chosen for the buildings was a vast pool of natural gas. A pipe sunk only a few hundred feet into the ground was able to supply unlimited fuel for heating. As winter yielded to spring, barracks, labs and offices sprang from the ground.

Experimental Station Suffield didn't get formal approval until August 26, 1941. In mid-summer Maass complained to

Davies about the "struggle," hinting that he should try to put on "a bit of a show" as soon as possible.[10] The problem was that only now, after two years of war, were the politicians finally trying to give shape and substance to a chemical warfare research program which the National Research Council had been running on a shoestring.

The Privy Council order, when it finally came down, called for two establishments. One was to be the huge tract of land near Medicine Hat which was to be jointly operated by Britain and Canada for field trials and the study of the offensive aspects of chemical warfare. The other, the Chemical Warfare Laboratories, was to absorb the existing work being done in Ottawa at the NRC and concentrate on lab work and defence. A Chemical Warfare Inter-Service Board would advise on policy and programs, and a newly formed Directorate of Chemical Warfare would look after day-to-day administrative liaison.[11]

The seeds of later problems were in this arrangement. By splitting responsibility equally between Canada and Britain, and then appointing Davies as the first chief superintendent, Suffield became, in effect, a direct extension of Porton through the British Ministry of Supply. The Directorate of Chemical Warfare exercised only nominal control through the provision of equipment and services and co-ordination with the Canadian military. For a while, this did not matter much, especially as the Canadians tended to defer to the broader experience of the British.

Wright of the University of Toronto supplied the materials for Suffield's first field experiment. He was one of the chemists Maass approached in 1939 to work on poison gases and had quickly zeroed in on metallic cadmium as a source of toxic smokes. After mixing it with various explosives, he was able to report that cadmium held promise as a "dual-purpose munition which will act as a surprise weapon." The toxic fume was odourless, had the appearance of ordinary smoke and its injurious effect (fibrosis of the lungs) was not obvious until after about 24 hours. Enemy troops would think they were being shelled by ordinary high explosive, Wright reasoned, and wouldn't put on gas masks until too late. In May 1941 Suffield test-fired cadmium mixed with the new super-explosive, RDX, in 25-pounder and 4.5-inch shells with rats in cages at 100 and 300 yards.[12]

Being first at Suffield was no small coup for Wright. Of all the Canadian scientists who did chemical warfare research, he was the most aggressively ambitious, juggling a wide variety of projects simultaneously. He was notorious for the appalling way he drove his graduate students, and for his sharp tongue in dealing even with his tenured colleagues. Most of his work later in the war focused on new explosives and it was not unusual for Wright's graduate students to be seen blithely decanting explosive compounds on the grass beside the chemistry building while they smoked and chatted. Amazingly, there were few accidents, although on one occasion passers-by were startled when the window of one of Wright's labs blew out. On another, flames flared above the roof from a flash fire in an elevator shaft. No one was hurt.[13]

Cadmium was probably first used at Suffield because the standard war gases were not yet available in quantity. There were no facilities in Canada to make them. Even mustard gas was made only in laboratory amounts with chemicals supplied at cost by Union Carbide.[14] The British were requested to send over what they could spare and the first shipment, mostly of mustard and phosgene loaded in shells, arrived in late July. The entire staff of the station, after suitable gas mask drill, pitched in to manhandle the munitions to a temporary toxic stores dump. Even though few buildings were up, Suffield was now ready for business.[15]

Maass also asked the Chemical Warfare Service in the still neutral United States if it could spare 200 pounds of chloropicrin, a standard war gas that is also commercially made as a fumigant and soil insecticide. That was in August 1941, and Maass received a polite suggestion that he procure his own supplies. It is testimony to the deteriorating relations between the United States and Japan that two months later, under order of the U.S. Secretary of War himself, the Americans sent Suffield 300 gallons of assorted mustard gases as well as the chloropicrin.[16]

The U.S. attitude changed because the country had begun to gear up for gas warfare. Britain was taking a beating from Germany on almost all fronts and Japan was making belligerent noises in the Pacific. It seemed inevitable that the United States would enter the war and in November, when Suffield senior staff did a mini-tour of the major U.S. universities, they found chemical warfare research well under way. At Chicago, Ohio State and at the Rockefeller Institute, scientists were studying ways of detecting the various war gases, Harvard was working on how to make them, and Penn State was trying to come up with new war gases based on fluorine.[17] The latter is especially interesting because it was parallel to a similar – and more successful – investigation by a team of young scientists at McGill University in Montreal.

In many ways, the fluorine line of inquiry was obvious. The very first gas used with deadly effect by the Germans in the First World War had been chlorine. Fluorine was a related but much more active element. It is used industrially, and by hobbyists, to etch glass, and it burns the skin on contact. In fact, it reacts so readily with most metals and other materials that it is expensive and difficult – and dangerous – to handle. Otherwise it would have been an excellent war gas.

Chemists during the First World War soon found they could improve upon pure chlorine by combining it with other elements to make phosgene, a choking gas that damaged the lungs more efficiently. By 1939 phosgene had become the king of the so-called attack gases, and throughout the Second World War canisters, bombs and shells filled with phosgene occupied immediate second place to mustard gas weapons in the chemical arsenals of the Allies. It seemed to follow, then, that the more active fluorine should make an even more deadly compound.

While Maass remained titular head of the chemistry department at McGill throughout the war, he was back and forth to Ottawa so much on other duties that he left a young chemist named Bob McIntosh in charge of his lab. Only in his mid-20s, McIntosh gathered around him a group of even younger graduate students and they set to work. In 1988, retired after a long career at Queen's University, McIntosh remembered: "We were simply trying to repeat work that might have been done by a German chemist by the name of Ruff. Otto Ruff. And, of course, our 'Intelligence' – if you want to put that in quotation marks – had told us that Ruff was working for the German chemical warfare. Therefore it became of some consequence to try to do the sort of work that he would be doing."[18]

McIntosh assigned two young graduate students to the problem, Richard Mungen and Templeton Hugill, and they began by burning various elements in fluorine gas. For the most part, the compounds produced were predictable, but on one occasion a gas that they knew to be innocuous failed a routine test for toxicity.

"When we tested the first samples we had on mice – which we got from Collip and his associates – the damn things just laid down and died. We knew that the compound we were making wasn't toxic, so there must be something else in there. And it was a pretty good piece of work to isolate what was doing it."[19]

What was "doing it" became known as Compound Z, or Compound 1120 to the Americans. It was three to four times more poisonous than phosgene and the only new lethal gas of any consequence discovered by the Allies during the Second World War. It was the object of intense study in Canada and the United States, and as a non-persistent attack gas it was only rivalled after the war by the German nerve gases. The Chemical Warfare Labs in Ottawa undertook to build a pilot plant to mass-produce it and Suffield gave it top priority for field trials. By 1944 Compound Z was cited in secret correspondence as one of Canada's most significant contributions to chemical warfare.[20]

Z also has been one of the war's best kept secrets. After forty-eight years, this is the first published description of its existence. When the McGill breakthrough was reported to Ottawa, orders went out that exceptional security precautions were to be enforced in Canada and in Britain. "Actual formula and scientific title for Z will not be used in any documents whatsoever," it intoned.[21] The power of that order was such that even now, some of those who knew of Z during the war still automatically lower their voices when they speak of it.

The discovery caused excited debate in Ottawa, particularly at meetings of the Chemical Warfare Inter-Service Board. Chaired by the Director of Chemical Warfare, to which post Maass was named at the beginning of 1942, it included his immediate deputies, Flood of the Chemical Warfare Labs and Davies of Suffield. The armed forces were also represented and the NRC by its new head of chemistry, E.W.R. Steacie.

On November 7 discussion turned on whether the Germans knew about Z or not. Maass suggested that some papers Ruff published just before the war were a deliberate attempt to throw the Allied chemists off the trail. Steacie, formerly Maass's deputy at McGill, argued that Ruff was "brilliant but erratic" and could have easily overlooked the "practical toxicity" of the fluorine compounds. Both men could speak with some authority about Ruff because both had studied chemistry in Germany and knew the German scientists at first hand.[22] In those days, a scientific war could be fought on a very personal basis.

Z put Canada on the chemical warfare map. It appeared to be the perfect attack gas because it was colourless, and therefore invisible, and heavier than air, so it would hug the ground. As far as anyone knew without actually risking death, it was odourless. This was important because all other war gases had characteristic odours which usually warned of their presence in time for a gas mask to be put on. Z was so toxic that no one knew whether it smelled or not because it was believed one whiff would kill.[23] The Americans at Edgewood threw themselves into the study of the new compound with characteristic energy, although the British appeared to hang back. Throughout the war, they were often reluctant to pursue vigorously the technical or scientific discoveries of their allied colleagues.

Despite its promise, Z was a long way from being a practical weapon. As an impurity in the production of an innocuous compound, ways had to be found to increase the percentage of it produced, and to separate and purify it. It was also expensive, costing $2.25 a pound versus 9 cents a pound for mustard. The McGill chemists and those in Ottawa worked at the problems. McIntosh became so concerned about security that he barred cleaning staff from the McGill lab and for two years the young scientists there worked in accumulated squalor.

In 1940 Fred Lossing arrived at McGill from the University of Western Ontario to do graduate studies and work on Z.

I was shocked by the primitive conditions of the laboratories. God, you can't believe the filthy, understaffed, undercleaned mess. It was a disgusting place. At Western I'd been used to good labs, but not such good chemists. At least, the labs there were clean and we had all the necessary fittings.

But in Room 401 at McGill, which we were supposed to inhabit, there was DC electricity, no AC electricity, no hot water, no steam line, no compressed air. There was one terribly backward little fume hood which had no suction on it.

The guy that was supposed to be in charge, and I guess he was in charge, was Otto Maass. During the two years I was there I met Otto once and smelled his cigar twice. That was the limit of his participation, as far as I know, in our lab work. Bob [McIntosh] did the whole thing.[24]

In the meantime, the Allies continued to rely on that old standby – phosgene. In September 1940, probably in response to Churchill's urgent demand for the production of more poison gas, the British Ministry of Supply asked if it could build a phosgene plant in Canada. Windsor was the suggested location because chlorine was readily available from the chemical company, Canadian Industries Limited. Not only did Canada oblige, but it took over the project in the following December.[25]

Canada's first poison gas factory was built on two and a half acres that included land owned by the Mullen Coal Company between Euclid Street and the Detroit River in Windsor. It was right next door to the CIL plant. Mullen somewhat unpatriotically resisted the expropriation but finally gave way when it was promised first option to buy the land back after the war.[26] Work on the plant proceeded slowly, so production of phosgene did not start until late 1942.

Looking back over forty years, it is important to remember that in late 1940 Canada, like Britain, felt threatened by Germany. With France gone, the government had to consider the country's position if Britain were defeated. It would mean a triumphant German Navy cruising the sea off Nova Scotia with the real possiblity of attack on Canadian shores. In August, at Franklin D. Roosevelt's invitation, Mackenzie King met the U.S. president at the border town of Ogdensburg, where they concluded what was essentially a North America mutual defence pact. Then, on December 7, 1941, Japanese bombers smashed the U.S. Pacific Fleet at Pearl Harbor in Hawaii. Canada now had two major enemies, one for each coast.

A month after the Japanese attack, the Canadian Chemical Warfare Inter-Service Board proposed that Canada start manufacturing mustard gas as well as phosgene so that it would be "in a position to retaliate."[27] Up until then, most of the mustard gas in Canada had been imported in relatively small quantities from the United States or Britain. Now the U.S. Chemical Warfare Service offered to lend Canada substantial stocks of mustard gas to tide it over during the emergency. In June the War Cabinet also ruled that Canadian poison gas production should only be for Canada's own use.

CIL began construction of the mustard gas plants in Cornwall in the spring of 1942 with the help of equipment from both the United States and Britain. Two plants were to be built, one producing HT, the high-quality mustard gas favoured by the British, and the other HS, the more unstable but easily made mustard gas that the Americans liked. It was hoped to have the HS plant running at about 100 tons a week by that summer, and the HT plant operational the following spring. On-site facilities were to be built for loading the mustard into shells and bombs.

While Roosevelt and Churchill were publicly proclaiming that the Allies would retaliate with gas should the Germans or Japanese use it on Russia or China, Maass calculated Canada's needs. The aim, he decided in a memo of June 3, 1942, was to have 10,000 tons of mustard on hand by the following March, plus 1,000 tons of phosgene and 2,000 tons of Lewisite. Canada couldn't possibly produce that kind of tonnage, so it was proposed to buy it from the United States. Both the Americans and the British also suggested the creation of a kind of "Allied Reserve," but the War Cabinet ruled that Canada's needs must come first. Maass then suggested that the Americans should store much of their gas at Suffield as a "strategic" depot for the defence of the West Coast.[28]

In the end, the United States sent Canada about 3,000 tons of mustard and 750 tons of phosgene. The Windsor plant was to supply 250 tons of the latter and it took almost to the end of the war to do so, and not without incident. As the gas was made it was loaded into reusable chlorine cylinders and shipped by rail to Suffield for bulk storage. The same numbered cylinders were used repeatedly and careful track was kept. Toward the end of the war, two were found to be missing and a frantic search was launched to find them. They were never located and it was concluded – somewhat optimistically perhaps – that there had been an error in paperwork.[29]

Suffield, however, was the real beneficiary of all this attention to poison gas. The Cabinet War Committee approved $500,000 for the setting up of a chemical warfare training centre and 300 of the new Ronson flame-throwers were earmarked for the station. Bulk storage tanks for "lethal CW agents as an operational reserve for Pacific Command" were ordered built to replace the open-air toxic stores dump, which had narrowly missed disaster the previous summer when one of the station's

Lysander aircraft crashed 100 yards away. Best of all, there was a "great increase in experimental and test programs, due in part to the special interest of General McNaughton."[30]

Davies, the Suffield chief superintendent, rose well to the situation, finally putting on the "big show" Maass had asked of him. He scraped together 95 tons of phosgene in 280 oil drums with a stick of dynamite in each. Then he fired the whole thing off in one big bang, ostensibly to test a fear expressed by McNaughton that current gas masks could not outlast a really big cloud. The one Davies created rolled over the prairie for seventeen miles. Everyone was impressed, including C.J. Mackenzie to whom Maass reported the experiment over lunch. In his diary Mackenzie wrote:

> For the first time, as far as the united nations are concerned at any rate, a field test was made using over 100 tons of phosgene in one place. . . . The Suffield test showed that at one-half mile the dispersion was so great that the ordinary gas masks were not appreciably affected and that there was no danger. The Americans co-operated, gave gas, sent a large delegation up. There were officers from the Air Force, Navy and Army from the Atlantic and Pacific coasts and altogether it was a remarkable show. Probably the most expensive experiment ever performed in Canada – probably $200,000 spent in something like a couple of hours but the results are well worth it. They are going to continue the experiments and do the same thing with mustard.[31]

Maass could be proud. It was due mainly to his energy that Canadian chemical warfare research in 1942 had been brought to the point that Canada could rightfully sit in on the scientific and strategic planning of the much more powerful Britain and United States. It was Maass who had guided the early work at the universities, and who had orchestrated the grants from the War Technical and Scientific Development Committee. He had also championed the Chemical Warfare Labs and Suffield. Consequently, when the Americans entered the war, plunging in with their characteristic all-or-nothing abandon, they found their northern neighbour to have a sophistication in chemical warfare out of proportion to its small size. The Americans were genuinely impressed and the co-operation in military science that resulted has persisted for more than four decades.

Mackenzie noted in his diary that "Maass, strange as it may seem, is becoming not only the scientific but the operational executive in chemical warfare."[32] There were suggestions that he be "put into uniform" but Maass stubbornly clung to his civilian status. That summer Maass's staff at the Directorate of Chemical Warfare was enlarged to twelve, with uniformed officers from the three services being assigned to it. His job was now defined as being the adviser to all three services on chemical warfare matters, short of issues of high policy. Even that was no limitation because Maass had so many contacts that he could get his ideas fielded at the Chiefs of Staff level or even before the Cabinet War Committee. If there was a dark spot at all in his success, it was the fact that he drank often and heavily. Maass was an alcoholic.

It was the enormous energy of the man people most admired, no matter what they thought of his weakness for alcohol. His appetite for chemical warfare matters was enormous and the files show he was constantly on the move between Canada, the United States and Britain to wave the flag and check progress. Though his home remained in Montreal, he spent more time in Ottawa at his office in the army's great wooden headquarters building opposite the Lord Elgin Hotel, or at the Chemical Warfare Labs at the NRC. He remained head of chemistry at McGill, but for that he had little time to spare.

He was also a man of considerable personal courage. After the war, Alison Flood told how Maass would insist on volunteering for dangerous experiments if he happened upon them:

"On at least one occasion I very nearly lost my job because I insisted an experiment be stopped, as he was exposing himself to a dangerous amount of gas, exceeding by a large factor what was considered an endurable limit.

"I can see him quite clearly. A Buddha-like figure, sitting stolidly with Germanic immovability, gradually turning purple, as though by sheer force of will he could throw off such minor hazards as gas."[33]

Many of the scientists working on chemical warfare were in their twenties, some of them his former students, and the much older Maass liked to cast himself in the role of "hardened old sinner." He played poker with them after work, and his favourite expression was a quotation from the eighteenth-century satirist, Jonathan Swift: "Many have suffered death rather than eat their eggs from the smaller end."[34] He was also fond of chess, and could play it well, drunk or sober, with or without a board. It was sometimes disconcerting for visitors to the NRC to see Maass and Flood eating their lunches in silence across an empty table, then to hear one of them mutter, "Pawn to King five" and the other answer, "Knight to Bishop three."

Maass was also fortunate in that he had excellent deputies, particularly Flood in charge of the Chemical Warfare Labs. This unit consisted of the laboratories in the NRC building at 100 Sussex Street, and the so-called container proofing facility in the disused lumber mill next door. Dubbed the John Street Annex, it was used to test the charcoal filters of gas masks which by then were being assembled in Canada. It was sometimes dangerous work.

"To impress on me the hazard of hydrocyanic acid, they took a goat which they said weighed 150 pounds and they took an eyedropper and they put a drop in the eye of the goat," recalled Dr. Richard Tomlinson, in 1988 one of Canada's senior nuclear scientists but then a fresh-faced young lieutenant. "In 15 seconds the goat was bellowing, in 30 seconds it was lying on the floor and kicking, and in 45 seconds it had expired. And the message I was given was that the eye, of course, absorbed the thing very quickly, but if six square inches of your skin got covered, you were out of luck. The jig was up."[35]

Working on gas masks may seem like a prosaic task, but for the scientists involved it was exciting. From intelligence reports, and their own imaginations, they tried to anticipate what new gases the Germans might be working on, and devise means of protection. It was like a chess game in which you could not see your opponent's actual moves.

After Banting and Rabinowitch returned from Britain in 1940, a regular exchange program was set up between Porton and the Canadian chemical warfare scientists. One of the first to go over was Dr. Tom King, who later was put in charge of Canada's gas mask production. At Porton, a regular job was to read prisoner-of-war reports, and those from intelligence agents landed in Occupied France.

"These French chaps would go over at nighttime during the darkness, go across the Channel," King recalled. "And they'd come and tell the British forces that they're moving a train from A to B with such and such in it, and B was a chemical production plant. Another train from C to B and it was for some other chemical. Put two and two together, and we tried to see what we could make of it."

The chemical ingredients added up, King and the Porton scientists believed, to a German attempt to stockpile the cyanogen gases. This was alarming because the gas masks of the Allies offered no protection and the hunt was on for a chemical that could be combined with charcoal to neutralize the new gas. Canadian and American scientists worked together on the problem, finally solving it.

"We came out with another process," King explained. "A chromium treatment that killed off the cyanogen gases. And the Jerries never found out. They knew what we had in there. They knew it was chromium, but they never found out how it was done."

King remained convinced long after the war that the failure of the Germans to develop protection against the cyanogen gases was the reason they never resorted to chemical warfare. There are many such theories, but even though the Germans had already developed the much more toxic nerve gases, there may be something to his theory. An attacker with a gas for which only he has protection has a powerful advantage. And while the cyanogen gases were not as deadly as the nerve gases, they still could kill.

And so it went. The entry of Japan and the United States into the war galvanized Canada's chemical warfare effort. One way or another, through Supply Minister C.D. Howe or the largesse of the British, after mid-1942 there was never any shortage of cash to pursue a chemical warfare idea. While Suffield's field trial program expanded to a broad range of weapons from all three Allies, the Chemical Warfare Labs undertook to develop all kinds of gas-proof equipment – masks, goggles, capes, ointments – both for the Canadian forces and other Commonwealth allies.

"Geez, Tom, do you know why I'm here? All hell's broken loose. I've been flown over here. The containers are all faulty. They're being destroyed."

The speaker was a Canadian officer who had flown back from Britain and had burst in on King at the Chemical Warfare Labs to tell him that thousands of gas mask containers produced at the John Street factory were being dumped into the North Sea. Apparently they tended to burst apart when roughly handled. As they were supposed to be interchangeable on British and

American gas masks, Canada's allies took no chances and simply threw them away.

The Canadian scientists had much to learn about quality control. At about the same time the South Africans sent 50,000 tins of Canadian-made anti-gas ointment to the bottom of the South Atlantic. This caused a real panic. The Canadians were afraid South Africa would do the same thing with the 200,000 gas masks it had bought. Canada grandly offered to replace the faulty ointment free of charge.[36]

Civilians living in a nuclear age can take comfort in the fact that if all-out war breaks out, death will be swift. They have no enthusiasm for gas masks. But in 1943 scientists like King envisaged their homes and neighbourhoods suddenly blanketed in grey clouds of phosgene or hydrogen cyanide. What happens then to the children in the playground, or wives at home nursing infants? The danger was greater in Britain, but Canada's coastal cities like Halifax were vulnerable, and with Japan's entry into the war so was Vancouver. The chemical warfare scientists tried to find the answers.

It would be an interesting footnote to history to know who dreamed up the Mickey Mouse mask. Gases like phosgene do not hurt when breathed; the fatal damage appears later. The problem, then, was how to persuade a squalling 4-year-old to tolerate the claustrophobia of a gas mask. The famous Walt Disney character was the answer. Similar ingenuity was used to devise protection for infants, and for other specialized problems.[37]

But this was war. The civilians came second to the troops and the wartime files overflow with memos, notes and diagrams dealing with military masks and equipment. Strangest of all is the research that went into providing for horses – goggles, gas-proof hoof covers, capes, masks, and so on. This was especially of concern in Germany.[38] After the war Hermann Goering, Hitler's deputy, told his Nuremberg inquisitors that the Germans hesitated to use gas against the Allies for a novel reason:

Q. We know you had Gas Blau (nerve gas) which would have stopped the Normandy invasion. Why didn't you use it?
A. The horses.
Q. What have horses to do with it?
A. Everything. A horse lies down in the shafts or between

the thills as soon as his breathing is restricted. We never have had a gas mask a horse would tolerate.

Q. What has that to do with Normandy?

A. We did not have enough gasoline to adequately supply the German Air Force and the Panzer Divisions, so we used horse transport in all operations. You must have known that the first thing we did in Poland, France, everywhere, was to seize the horses. All our material was horse-drawn. Had we used gas you would have retaliated and you would have instantly immobilized us.[39]

The Chemical Warfare Labs were not by any means confined to defensive projects. In the summer of 1942 they were actively pursuing their own line of research on Z, experimenting on a new blister gas which had been developed at Porton and Britain's Manchester University, and trying to develop new lethal gases, smokes and weapons. The Hand Fireworks Company reported it had made good progress in perfecting a device that would create a dense cloud of poisonous sulphur dioxide, while CIL politely declined to make 80,000 glass bombs filled with the same substance unless the Chemical Warfare Labs would take responsibility for their safe transportation. In view of the wildly dangerous nature of this weapon, the idea was dropped.[40]

One promising line of inquiry had embarrassing consequences. Hydrogen sulphide, or H_2S to give it its chemical formula, is familiar to many high-school students even today as "rotten egg" gas. Producing it is a common classroom experiment and most chemistry teachers mention that it is also quite poisonous. The reason no one ever gets hurt is that it is incredibly smelly even in trace amounts. One would be forced to stop breathing because of the stench long before it could cause any harm.

The chemists in Ottawa reasoned that if one replaced sulphur in H_2S with more active related elements on the periodic table, one should get gases that were even more poisonous – and they did, except that the new gases smelled even more fiercely. Unfortunately, if even minuscule amounts of these gases were breathed, they soon worked themselves out through the pores of the skin, making the individual smell as well. As a gesture of consideration to the people of Ottawa, the scientists and technicians working on these substances usually elected to take the late streetcars home. What their wives must have thought is not recorded.[41]

While Flood was one of Maass's key deputies, young Dr. McIntosh was another. Not only was he in charge of the Z research at McGill, but Maass made him responsible for monitoring work at all the universities. Everyone, including Wright at Toronto (probably to his chagrin) had to send regular reports in to him, and once a month a meeting of the university chemists was held in Ottawa to discuss progress.

In early 1943 much of the work at the universities dealt with the study of the characteristics of the various toxic compounds and ways to neutralize them, the study of activated charcoal – the main ingredient of gas masks – and the study of the physiological effects of the poison gases on animals. Almost every chemistry lab in the country had a shelf of deadly chemicals, although there were few accidents and none of them (as far as we know) serious. There were also some novel ideas being pursued, like the balloon being designed at McGill to pop in the presence of mustard vapour. Even the small Baptist college, McMaster in Hamilton, soon had new locks on the laboratory doors behind which Ron Graham and his students studied ways of detecting the poisoning of water reservoirs.[42]

Some of the work at McMaster was being done in cooperation with Fred Beamish's lab at the University of Toronto. Wright was all flash and panache in comparison to the gaunt and scholarly Beamish, and the work in his lab prosaic in comparison to the panoply of poisons and explosives being developed by his colleague. But Beamish had the best operation for chemical analysis in the country and was one of the Allies' leading producers of chemical detectors for toxic compounds, an essential function in chemical warfare defence. As fast as his team received the assignments, it produced papers and paints which changed colour in the presence of specific poison gases, the idea being to give early identification in a gas attack of the agent being used. Beamish's lab even developed a detector for the invisible and odourless Compound Z.[43]

At Royal Military College in Kingston, R.S. Brown worked on developing a mustard gas foam which would float on water for the defence of beaches. At Western University, C. Sivertz worked on methods of creating dense tear gas clouds. At the University of Alberta students walking across campus in mid-winter were treated to huge sheets of flame leaping up behind the chemistry building. This was E.H. Boomer testing flame-thrower fuels, the idea being to measure the length and shape of the snow that melted. Every chemistry department at every university had some kind of assignment.[44]

One of the biggest problems was getting competent graduate students. They were the navvies of research, and in chronic short supply. Sometimes they also fell short of expectation. Dr. C.C. Macklin, studying the effect of poison gases on the lungs of animals at Western, had some curious problems with one of his assistants. He wrote as follows to the man's former professor:

> Mr. X——— has shown a curious tendency to absent himself from the laboratory for considerable periods of time. Out of 15 working days he has lost time from 6. In all he has lost some 21 hours of time. Yesterday, Feb. 17th, he was away all day, and his landlady phonèd at 2.15 p.m. to say she thought he would not be down. He was reported to be heard "muttering" to himself in bed. I called to see him early in the evening and he seemed fairly rational, face a little flushed, tongue coated, eyes watery and bloodshot, flesh clammy. His landlady was greatly disturbed about him.
>
> This morning, Feb. 18th, she phoned again to say that he was still in bed. One of our practising physicians called to see him in the middle of the morning. However, he got up and appeared in the laboratory at about 11:15 looking fairly well, and went to work. He has been working ever since to the present, about 3 p.m.
>
> Last night he said he had the "flu" he thought. Today he blamed the condition on his teeth.
>
> He is said to be very irregular in his eating, living largely on pastry and cream puffs. . . .
>
> I have tried to get him into some social life. Last Saturday night I had him accompany me as my guest to our local Chamber Music Club, and he seemed to enjoy himself; but apparently the following night (Sunday) he was out until after 12 o'clock somewhere. . . .
>
> I am wondering if he showed these peculiarities while with you. . . .[45]

While leaders like Banting, Maass and Mackenzie were into their late forties or early fifties, many of those who did the frontline research were in their twenties. Ordinarily, they might have been in the army or navy, except that General McNaughton himself had publicly insisted that they could better serve their country in its laboratories. There was often risk in what they did, and they approached their work, and their lives, in much the same way as soldiers. Nowhere was this more evident than at McGill.

In 1988 Dr. Lossing was retired from the NRC and teaching part-time at Carleton University in Ottawa. He recalled his two years working on Compound Z as among the best of his life.

The first year I demonstrated to a class for which I was paid $750. My wife was living there as well. I was a married post-doc, you see, which was unusual. Many professors prophesied terrible doom but it worked out all right. My wife isn't afraid of anything.

We had a great time. We had a small apartment in Montreal and a rotten old car that ran sometimes – an old Chev, an old rattletrap. We lived out in the west end on Sherbrooke, near Trenholme Park. I used to drive to work. I used to climb the hill up University Avenue, then I could coast all the way down by turning off the motor halfway home.

For 25 cents you could go to the System Theatre which was downtown, at the corner of Sherbrooke and University. You could see a double feature, and maybe a triple feature, and take in sandwiches. A cheap lunch and entertainment when I should have been studying.

The building at McGill was secure after hours. There was guard and when he wasn't asleep he would stop you coming in if you didn't identify yourself. You had to sign in.

The lab itself was certainly marked No Admittance. Nobody got in that lab. One time one of the professors, Archie Ross, came in and he was shepherded out. Nobody was allowed in there except the people who were involved.

But if someone really wanted to get in there, he could have practically crawled in through the cracks in the floor. You never saw such a place . . . wooden floor, long boards, and when the sun shone through the window – which was seldom because it was so dirty – you could see mercury gleaming in the cracks in the floor. I'm sure if you spilled 100 cc of mercury on the top floor, 100 cc would come out in the basement. The building was saturated. Incredible. But, you know, you're young and in those days people didn't worry much about the bad smells and dangerous compounds.

Our whole group, I think including Maass, had the belief that (because of Z) we were way ahead of the Germans in gas warfare – which was not the case. They had nerve gases. So we were damn lucky we never tried to use this stuff. We would have got wiped out.

We had quite an esprit de corps there, you know. We were working with the most dangerous compound and we enjoyed the thrill. Morale was good. We weren't doing something that was just run of the mill.

It was a happy time. My wife and I look back with considerable pleasure.

She knew I was working with a war gas. She didn't know what it was. She didn't know any chemistry so it wouldn't have mattered if I had told her. But we did not tell our wives and girlfriends what the gas was.

In fact, though, one night we sneaked Jim's girl friend and Frances, my wife, and another who was Dick Mungen's girl into the lab. Unfortunately, we had been at our place drinking in the way we did in those days – which was to buy a gallon of wine and add a slug of 35 OP (overproof) Demerara rum to it. And we had got pretty frisky. . . .

Geez, when I recollect. . . . We drove down Sherbrooke Street zig-zagging side to side and parked at McGill. We browbeat the dragon at the desk to let us in. We took the girls up to this room, showed them where we worked. It was strictly illegal. Bob nearly had a haemorrhage when he heard about it.

At one stage there was considerable pressure put on for us to go into uniform but we didn't trust the compulsion that might follow. . . . We got together and discussed this and said, "Look, let's stay the way we are. We're quite happy with Bob. He doesn't try to get us to do anything we don't want to do. We're willing to go along with everything he's suggested so far. What's the problem?" And we stayed out of it.

We might have been ordered to do things that we didn't want to do, that we thought were dangerous. Ever try to convince a major up the line that something is dangerous? He's going to say, "Well, you're a soldier, man. Get in there and do it."

I remember toward the end of the project the people here in Ottawa at the gas mask plant wanted a sample of 100 grams. We had never made more than five at a time. So we worked shifts, and we got Jack Davis in (from another project), and we ran this thing 24 hours a day until we had 100 grams of this stuff.

And I was the guy who drew the short stick when it came to taking it up to Ottawa.

So – this has nothing to do with science – I blew a special glass container. I wanted to make sure so I made it myself, with a little tip on the end. And we condensed the stuff in that and packed it into a Dewar flask with dry ice – made a nice looking parcel of it.

And I got a ticket on the train to Ottawa. This thing sat beside me in the parlour car with white smoke coming out of it, and all these old guys were reading their Montreal Gazettes and looking. . . . (laughs) There was enough there to kill the whole train.

Anyway, the next morning I walked in very proudly with this sample and it was Stan Mason, I guess, who greeted me. I said, "Well, Stan, here's the sample." And I pulled this great bottle of the stuff out and Stan turned white as a sheet. "Whaat! Whaat!" (laughs)

And here's another funny thing. The night before I stayed in an old hotel on Market Square right behind Freedman's store. And I put this stuff in the bathroom and shut the door. It was early spring and I thought it would be cool in there.

I woke up in the middle of the night choking on something. I thought, "Jesus, Z's loose!" I rushed over and threw up the window. I put my head out and inhaled a whole lot of fresh air.

Then I realized they were working on the road right down below. They were melting tar.

I was pretty rattly by breakfast time, I can tell you.[46]

Lossing, of course, could have been killed. But his memories were not of fear. Instead, he told of young men larking in the lab, listening to Radio Berlin on short-wave radio, carrying drunken comrades home after a night on the town, playing pranks on one another. In early 1942 none was older than 26. It was much the same in Toronto, in Ottawa, or wherever. On the battlefield, in the air, or in the laboratory, it was still a young man's war.

C·H·A·P·T·E·R

F·O·U·R

Germs in Earnest

Banting crawled out of the downed bomber that freezing day in February 1941, and stood up, alone in a desolation of rock and stunted firs. Numbed and hurting from a head injury and a punctured lung, he would not have known that the pilot was still alive, and had gone for help. Inside, there had only been the silence of two dead crewmen, slumped in the wreckage. If Banting could think at all through the haze of injury, then it must have been to realize that his awful premonition of death was coming true. He staggered forward, the drift sucking at his flying boots, step by step. Then he fell, face down.

Something else, not just the living spirit of a determined man, faded in the cracking, sub-zero air. His ambitions, the dozens of research ideas that had tumbled through his brain, also slowed with the cold. And stopped. When the rescuers arrived, and gathered up his body, they found his precious notebooks. In his breast pocket was his daily diary, with his last bravely optimistic jottings about a flight finally to begin, and in the aircraft, the more formal notebook describing what he planned to do on arriving in England. On the last page there was a list of sixty-eight people he intended to see: Hankey, Rothschild, McNaughton, Sir Joseph Barcroft, Mellanby, A.V. Hill, Sir Henry Dale, Lord Beaverbrook, and so on. Not now. Not ever.

Banting's death, of course, was big news. Back at the NRC, Mackenzie first heard only that his plane was missing after leaving the airfield in Newfoundland. He immediately took the train to Toronto to break the news to Lady Banting. There Miss Gairns, Banting's secretary, spoke of his premonition. In all the years she had worked for him, this was the only time he had been worried, she said.[1] Mackenzie returned to Ottawa to news that wreckage had been spotted and there appeared to be a survivor. The next news was that it was not Banting; it was the pilot. At Porton, where Don Dewar was doing duty as the first Canadian scientist on chemical warfare exchange, the flurry of preparation for Banting's VIP visit suddenly evaporated. Dewar did not know why. Banting just failed to show. Much later, he found out why.

Elaborate ceremonies were held in Toronto a year later commemorating Banting, with Lady Banting swathed in black and appropriate euolgies from University of Toronto dignitaries from President Cody on down through the city's academic and social hierarchy. Mackenzie went, and Charlie Best was there, as were most of the staff and scientists from the Banting Institute and the faculty of medicine. Press coverage was heavy. Banting had had his wish. He had died on active duty for his country. Few knew, however, the nature of that duty.

If, through the muddy swirl of time and academic sniping there remains doubt about Banting's real contribution to Canadian science, in 1941 Mackenzie had none. Because almost everything Banting had been working on was a war project, there was only one forum where his most recent contributions were adequately appreciated, and that was the War Technical and Scientific Development Committee. Within days of Banting's death, at the meeting of February 25, Mackenzie told Bronfman, Duncan and the rest that "there was nothing which he could say which would adequately express the extent of loss Canada has suffered, particularly in relation to war research, through the death of Sir Frederick."

These were not idle words to flatter the men who were bankrolling the NRC's research. The money was already long committed and the tycoons could not have pulled back had they wanted to. It came straight from the heart. "When the time arrives," Mackenzie said, "to make known the details of Canada's war activities, it will be realized that Sir Frederick's work on insulin, great as it was, has been surpassed by the work which he has done since the outbreak of hostilities."[2]

One can imagine sage nods, perhaps, and a round of applause – a little short, to be sure, of the "honours" Banting had envisioned for his efforts but that was the price of secrecy. Only four copies of the minutes of the meeting were made. Mackenzie's little speech would have been lost except, amazingly, two survived.

After voting to send a message of condolences to Lady Banting (moved by Bouchard, seconded by Bronfman), the meeting carried on into debate about the financing of the various war research projects. By now the list was already formidable, ranging over radar, ballistics, explosives and poison gas, but there was nothing further to be said of the project that had most consumed Banting, bacteriological warfare.

The prospect of raining death from the sky, of sowing germ-laden sawdust from low-flying aircraft, appeared to have died in the snow of Newfoundland. Work in Canada on the weapon Banting feared could win the war for Germany abruptly stopped.

The mantle of M-1000 had fallen to Greey. At a meeting in May, Mackenzie urged the Toronto bacteriologist to take over the project and administer the $25,000 that had been allotted to it. Greey was reluctant, even though the only experiment since Banting's death had been a qualified success. In March Dr. Donald Fraser, head of the university's School of Hygiene and an associate professor at the Connaught Labs, reported that typhoid bacteria dried on sawdust – Banting's "sinker" – were capable of being restarted up to six months later. Unfortunately, the surviving bacteria seemed to lose their virulence. Greey told Mackenzie that he doubted it was practical to produce infectious bacteria on a large scale. He indicated they would continue trying.[3] They did not.

Fraser's work with sawdust and s. typhi murium – which causes salmonella poisoning – appears to be the first-ever attempt among English-speaking nations to cultivate a bacterial agent specifically for use against humans. At the time he started his experiment, late October or early November of 1940, the British at Porton had confined their bacteriological warfare efforts to defensive research, chiefly aimed at the mechanics of airborne infection and the way bacteria are spread. It was not until early 1941 that Porton began to study the weapon potential of germs, and even then this appears to have been aimed at livestock. The Americans, meanwhile, had done only theoretical studies and were over two years away from actual experiments.[4] As for the Germans, Russians and Italians, as far as we know they appear to have been doing very little. Only the Japanese, according to postwar interrogations, had by this time developed practical methods for breeding and spreading deadly diseases.

Greey's unwarranted pessimism is reflected in Fraser's handwritten report on the experiment which appears hastily, even sloppily put together, as though he had been asked to put something down in writing to prove he had actually done the work. Even if his results had been less promising than they were, one experiment would have been poor justification for dropping the program. Looking back nearly half a century, Dr. O.M. Solandt, in 1988 one of the few living contemporaries of Banting, Fraser and Greey, speculated that the two abandoned the bacterial warfare project on Banting's death because they had little faith in it in the first place. Banting, according to Solandt, was at "his worst in the eyes of scientists" just before the war. "He just had a whole series of screwball ideas. . . . "

"They [may have] dropped out quite happily for two reasons. One, the ordinary university bacteriological lab was totally unfitted to handle these things. It's lucky they never did get into production. They would have killed a lot of people. . . . The Connaught Lab, of course, was much different. It was much better. They had experience in sterility, in containing bacteria. I think that would explain why the thing dropped. I don't think anyone under Banting took fire, so to speak."[5]

Solandt may be right, but only partly. Banting's original plan had been to use the Connaught Labs as a major war-germ production facility and it is almost certain Fraser did his experiment there, probably at the farm facility where Craigie was already working on typhus. Greey, moreover, in his private correspondence shows that he admired Banting. The more likely answer is that they both got cold feet. Both were medical doctors who had taken oaths to preserve life, not take it. Banting rationalized himself out of this dilemma but they may have had more difficulty. Greey also was in the midst of experiments with the newly discovered sulpha drugs which were curing rather than killing. Fraser's mandate at the School of Hygiene was specifically preventative medicine. Both men undoubtedly felt a lot more comfortable working in the traditional areas of medicine.

And so, throughout the spring and summer of 1941, Canada's foray into bacteriological warfare languished. The records of the War Technical and Scientific Development Committee show that there was no further demand for M-1000 funds beyond the original $1,273 spent on the first experiments. Banting's idea of a germ weapon of retaliation which could spread death and despair to "millions of Huns" appeared dead. Not for long.

The year 1941 was a grim one for Britain. In May Canadians had thrilled to read of the Atlantic chase of the German pocket battleship *Bismarck*, but it was destroyed only after it had first sunk the pride of the Royal Navy, the giant battleship *Hood*, and mauled the brand-new *Prince of Wales*. Moreover, German U-boats roamed the ocean virtually at will, and the toll on merchant ships soared disastrously. In North Africa, General Archibald Wavell had massively defeated the numerically superior Italian army, but in March and April public elation plummetted when he in turn was thrown back to the very frontiers of Egypt by an obscure German general named Erwin Rommel, later to become famous as "The Desert Fox." And the German invasion of Russia in June, which at first seemed folly on Hitler's part, rolled across the steppes toward Moscow with apparently unquenchable fury.

Churchill's messages to Roosevelt in this period reflect his growing desperation. The president stepped up his under-the-table help to Britain with the Lend-Lease Act in March followed by covert arrangements between the navies of the two countries which saw U.S. warships taking reponsibility for protecting the vital convoys as far as Iceland, even though the United States was not yet at war.

The Americans, however, had their own special worries. Since the previous fall they had been regularly reading messages between the Japanese embassy in New York and the Foreign Office in Tokyo, having broken the Japanese diplomatic cipher in mid-1940. What was increasingly apparent from their eavesdropping was that Japan was a nation preparing to go to war, with the United States the number one enemy. As early as the spring of 1941 the Americans were reading the reports to Tokyo of spies in Seattle and Los Angeles, followed by specific requests to the Japanese consul in Honolulu in September to report on the deployment of the U.S. Pacific Fleet in Pearl Harbor. By that autumn there could have been no doubt in the minds of Roosevelt and his cabinet that the United States would soon be at war with Japan.[6]

It is in this context, of a nation hurtling toward armed conflict, that on October 1 the U.S. Secretary of War, Henry L. Stimson, sent the following letter to Frank B. Jewett, president of the U.S. National Academy of Sciences:

> Because of the dangers that might confront this country from potential enemies employing what may broadly be described as biological warfare, it seems advisable that investigations be initiated to survey the present situation and future possibilities. I am, therefore, asking you if you will undertake the appointment of an appropriate committee to survey all phases of this matter.[7]

This letter marks the beginning, both formal and actual, of the U.S. biological warfare program, which sped down an ever-widening highway of research and production to culminate in a veritable arsenal of bacteriological weapons by the end of the war.

Jewett immediately sub-let Stimson's request to Dr. Edwin B. Fred, former president of the Society of American Bacteriologists and a distinguished professor at the University of Wisconsin. He canvassed U.S. scientific circles for a blue-ribbon committee of experts in plant and animal diseases. Representativies from the U.S. Army's Chemical Warfare Service and from Naval Intelligence were also invited.

In Canada, meanwhile, someone less exalted than Stimson or Roosevelt was aware that the Japanese diplomatic code was broken. Mackenzie of the NRC was reading, and marvelling, at the exchanges between the Japanese in Washington and in Berlin, as well as at messages to Berlin from the German consulates in South America.[8] A year earlier, following a request from the British Admiralty for help in monitoring enemy transmissions, the NRC had set up facilities for intercepting German and Japanese radio signals. By the summer of 1941 the Canadians were systematically monitoring Axis transmissions and deciphering many of them.

It is hardly surprising, then, that in early November Collip, chairman of the Associate Committee on Medical Research since Banting's death, called a meeting of the apparently defunct M-1000 Committee. It was held at the NRC building on November 13 and was attended by most of the original committee members plus Mackenzie and Collip, and Otto Maass and Alison Flood from Chemical Warfare.

Mackenzie was the first to speak. He gave a brief recitation on how the project had begun, describing Banting's futile trip to England where "none of those in authority seemed at all concerned" and then how he had involved Colonel Ralston and how they had obtained research money from the War Technical and Scientific Development Committee. Greey was next, and he told how Banting had got him and Fraser started on trying to develop an "infectious agent" for aerial distribution but how the project foundered when they were unable maintain the virulence of dried typhoid bacteria.

Reed of Queen's chimed in to say that he had tried suspending typhoid bacteria in oil, and while the total number declined, they remained infectious. Then Professor Murray of McGill added that he still thought releasing rats infected with plague had promising possibilities, as did fleas, lice, ticks and mosquitoes. It was basically bold talk. Murray apparently had not done any research on the subject since the meetings with Banting the previous December.

It was left to the chemists, in particular Alison Flood who was now in army uniform, to make the most original suggestion. What about botulinus toxin?

Of all the poisons then known to man, one of the most deadly was familiar to all housewives who did their own canning and preserves. They knew it by a prosaic title. Food poisoning. It is caused by botulinus bacteria which are widely dispersed in the environment and are common in soil, on food, and in the very air we breathe. But it is only when they are closely confined in an airless environment that they become a hazard, multiplying surprisingly quickly. In a few days, improperly preserved food, particularly in sealed but faultily sterilized cans or jars, can become deadly. It is something that is forgotten today with our "cover-it" mentality and refrigerators everywhere, but almost everyone knew about it in the 1940s.

Like the penicillin mould, botulinus bacteria produce a substance that can be extracted. Unlike penicillin, with its life-saving properties, these bacteria produce a poison, a toxin, that can kill in trace amounts. As Flood told the meeting, the toxicity of botulinus, or tetanus for that matter, was greater than any chemical.

Maass and Flood proposed that work be done to produce a sufficient quantity of dried toxin to run field experiments. They wanted to see if it killed on contact, or by inhalation. They pointed out that a large experimental station was being built in western Canada to test chemical weapons, and it could easily accommodate bacterial warfare work. The others were doubtful. Something that killed when you ate it did not necessarily kill when you breathed it. Besides, as someone pointed out, field experiments might be dangerous unless there was an ample supply of anti-toxin on hand.

Most of the remainder of the meeting dealt with animal diseases, particularly rinderpest, a disease of cattle that was rampant in the Far East and in Africa but which was unknown in North America. There was no really effective vaccine against it, although it was thought the Germans may have developed one. Dr. Watson, of the Animal Disease Research Institute in Hull, suggested that its introduction into Canada by enemy agents would be "devastating."

The discussion then turned to anthrax, plague, typhoid and cholera. It was noted that experiments to determine whether anthrax was infectious by inhalation "would be useful," but it was plague that got the lion's share of the debate. All agreed that dropping large numbers of infected rats on enemy territory had possibilities, although it was Flood who again got down to practicalities. "Mice can be thrown out of an airplane without damage, but not rats," he said. But it would not take long, he added, for the new experimental station at Suffield to determine the optimum size of parachute necessary for releasing rats.

Possibly with visions of thousands of rats descending on Germany beneath miniature parachutes, the meeting turned to plans of action. Reed would do experiments on the killing power of botulinus toxin by inhalation, Fraser would see if the Connaught Labs could mass-produce it, Watson's animal disease colleague Charles Mitchell would study anthrax and Murray would check out plague. As a general recommendation it was decided that the NRC should formally set up a working committee on bacteriological warfare under the M-1000 label.[9]

Within three days Collip had sent a letter to Murray at McGill. Would he agree to be chairman of the newly reconstituted M-1000 Committee? Murray does not appear to have hesitated. On November 26, according to his own notes, he arrived in Ottawa to be steered by Collip to the deputy ministers of health and agriculture, then over to the Department of Defence where they were "pleased to know of M-1000 and were willing to inform Intelligence of it." He also stopped in at the office of the NRC secretary, S.P. Eagleson, and was informed he would now be allowed to see the secret M-1000 file. And did he need any money for immediate expenses? Murray was given $500. One of the first things he bought – for $70.20 – was a large steel safe.[10]

E.G.D. Murray was a good choice as the new head of Canada's fledgling biological warfare program. The 52-year-old bacteriologist cut a striking figure with a bristling mustache and beard that earned the nicknames Iron Whiskers or Electric Whiskers, from the soldiers and staff who knew him during the war. Later he was also known as E. Goddammit Murray from his habit of peevishly interrupting postgradute students stumbling through their oral examinations with: "Come on, hurry up, Goddamn it!" To his colleagues and intimate friends, however, he was known simply as Jo'burg, a reference to his Johannesburg birthplace.

Reed, the Queen's University bacteriologist, might have been a good choice, too, except that he was a keen and practical research scientist. He already had definite ideas he wanted to explore. Greey, on the other hand, had had his chance. The only other reasonable choice was Mitchell, the animal pathologist of the Department of Agriculture. He also was a biological warfare enthusiast but because he was late arriving at the November meeting he apparently did not make a deep impression on Collip or Mackenzie.

Murray had other qualifications as well. He had studied and then taught for ten years at Cambridge, a fact that was bound to be useful in dealing with the sometimes snobbish British, and he was the author of innumerable academic papers. He had also served as a medical officer during the First World War, first in Britain and then in the Middle East on special duty treating dysentery. There he not only saw first-hand how disease could play havoc with troops, but almost died of dysentery himself. He came to McGill in 1930.[11]

Murray held his first meeting as M-1000 chairman at the NRC the following day but it was a small affair. From the previous meeting there was only himself, Mitchell, Watson and Collip. It was held primarily to introduce three newcomers, all from the

Department of Agriculture, who were needed to round out the project's expertise. They were Dr. A.G. Lochhead, Dominion agricultural bacteriologist and a specialist on plant diseases, Dr. J.M. Swaine, director of science services, and Dr. A.E. Cameron, veterinary director general.

After explaining the origin of the project, Murray quickly steered the discussion to the question of rats and plague. Swaine said there would be no difficulty in breeding sufficient quantities of inflected fleas. As an outbreak of plague in ports like Vancouver or Halifax could seriously interfere with shipping, it was agreed that Canada might be wise to get estimates of the numbers of rats in these cities. It was also suggested that plague could be spread by wild animals.

The subject of enemy agents and fifth columnists came up. They could be used to spread rinderpest and foot and mouth in cattle, crop diseases or even get into a canning plant and contaminate food. In an echo of the great Tylenol scare four decades later, when the deliberate cyanide poisoning of a few capsules of a headache drug resulted in damage in the hundreds of millions to the U.S. pharmaceutical industry, it was observed that the danger was not in the number of people killed by booby-trapped food, but in the public doubt it would create in existing stocks, and in the cost of checking production for infection.

Murray also noted: "Dr. Watson and Dr. Mitchell mentioned an ex-worker in their laboratory who was of doubtful character though skillful and clever, and of foreign origin. This man is now preparing and selling 'biologicals' for veterinary use. Such persons could be ... a source of infective materials to less skilled enemy agents used as distributors." Dr. Cameron further suggested that all labs were in danger from "undesirable" employees and the group agreed to undertake a secret review of laboratory staffs. Later the Department of National Defence was asked to screen all lab employees.[12]

Murray's next move was to visit the U.S. National Research Council in Washington. There, on talking with Dr. Lewis H. Weed, chairman of the medical committee, he learned of the existence of a U.S. counterpart to M-1000, the group formed under the order of Stimson which had named itself the WBC Committee. The letters stood for Biological Warfare Committee but had been deliberately scrambled and the word "committee" tacked on again to disguise its purpose. Its mandate was exclusively study, Murray was told, and "it had not yet been directed to undertake experimental investigations."[13]

Murray could not have failed to be impressed by the Who's Who calibre of scientist the chairman, Dr. E.B. Fred, had assembled. The secretary was T.B. Turner of Johns Hopkins University in Baltimore, and the others were Thomas Rivers, director of the Rockefeller Hospital in New York City, Stanhope Bayne-Jones of Yale, J. Morgan Sherman of Cornell, William Hagan of the New York Veterinary College, Louis Kunkel of the Rockefeller Institute at Princeton, and William Hay Taliafero of the University of Chicago. Most were senior professors or deans. A high-powered group of scientific minds, indeed.

"I gathered," Murray wrote, "the committee had only recently been formed and that they had not had time to get very far. The opinion was expressed that they had not covered quite as many possibilities as M-1000 had." He was also told that the U.S. research council had gathered extensive files, but nothing so far received from Britain related directly to biological warfare. Murray did not know of anything in Canada from Britain either.

After phoning Dr. Fred and introducing himself as the chairman of a parallel biological warfare committee in Canada, and receiving an invitation to attend the WBC's meeting later that month, Murray took the long way home. He stopped at Baltimore to see Turner at the Johns Hopkins School of Hygiene, where "he showed me the specifications of an invention which had been referred to their committtee. It was a bullet designed for bacterial warfare. The case was filled with absorbent material to be charged with culture or spores and was perforated with numerous holes to secure infection." This was exactly what Banting had proposed in his memo to the British a year earlier.

On December 6 Murray dropped in on Rivers in New York and had an instructive discussion on the possibilities of spreading yellow fever by breeding and distributing its mosquito carrier, *aedes aegypti*. Then he headed home, brimming with enthusiasm. "All I spoke to welcomed closest cooperation with M-1000," he confided to the file.[14]

The next day, Japanese aircraft bombed Pearl Harbor. The United States was at war.

Like millions of Americans, Canadians and Britons, Professor Murray likely spent the next few days glued to the radio listening to reports of the U.S. Pacific Fleet in flames. Newpapers such as the *Toronto Daily Star* bannered headlines like "1,500 Killed in Honolulu Area: Declare War On Jap, FDR Asks Congress" and featured artists' renderings of Japanese aircraft carriers launching their planes. It was exciting and dramatic and it must have made Murray feel that he was as much involved in the war as any sailor on a U.S. warship, or British soldier defending Singapore.

Within the week, Murray was on his way down to Toronto, where he met Greey at the Banting Institute. They went over Banting's notes. Then the Toronto bacteriologist warned Murray that he was very busy right now and "might not be able to devote much time to M-1000." If Murray was disappointed he didn't record it, but he took the Banting files – except those personal notes that Greey withheld – and went directly down to Kingston to see Reed at Queen's.[15]

Reed was of a different stamp altogether to Greey. An inveterate chain smoker, an impatient, searching man, he was to prove one of the most ingenious of all the Allied scientists who worked on biological weapons during the war. He had a plan for Murray, which he had originally mentioned to Banting, that was positively diabolical in its simplicity. The first line of defence against bacterial warfare, he pointed out, was the chlorination of water supplies. What if one could coat dried organisms with some sort of nutrient gel? Then they would be resistant to chlorine, maybe even to boiling. Sprinkle them over an open reservoir in enemy territory, the people drink the water from the taps and . . . Presto!

Murray liked the idea. They worked out the cost, including work Reed was to do on the effects of botulinus toxin dispersed as a mist or a dust. It came to $800 for materials and supplies, $1,600 for two technicians. Murray promised to push through the grant application.[16]

Back in Ottawa, Murray now had time to read through the M-1000 file. There he found notes that Banting and McNaughton had both kept of their discussion about bacterial warfare in 1937, and Banting's first memo on the subject, plus the more elaborate outline he had given the British in 1940. He also found some unexpected gems put there by Maass and Mackenzie – reports from the Ottawa Experimental Farm in the summer of 1940 on the destruction of crops by plant hormones.

Plant hormones are a family of organic compounds that had recently been discovered and had been found to be extremely toxic to plants in very dilute amounts. The 1-naphthyl acetic acid used by N.H. Grace on his test plots of wheat, cabbage, sugar beet and potatoes – the principal crops of Germany – was the harbinger of herbicides such as 245T (apparently developed by Maass) which were later sprayed by the British on suspected guerilla crops in Malaya during the Communist insurgency of the early 1950s, and later by the Americans in their attempts to defoliate the jungles of Vietnam. Grace's tests were a success, reducing germination by as much as 85 per cent and giving rise to the conclusion that if sprayed from aircraft, the chemical "would seriously affect food supply."[17]

Murray also stumbled across the letter of a year earlier from Dr. M.V. Veldee of the U.S. Public Health Service which he had sent to Defries, the director of the Connaught Labs. In it he wrote that he was chairman of a committee studying bacterial warfare and he had heard "Canada had a similar committee." This was the letter that gave Banting such a scare because he could not figure out how the Americans had heard about his super-secret germ warfare go-ahead so quickly. There was nothing in the file to explain either that or what had become of the Veldee committee. The WBC group had apparently never heard of it.

As luck would have it, this very Dr. Veldee was due in Toronto within the week to attend a meeting of the Canadian Public Health Association. Murray buttonholed him. What was the story? The surprised visiting professor said his committee had made its report, all two pages of it, a year ago. They had recommended no action be taken. The actual report, which Murray subsequently obtained, said: "It is evidently the belief of this group, or committee, that the chief danger lies in irresponsible actions . . . and for that reason they recommend against elaborate consideration of this field in order that as few persons as possible have the possibilities suggested to them."[18] After his experiences with the British, had Banting been aware of this rather convoluted conclusion, he would have cringed.

When Veldee returned home, he told his superiors of Murray's query and in early January the latter was sent a copy of the letter that had started it all. It was from Dr. Vannevar Bush to Dr. Weed of the medical committee of the U.S. Council of National Defense. It is dated September 28, 1940, and is worth quoting.

Dear Dr. Weed,
The subject of so-called bacteriological warfare has been
brought to my attention and I have discussed it with General
Strong of the General Staff. . . . I feel it properly comes
within the range of your committee, and hence the suggestion that it be there considered. . . . I would assume that
there would be included a consideration of offensive and
defensive measures in the field of human, animal and plant
diseases. The primary attention without doubt will be found
to rest on possible sabotage by irresponsible individuals.[19]

In scientific circles in the United States, this was power talking.
President of the Carnegie Institute and a formidable scientist
and inventor, Bush clearly saw that the German conquest of
France in the spring of 1940 inevitably meant that the United
States would be drawn into the war. With that in mind, he persuaded President Roosevelt to allow him to set up the National
Defense Research Committee, a small group of the most important scientific leaders in the country – the crème de la crème –
charged with steering the nation's military research effort. It was
given independent funds and had the direct ear of the country's
top soldiers and politicians. Led by Bush, it included Frank
Jewett, Karl Compton and James Conant, president of Harvard,
and was to become instrumental in the massive research effort
that led to the development of the atomic bomb.

Bush's interest in bacteriological warfare in the fall of 1940
also seems to lead back to Canada. The NDRC was set up the
previous June, just as German panzers were finishing off France,
and was in place to receive the Tizard scientific mission that
September. On their way to Washington the British delegation
passed through Ottawa and picked up Mackenzie. It was the first
of several visits he made to Bush and his committee that fall and
he found "extra-ordinary pro-British sentiment in such quarters.
Scientifically and technically they are at war as much as we
are."[20] Mackenzie had been in Washington only a few days before
Bush sent his letter and must have mentioned that Banting had
got the go-ahead to explore germ warfare. That seems the only
explanation for Veldee knowing so quickly about the Canadian
involvement.[21]

The next meeting of M-1000 was held on December 19 and
Murray reported on the WBC Committee and his reception in the

United States. The group was then made to swear oaths of allegiance and of secrecy: "I do solemnly swear that I will be faithful and bear true allegiance to His Majesty King George the Sixth. . . . " There was some discussion about asking Defence to check out non-Canadians working in labs and biological supply houses, more suggestions regarding agents that might be used against humans, notably psittacosis and tularemia (rabbit fever) and the need to be somewhat circumspect when making written application for funds from the War Technical and Scientific Development Committee, now renamed the Sir Frederick Banting Fund. Reed then described his idea of coating bacteria and presented his grant application. When the meeting broke up, everyone had an assignment. Even Greey promised to look into the prospects of combining mustard gas with bacteria.[22]

On Christmas Day, having fought bitterly and bravely against the Japanese, the remnants of the two Canadian battalions at Hong Kong were overwhelmed. For the previous two weeks Canadians had followed reports of fierce fighting on the island as the desperate garrison was driven into two pockets and final, bloody surrender. The *Toronto Daily Star* interviewed the families of the thirty-two Toronto men known to have been in the battle, but about which there was no word. A few days later, on December 28, Murray and Reed were in Baltimore.

In a Washington archive somewhere, probably in a file box still marked secret, the minutes of the first formal U.S. meeting on biological warfare research may still exist. Or they may not. The subject was so secret, both during and after the war, that they may not have been taken, or they may have been destroyed. Up to now, certainly, they have escaped the notice of historians panning for treasure in the U.S. biological warfare documents so far declassified. But E.G.D. Murray to the rescue. In a cramped, tiny hand on ten foolscap pages he recorded the progress of the meeting in exquisite detail.

It convened at 10 a.m. in the Lord Baltimore Hotel. The Americans got right down to brass tacks. They were not there for academic debate, Dr. Fred told the assembled scientists and representatives of the army and navy. Their job was to supply some practical answers and "Speed, Accuracy and Secrecy have to be the guiding principles." The subjects to be considered were human diseases, animal diseases, plant diseases, food products and water supplies. They were to report on the need for research and what could be gained from it.

The Canadians were then asked to speak and Murray made a brief speech on the history of M-1000, stressed the need to explore every possibility – "nothing is too foolish" – and proposed setting up an information exchange between the two committees. Short reports and frequently, he added, and not so much secrecy that action gets hobbled. He also held out the carrot of a 900-square-mile experimental station in western Canada where the Americans could test out their theories with actual field trials.[23]

Next came botulinus toxin. The U.S. Chemical Warfare Service had tried spraying it but so far with uncertain results. Rivers insisted that the experiments be continued, while Bayne-Jones of Yale suggested dumping a large quantity in a water supply and seeing what happened. Sherman, the Cornell bacteriologist, pointed out that the acetone/butyl alcohol industry could be easily mobilized to produce vast amounts. "Quantities of 50,000 gallons could be produced in pure culture and quantities of 250,000 gallons not completely free of contamination present no great difficulty." One could even use the tank cars of the commercial solvent industry, he suggested.

Murray and Reed must have really thought this was thinking on a grand scale. More was to come. Much more.

The findings on plants were presented by Louis Kunkel of the Rockefeller Institute, with the assistance of a colleague who displayed maps showing the world-wide distribution and growth density of potatoes, soybeans, rice, wheat and so on. His group felt the aerial spraying of fungus spores might not be very rewarding, while rusts could boomerang on friend and foe alike. But there was a devastating pest of rice in the western United States ("I did not gather what it is," Murray scribbled) which was unknown in the Far East and which could cause a lot of trouble. Also, the University of Chicago, like the NRC in Canada, had started experiments with toxic plant hormones which looked promising.

Hagan spoke for the animal disease specialists and they put the cattle disease, rinderpest, at the top of the list followed by the sheep sickness, Rift Valley fever. The latter virus dried well and was very infectious to man. It might be spread by releasing infected mice and other small animals, it was suggested, and be confused in man with influenza or dengue fever. It was not deadly but it could be sprayed over a city and might incapacitate the population, or an army, for up to two weeks.

But rinderpest was seen as the number one threat to North America. It spread rapidly and killed up to 80 per cent of the herds it afflicted. There was only a very inferior vaccine against it, and that only in small quantities. An enemy attack with rinderpest would be devastating and the group urged that research to combat it be given the utmost priority. Hagan, in deference to Murray and Reed, also noted that the Canadians had come to the same conclusion.

Other animal diseases like foot and mouth, pleuropneumonia, African horse sickness, glanders and anthrax were also touched on. Anthrax was considered a possibility, particularly because it could be produced easily and in the spore state was very tough, but Hagan was not keen on it. It did not spread from animal to animal; you had to literally score direct hits on individual farmyards and then you could not get rid of it. It persisted in the ground indefinitely.

Rivers, reporting for the group on virus diseases in man, thought especially highly of the tropical diseases, malaria and yellow fever, particularly if a new mosquito carrier could be found which thrived in the northern climate. This sparked some brisk debate. The insect specialists argued that the appropriate eggs could be dried on blotting paper and introduced in any climate where mosquitoes already existed – Canada, for example. A lot more research was required.

The Rivers group dismissed the various forms of encephalitis, but it seemed the current cowpox vaccine did not protect against the Far Eastern strain of smallpox, which lent itself to being spread as a kind of dusting powder. Bayne-Jones volunteered that it could be used to tip poison arrows while Murray offered the more practical possibility of it being used by enemy agents to contaminate mail.

Psittacosis was dealt with last. The Rivers group said that a dried infective powder could be produced in very large amounts. It had the further advantage that it did not spread naturally among humans. There was no known vaccine.

Bayne-Jones spoke for human bacterial diseases, running down a long list that included diphtheria, tetanus, salmonella and, Murray's favourite, plague. His group was of the opinion that human bacteria could cause a lot of disorganization and demoralization in a population, but "great killing" was unlikely. On that note, the meeting concluded.[24]

To say that Murray and Reed were impressed is undoubtedly an understatement. In the month that followed, Murray frequently spoke admiringly of the work of the WBC Committee in his correspondence with its chairman, Dr. Fred. There is a current of anxiety, in fact, a sense of urgent desire to stay ahead or at least abreast of the Americans in everything he subsequently writes or does that spring of 1942. He wanted to do his bit, in a big way. He soon got his chance.

Fred, an agricultural bacteriologist, did not have to wait for the formal meeting of the WBC Committee to recognize the threat of rinderpest. He had read Hagan's report and acted on it the day before by raising the alarm in a letter to Dr. Jewett, the man who had ordered the germ warfare survey. He stressed the urgency of immediate research but, because of the danger of accidentally introducing the cattle disease in North America, he proposed that an isolated spot be found, an island perhaps, where experiments could be safely undertaken.[25]

Murray assured Fred that M-1000 would back his request to Jewett but when he was next in Ottawa he must have talked up the problem. A month later he could hardly contain his excitement when he wrote Fred that Collip and Dr. R.E. Wodehouse, the Deputy Minister of Health, had suggested the disused quarantine station on Grosse Ile, a small island in the St. Lawrence downstream from Quebec City. From what he was told of it, it appeared to be made to order for joint experiments "on Rinderpest, Plague and Enemy Agents." The capitalization is Murray's.[26]

Fred snapped up the offer. Subsequent surveys of possible sites in the United States failed to turn up anything as ideal as Grosse Ile, which had an array of buildings, its own power plant, was difficult of access and was completely deserted. In the months to come there was much toing and froing and as Murray struggled through Ottawa red tape to get the okay. The Americans remained steadfastly enthusiastic.

Meanwhile, the M-1000 Committee marched steadily on. Grosse Ile and Murray's report on the WBC meeting dominated the committee's next meeting in January, but some of the research seemed to be making progress. Reed, who had got his grant earlier that month from the WTSDC, said he was not having much luck with botulinus toxin released as a spray, but it appeared to persist in water and resist chlorination. Swaine had a survey of mosquito types under way and was looking for a suitable way of carrying them for release from aircraft. Lochhead was studying how well micro-organisms survived on peat. Fraser confirmed that the Connaught Labs could produce toxins on a large scale.[27]

Also at the meeting were three invitees from the WBC group, Drs. Hagan and Sherman, plus Captain C.S. Stephenson of the U.S. Navy's medical division who also was the link to Naval Intelligence. A man who played the part of sailor to the hilt, to whom women were wenches and a warm bed best when jointly occupied, Stephenson made an excellent impression on Murray. The professor actively sought his friendship and this may explain some rather odd things that found their way into their own acid-free folders in the National Archives collection of Murray's papers. Labelled "humour," they consist of a typed copy of some bawdy specifications for a pilot's girlfriend, cockpit for joystick and the like, and "The Ballad of Chambers Street," a lengthy poem about the misfortunes of a Boston prostitute. Murray was well-known for his taste for the salacious and one can imagine the snorts of laughter as the worldly wise sailor and middle-aged academic poured over these lines of doggerel.[28]

Murray, however, had much more serious reading to do at this time. The *Globe and Mail* ran a story saying the Japanese were believed to have dropped bags of rice in China laced with fleas carrying bubonic plague. And a refugee German microbiologist, Dr. Helmuth Simons, sent through a report that the Germans were actively working on toxins in powder form and had done live-animal trials on an island off the coast of Spain before the war. The Pasteur Institute in Occupied France was said now to be involved and there was supposed to be an actual factory in production at Briacon, near the Italian border "where 300 refugees are being held prisoner and forced to work in this line. No one can approach this building and no one of these prisoners has ever come back." Even if both reports were only half true, it was scary stuff.[29]

Murray and Watson attended the next meeting of the WBC Committee. It was held at the National Academy of Sciences in

Washington, February 15, and it was to finalize the wording of the recommendations in the full report to be submitted to Jewett. The mood was sombre. The biggest surprise hadn't been the attack on Pearl Harbor but the way in which the Japanese were systematically kicking the stuffing out of the British and the Americans. As the scientists gathered, supposedly impregnable Singapore – Britain's Gibraltar of the Far East – raised the white flag. Bataan and Corregidor in the U.S.-held Philippines were obviously next in line.

The Canadians were again assured that the offer of Grosse Ile was most urgently welcome, particularly for the development of counter-measures against rinderpest. There was no place as well suited in the United States, they were told, and it may be that the Axis powers were just waiting until spring when cattle were out to pasture before striking with the devastating disease. They proposed to add a supplement to their main report calling for an immediate joint U.S.-Canada effort on rinderpest.[30]

Dated February 17, 1942, the final report of the WBC Committee was monumental in size. It began by saying the committee considered biological warfare a distinct possibility and U.S. authorities should formulate both defensive and offensive measures. These were mainly to be according to the priorities discussed at the previous WBC meeting in the categories of botulinus toxin and diseases to man, animals, plants and food supplies. Each group submittted a full report. Steps were also outlined to mobilize the public health system in the event of attack and to secure water supplies and biological laboratories from possible sabotage.

Attached to the main report was a world-wide collection of 230 articles published on biological warfare: 61 French, 60 German, 40 English and American, 27 Italian, 5 Russian, one Japanese and so on. "An analysis of the opinions expressed by the authors of the articles under consideration reveals that the great majority believe that Biological Warfare is possible or probable in the future. In addition a significant number assert emphatically that this arm will be used." Industrial methods of bacteria and toxin production were also advocated.[31]

The observations, individual reports, comments from experts all over the United States, and the reprinted articles and abstracts made for a weighty tome, but Dr. Fred and his associates had been determined to cover the subject exhaustively. Their work, after all, was to be the basis of U.S. policy. As Jewett commented when he sent the bulging volume along to Secretary of War Stimson: "The first and most important question is that of high national policy as to whether and to what extent, if at all, this country should interest itself along the lines suggested in this report." It was a decision for the president himself.[32]

The scientists sat back and waited. The Americans returned to their regular work and Murray went back to Ottawa to clone a similar report for Canada and press for a decision on Grosse Ile. Meanwhile, considerable interest had been kindled in U.S. Army circles. Lieutenant-Colonel James Defandorf, the observer on the WBC Committee from the Chemical Warfare Service, had earlier mentioned to Murray that he would like to look over the M-1000 files. They had already been studied by Hagan, Sherman and Captain Stephenson, but since then a number of documents had been received from Britain. In the event, because Defandorf left for Britain and a tour of the biological warfare facilities there, in late February his aide, Lieutenant Luman F. Ney, came to Ottawa instead.

Banting's memos on germ warfare were about to find a truly enthusiastic audience. Ney was given a spare copy of Banting's 1940 proposal to the British, and he made notes of a lot of the other material. Some documents were so lengthy that he asked that copies be made and sent to him. These included Banting's 1937 memo to the NRC on bacterial warfare, a review of the possibilities of germ warfare sent to Banting in 1938 from the Canadian Army Medical Corps, and a February 1941 summary of British experiments to date. Most important of all, Ney wrote, were the NRC reports on the use of plant hormones to kill crops and Banting's report on the airplane dispersal of sawdust over Balsam Lake. "They could be useful to us in getting some aggressive work underway."[33]

Murray blithely assumed that Ney and Defandorf were acting on behalf of the WBC group, and sent the requested papers to that committee's administrative secretary. A few weeks later, he received an anguished letter from Ney, under War Department letterhead from the Office of the Chief, Chemical Warfare Service. He had intended, Ney said, that the papers be sent here, not to the WBC. The Chemical Warfare Service "can get more active use out of them." Would Professor Murray please ask the WBC to release them? One can imagine the rocket poor Lieutenant Ney got from the hatchet-faced Defandorf. Murray primly replied that he was only authorized to release secret documents to the WBC Committee. Ney would have to get them from there.[34]

The exchange is significant. By this time, the Chemical Warfare Service's research on the aerial spraying of mustard gas was in full swing. The chemical destruction of crops offered a bright new vista, which the U.S. Army ultimately exhaustively and successfully pursued. Oddly, Defandorf and Ney overlooked excellent intelligence on the subject that was right under their noses. A little later Murray asked Captain Stephenson if he could obtain data on prewar crop-dusting by the Tennessee Valley Authority, the massive agricultural reclamation project that Roosevelt initiated with his New Deal during the 1930s. The Navy man promptly obliged.[35]

The incident must have made Murray realize, too, that the U.S. Army types weren't falling over themselves to co-operate with the scientists. Defandorf neglected to send the WBC copies of the British documents Ney had taken, so Murray did so, forwarding a complete set in early May that included recently received "Most Secret" reports on experiments done at Porton. These are still withheld in Britain under a fifty-year embargo – if, indeed, they still exist.

British historians trying to reconstruct the history of that country's biological warfare program have been banging their heads against the wall of official secrecy for years. All published accounts have been pieced together from expurgated official histories, fragmentary mentions in diaries and War Cabinet minutes, and the occasional recollections of major and minor participants. As a result, British writers like to assume that Britain got into germ warfare research early, before the war, and that this is one of the nation's guilty secrets. Not so.

The only thing the British have to hide in their early research work on germ warfare is tardiness in time of crisis. Lord Hankey, the so-called Man of Secrets according to his biographer,[36] is usually credited with being the father of Britain's biological warfare program. It is not true. For the longest time as chairman of the Microbiological Warfare Committee he was in charge of keeping an eye on bacteriological warfare developments, but that is all he did. If anything, since 1936 he had stood in the way of actual research, and by the time war broke out – other than planning for an emergency public health laboratory service – nothing had been done.

Banting and Rabinowitch, both of whom toured Porton in great detail, as we have seen, found no evidence of bacteriological research. The Porton documents obtained by Murray confirm that by the spring of 1940 there had been no appreciable research effort. Even in September 1939, when the War Cabinet of Neville Chamberlain expressed alarm about the possibility of a germ warfare attack and reconstituted his committee as the Bacteriological Warfare Committee reporting directly to cabinet, Hankey vacillated.[37] He requested and received from the like-minded Mellanby the October report that Banting complained about. It said, in effect, there was no real danger. And while he did "mention" Banting's memo on bacteriological warfare to the War Cabinet in February 1940, Hankey didn't actually present it or press its recommendation for research, saying instead that the Canadian took a "somewhat alarmist view" which his advisers disagreed with. To cover himself he said he might – he just might – ask for authority to pursue a program of further experiments in the future.[38]

The German invasion of Norway and the fall of France changed everything. In that moment of high crisis, when the world seemed to be falling apart, the British Parliament kicked out Chamberlain and replaced him with the old fire-breather, Winston Churchill.

Hankey knew Churchill from way back. Both had been the bright young(ish) men of Britain's war councils of the First World War, Hankey serving in the Imperial War Cabinet and Churchill as First Lord of the Admiralty until dismissed because of his support of the ill-fated Dardanelles attack. Hankey, who all these years had managed to remain a comfortable senior bureaucrat no matter what government was in power, knew that Churchill was as different to Chamberlain as bangers were to beans. And Churchill, who wrote years ago of the dangers of germ warfare, liked men of action, not talk.

With Churchill in power, Hankey must have immediately felt his neck. There was a sudden flurry of interest at Porton in bacteriological warfare. The Tizard mission to the United States was sent out with a questionnaire directed to the U.S. Chemical

Warfare Service. Question 19 asked: "Has serious consideration been given to the possibility of disseminating bacteria or spores? Any experimental data?" The Americans replied in the negative. "Has consideration been given the destruction of crops by chemical means?" No known weed killers good enough, the Americans said.[39]

The questions were probably framed by Dr. Paul Fildes, one of Britain's senior bacteriologists, who had just been assigned to Porton to put some motion into BW research. A hard-minded sort of person, he wasted no time. Porton documents sent to Murray show that in early 1941 Fildes began a series of experiments on spraying bacteria from aircraft, quickly leading to field trials assisted by Drs. David Henderson and Donald Woods involving the aerial spraying of cattle with anthrax. This was the very use of anthrax that the American specialist, Dr. Hagan, had warned against, citing the longevity of anthrax spores. And while the Americans and Canadians were casting around for an isolated island where they could conduct rinderpest experiments in safety, the Porton scientists were feeding the virus to cattle. Other animals were also dining on hay and animal cakes, bran or whey, sprinkled with foot and mouth, either fresh or dried, and the bacteria of undulant fever.[40]

If they were also working on diseases against humans up to the end of 1941, the British did not tell the Canadians. It's doubtful. The Porton effort was still tiny and a year-end summary entitled *Defensive Measures Against Possible Bacteriological Warfare* concluded that bacterial warfare against the civilian population was still "not likely" and would not be as destructive as a gas attack. The natural spread of disease resulting from the dislocation of the population from bombing was a more serious problem. If the enemy was going to use such methods at all, it would be against livestock and plants. The report smacks of rationalizing previous inaction.[41]

The roadblock appears still to have been Hankey. He was the ultimate committee man who preferred "watching briefs" with establishment intellectuals and writing lengthy "appreciations of the situation" to actual action. He also had a gentlemanly horror of bacteriological warfare and instructed his subordinates as late as March 1942 to make it clear to visitors "that we should under no circumstances initiate these forms of frightfulness, although the possibility of retaliation, e.g., under pressure of public demand, could not be excluded."[42] Churchill fired him that same month.

The man who must have taken the most satisfaction out of that move was Fildes. After a year and a half of operation, the total biological warfare establishment at Porton consisted only of himself, eight technicians and a handful of helpers. A small twenty-room laboratory had just been built but he wasn't even provided with his own clerical staff. The only "weapon" he had so far developed was a pellet made of linseed or cottonseed meal with a hole bored in the centre to be filled with a suitable poison. The idea was to drop these on enemy pastures to kill livestock.

With Hankey out of the way, Fildes was clear to do more aggressive research. By early March he had rejected botulinus toxin as not "sufficiently effective when used in the form of a dust" and had directed almost the entire effort of his team toward developing anthrax as an offensive agent, particularly in bullets or shells. He had concluded that anthrax spores were ideal because of their resistance to heat and drying, ease of production and transportation, and deadliness to both animals and humans "by any route."[43]

Meanwhile, back in Canada, Murray laboured on his own projects, ruffling the feathers of the deputy minister of agriculture as he lobbied for a decision on Grosse Ile. Mackenzie managed to smooth things out and then pressed the cabinet to set up some kind of subcommittee to oversee biological warfare. There was great indecision. Even Colonel Ralston was hesitant to take sole responsibility for it, insisting it be shared with other ministries, particularly the Department of Agriculture. Murray discussed with Maass the possibility of his chemical warfare group taking charge. Maass promised his full co-operation.[44]

Also at this time word began to get around about M-1000 and Murray received offers of fleas "by the bucketful" and helpful suggestions like one from McGill's Institute of Parasitology by which it was proposed to paint propaganda leaflets or counterfeit money with a fly attractant and then dump them out over enemy territory along with dysentery-infected flies. A mixture of bran, alfalfa, dextrose and brewers' yeast was recommended for breeding "more or less uniform flies." Murray fired back a letter asking whether the writer knew of anything that was particularly attractive to flies but not repulsive to humans.[45]

Dr. Fred continued to wait impatiently for a reply to his report from the U.S. Secretary of War. There was nothing, only silence. Murray commiserated. The hangup was Stimson, who had sent the report to the Joint Chiefs of Staff for comment. They were in favour of a biological warfare program but felt that it was better that the military not have direct control "to help in preventing the public from being unduly exercised over any idea that the War Department might be contemplating the use of this weapon offensively." Stimson only finally sent Roosevelt a lengthy memo on the WBC's findings on April 29, recommending that the program be set up under a civilian agency and pursued with "secrecy and great vigor." The memo then lay on Roosevelt's desk, unread.[46]

Murray, however, now had a powerful ally in Maass. Suffield was growing rapidly and so was the director of chemical warfare's influence. In April he was able channel $47,000 to Reed who was able to expand his lab, buy new equipment, bring in other scientists and build a separate building for experimental animals. His lab was also put on a war footing, with military personnel assigned to it both for security and to act as technicians.[47]

On June 11 Murray held his own big meeting. It began at 2 p.m. in the NRC's council chamber, an elegant pseudo-Edwardian room which remains today much as it was forty-six years ago. It is easy to imagine him taking his position at the head of the nineteen-foot conference table, Greey on his right as recording secretary, Collip at the other end, the rest in the plush, leather chairs ranged on either side, eight facing eight. The five American observers sat tight against the wall on each side of the huge fireplace of Italian marble, and below Canada's coat of arms set into the panelling. They included Dr. Hagan and Captain Stephenson, as well as the straight-backed Colonel Defandorf who had come this time for himself. The floor of polished teak creaked and groaned as people adjusted their chairs. The small talk died as all eyes turned toward Murray.

The Grosse Ile research station was first on the agenda and was quickly dealt with, the group voting unanimously for the joint U.S.-Canada project. Next up was discussion of Murray's draft report. Collip felt the preamble giving the history of M-1000 didn't indicate sufficiently clearly "that the late Sir Frederick Banting had been the moving spirit behind biological warfare." It was decided that this report, and all those that followed, would be routed through Collip to Maass and from him to Colonel Ralston, the Minister of Defence.[48]

The report itself, consisting of fifteen closely typed pages and containing much pedestrian detail, can be summarized as follows:

> Bacterial Warfare is unquestionably within the range of practical use. . . . The High Policy as to whether Biological Warfare should be initiated or used in reprisal, is not for this committee to decide. But it is important that every preparation for its immediate use be completely ready in case it is required . . . defence depends absolutely on a complete knowledge and understanding of the nature and the possible methods of using biological agents of disease and pests as offensive weapons. . . . Personnel, laboratories and facilities should be established immediately . . . for both defensive and offensive Biological Warfare.[49]

In pitching for a substantial expansion of M-1000, Murray had also given expression to science's standard moral position on weapon research in the days before the mass destruction potential of the nuclear age. The scientist's job was to make sure his country was prepared to do battle successfully against its enemies, in every way possible. How wars were started, and how new weapons were used, was up to the politicians and the soldiers. The scientist had no ultimate responsibility; the swordmaker was not splattered by blood from the sword. It is a position many might take, even today.

The M-1000 researchers had made significant progress. Dr. Lochhead told the group he had had excellent results keeping bacteria alive on peat. Dr. Swaine said he had nearly completed his survey of mosquitoes in Canada and Dr. Mitchell said "he was going to study the distribution of particles in the air of a theater by introducing the spores of a non-pathogenic mould into the ventilating system." Even Greey, who had been so reluctant, was able to report that anthrax spores survived quite well in distilled mustard gas, although he had not yet established whether the anthrax bacteria could gain entry into the body through the blisters caused by the gas. If they could, it would make a particularly deadly, dual-purpose weapon.[50]

Outside, it was a beautiful day. It was sunny, the maple trees dazzled in new green around and below the Parliament Buildings, while river tugboats nuzzled spring's first great rafts of logs toward the hungry saws of E.B. Eddy. There was the scent of lilacs; the sky was an innocent blue. In the faraway Pacific, Admiral Yamamoto's great battle fleet limped away from Midway island, having lost four precious aircraft carriers in a U.S. Navy ambush.

Now both the WBC and M-1000 committees were waiting. In the two months that followed – nothing. Dr. Fred sent a copy of the M-1000 report to Jewett. No reply. "This nebulous sort of thing is getting under my shirt," Captain Stephenson complained to Murray. "I had a long chat with the Chief the other day and he says he is going to do something." Murray, in his turn, ruminated about appeals to "Higher Authority," his code for the prime minister, while Mitchell – ever the one with a friend in high places – offered: "I will attempt to personally interview the PM and speed the matter up. As you know, I dislike doing things this way. . . ."[51]

There was movement. Unknown to the fidgety scientists, in mid-May Roosevelt had told Stimson that he hadn't had time to read the WBC report but to go ahead with a biological warfare program anyway. Stimson then conferred with the secretaries of Agriculture and Health. A plan slowly began to take shape. The United States would explore the possibilities of biological warfare but the rinderpest problem seemed to have particular urgency. It was always possible to find money for special projects. The scientists would be told soon. . . .

There were blips of concern. German submarines were reported in the Gulf of St. Lawrence. Would that affect Grosse Ile? Mitchell picked up a radio report which said that Banting had set up a committee studying bacterial warfare before he died. Otto Maass promised to get to the bottom of the leak. Eight alleged German spies were in custody in New York; Murray proposed that an exhaustive series of blood tests be run on them for anti-bodies of plague, botulism, and the rest. Captain Stephenson undertook to "smoke out" a mouthy FBI agent who had given an after-dinner speech on sabotaging food supplies. Murray took a break and went fishing.[52]

The beginning had ended.

C·H·A·P·T·E·R

F·I·V·E

Made in Canada

Anthrax. The possibility of using Grosse Ile to develop germ weapons, as well as vaccines, had occurred to Murray right from the start. By mid-August 1942 he had proposed working on this particular disease to Dr. Mitchell, his stalwart ally on M-1000, now reorganized under the Directorate of Chemical Warfare and renamed the C1 Committee. Mitchell responded enthusiastically, mentioning that he had already been discussing the prospect with members of his staff at the Animal Diseases Institute.[1]

By that time the Grosse Ile project was a go. In mid-July Murray had been invited to Washington to meet with R.A. Kelser – chief of the U.S. Army Veterinary Corps – Fred and Weed, who told him that Stimson, the Secretary of War, had finally approved the idea of a joint U.S.-Canada research project and was making $200,000 available for it. But he had expressly stipulated that their efforts be confined to the development of a vaccine against rinderpest. The American team did not have a mandate to explore other areas of bacterial warfare.[2]

Murray immediately invited his American colleagues to Quebec. On July 21, with Reed and Mitchell, they all met at the Chateau Frontenac, the beautiful old railway hotel overlooking the city, and then set out for the island. The Americans, certainly, must have been impressed by the site's isolation if they took the usual transport, a leaky, wooden tug from Montmagny which looked ready to slide beneath the water at any moment. The island itself, however, was perfect.[3]

Grosse Ile is about two miles long and a mile wide, with a heavily treed, rocky ridge rising not far from shore. The buildings of the former quarantine station cluster along the south shore and the visitors found what appeared to be a perfectly preserved ghost town – an empty village from which it seemed the people had disappeared but yesterday. There was a school house, the desks still in place, substantial Protestant and Catholic churches with hymn books in the pews, some excellent brick and frame single-family dwellings and several very large barrack-type buildings that had accommodated passengers from the immigrant ships of the nineteenth century.

At the eastern end of the island there was the large isolation hospital with kitchen stoves and a generator still in working order, a smallpox hospital, several barns and out-buildings – the medical complex of the island. At the western end there was a very large disinfection building and laundry, complete with steam engine and boiler. Just to the west of this area there was a large cemetery overlooking a small cove appropriately named Cholera Bay. There were also two monuments to the twelve thousand immigrants, mostly Irish, who had perished on this doorstep to Canada.

It was the disinfection building that was the real gem, particularly for men contemplating working with diseases that must not escape. It consisted of two huge rooms separated by a bank of walk-in steam chambers with iron doors at either end. Immigrants from the ships would strip in one room, put their clothes in a chamber, walk around through showers, and retrieve their clothes from the room on the other side after they had been sterilized. The chambers were, in fact, like over-sized autoclaves, the high-temperature sterilization ovens that were essential equipment in all bacteriology labs.[4]

The Americans were satisfied. Back at the Chateau Frontenac they proposed Dr. Richard N. Shope of the Rockefeller Institute as the scientific director, agreeing on a salary of $7,500 with General Kelser promising to look after the difference between that and the $12,000 (a fortune in those days) he was already making. They also agreed to pick up 75 per cent of the operational cost and hammered out other details of staffing and finance. Then the whole group went out on a tour of old Quebec. The Americans found this relic of eighteenth-century France, with its cobbled and narrow streets and cliff-top walls overlooking the St. Lawrence, absolutely charming.[5]

It was probably the walk-in disinfecting ovens that suggested to Murray the idea of producing anthrax at Grosse Ile and he soon got further support for it. A week after receiving Mitchell's letter, Murray got a note from Maass saying he had just come back from England with an "important report from Dr. Fildes in my head." It was so secret that he didn't want to write it down but he excitedly discussed it with Mackenzie as soon as he arrived in Ottawa, and later with Murray.[6]

Even though there are no documents available to researchers which describe Maass's information, we know what it was. Fildes had been concentrating almost exclusively on anthrax since early spring, trying to find a way of successfully combining the bacteria in a bomb or shell. That summer his research had taken a giant step forward. He did a series of open-air, live-animal field trials.

Anthrax is naturally nasty. It is known as woolsorters' disease because men working with sheep hides ran the occupational hazard of being infected by breathing the bacteria or having it enter their bodies through small cuts or scratches. When that happened, the bacteria would multiply rapidly, filling and plugging blood vessels and causing the tissue around the original black scab to break down. That kind of infection was not always fatal, but if the bacteria were inhaled or swallowed death was inevitable. When without a host to infect, the bacteria change into spores, a state of suspended animation in which they can live for years, for decades even. Moreover, these spores are extremely tough and hard to kill, and more likely than most other organisms to withstand the heat and stress of an explosive.

The trouble was, as the American scientists had pointed out to Murray, anthrax spores did not go away. Once spread on the ground, they just stayed and stayed, making an area dangerous indefinitely. That probably didn't matter to the British scientists; what they saw was the fact that anthrax could complicate a flesh wound and make it life-threatening. To test out the theory, in the summer of 1942 Fildes acquired a small, uninhabited island off the coast of Scotland. That island, Gruinard, subsequently became so badly contaminated that it was sealed off for more than four decades. No one, unless suitably protected, was allowed to set foot on it.

Despite the secrecy that surrounds the episode, British journalists have been able to get a fair picture of Fildes's experiments by interviewing the military personnel who witnessed them. And crude they were. Anthrax slurry was poured into stationary explosives while test animals, mainly sheep, were attached to stakes at appropriate distances. The bomb was detonated and then the scientists counted how many animals died. They repeated the experiments again and again, probably noticing then that anthrax is much more deadly as a cloud of spores than it is as a contaminate of bomb splinters. Instead of being a secondary cause of death from a munition, anthrax could be the primary one. The British had hit upon the first really practical germ warfare bomb.[7]

That fall Murray was exceedingly busy. There were a hundred and one administrative matters to see to before winter made Gross Ile inaccessible. Murray became a little annoyed at the Americans who did not seem to appreciate the urgency. That changed suddenly in October when he learned that Stimson had appointed George Merck, president of the famous pharmaceutical company of the same name, to head up a group called the War Research Service to organize a full U.S. biological warfare program. The actual financing and administration of individual projects was to remain the responsibility of existing army agencies like the Surgeon General or the Chemical Warfare Service, but Merck had the job of setting up the various offensive, defensive and research components and getting them to fit together. The Americans were now in the business in earnest, and Murray immediately arranged for Merck to visit Grosse Ile, and then go on to Ottawa and meet Maass.[8]

Reed was also busy. With Maass now officially holding the purse strings, Reed petitioned for an entomologist – a scientist specializing in the study of insects – so that the Kingston lab could establish a flea colony in order to develop "a technique to allow the use of Plague combined with Murine Typhus as an offensive weapon." He also suggested that the Dominion Parasite Laboratory in Belleville be invited to help. Maass apparently agreed to both requests.[9]

The Canadian germ warfare effort also got some rather unwelcome attention at this time. J. Edgar Hoover, head of the U.S.

Federal Bureau of Investigation and probably the twentieth century's most notorious busybody, contacted the RCMP to ask for its opinion of biological warfare research in Canada. Somehow the Mounties' reply, containing "many inaccuracies and expressions of opinion they are not qualified to give," fell into Murray's hands. He suggested to Maass that they let the Mounties know they didn't have any business commenting on something they knew nothing about.[10]

The anthrax question, however, stayed near the surface. As winter drew on it was apparently discussed frequently by Reed, Maass and Murray, and both Dr. Fildes and his boss, J. Davidson Pratt, controller of chemical defence development for the British Ministry of Supply, came out from Britain to add their suggestions and encouragement. Fildes, in fact, stayed for a time at Murray's home in Montreal and both men attended a conference in Washington later that month to discuss the setting up of a U.S. germ warfare research station. Finally, on December 8, 1942, Murray sent Maass a formal proposal to produce anthrax for the British. It is worth quoting in full. 'N' is the code letter for anthrax. The memo is heavily stamped SECRET and MOST SECRET:

> The G.I.N. project as we have planned it is entirely Canadian. It is designed to produce 'N' for the British authorities immediately in suitable quantities. If practice comes up to our calculations, we hope to produce 300 lbs. of 'N' spores per week; these would provide for 1,500 of the 30-lb. bombs a week. Should the U.S. want to join us in the 'GIN project' C1 would raise no objections, but there are no indications they are prepared to do so immediately.[11]

A few days later Murray again wrote Maass proposing field trials at Suffield once they had some anthrax bombs on hand, noting that "the precaution of double-fencing an adequate area will have to be observed, probably five square miles." Permission, of course, would have to be obtained from the Deputy Minister of Agriculture. He concluded by saying that "Davidson Pratt and Fildes will be pleased by this arrangment."[12]

Murray's next job was to convince the Americans to buy into the scheme. Setting up facilities to mass-produce deadly bacteria for use in bombs was a far cry from an operation originally designed to produce an animal disease vaccine. Indeed, it was precisely the kind of extension of the work at Grosse Ile that the

U.S. Secretary of War had expressly forbidden. As luck would have it, Murray was able to cash in on some creative American finagling.

The original agreement to share the expenses of the work at Grosse Ile was in every sense an international agreement between Canada and the United States and it should have been negotiated by the State Department and presented to the president and then to Congress for approval. Stimson, however, in the interests of speed had asked the State Department to steer clear and undertook to have the War Department pick up both the cost and the responsiblity. The question was how to do so legally.

After much discussion, the Americans asked the Canadians to put their new government agency, War Supplies Limited, in charge of Grosse Ile on paper. They then drafted a contract by which the Crown company would furnish certain secret reports at $15,000 each which would be sent twice monthly directly from Grosse Ile to General William Porter, the head of the Chemical Warfare Service. War Supplies officials would never actually see the reports but Porter would pay for them out of his service budget until he had met the agreed-upon American contribution. Thus there would be no U.S.-Canada effort on the books whatever; just a U.S. contract let to a foreign supplier.[13]

This put the U.S. Chemical Warfare Service completely in charge of American participation in Grosse Ile so it was only the army that Murray, Reed, Merck and Fred had to convince when they sat down at the conference table in Washington that January 15, 1943, to discuss Murray's proposed anthrax factory. Merck and Fred could not finance involvement but the army brass facing them across the table could. General Porter had come with most of his top aides and they liked what they heard. From chemical bombs to bacterial bombs – what could be more natural? Porter agreed to pick up two-thirds of the estimated $75,000 start-up cost by paying for regular reports in the same way as with the rinderpest experiments.[14]

By condoning the circumspect financing of the Grosse Ile project and then making the War Research Service financially dependent on the army, Stimson had set up an awkward political situation. It effect, it put Merck in charge of germ warfare on paper, but Porter in charge in fact – especially when it came to producing an offensive bacterial weapon. The reports went to him, not to Merck, so he was in a position to run the operation secretly without any checks whatever. The situation had echoes a generation later in the spectacular Iran-Contra affair.

It was Maass who undertook to get Canada's share of the anthrax factory approved without political fuss. He cheated too, although also entirely within the system. He simply sent a note to the Master General of the Ordnance, his immediate administrative superior in the army, asking for extra money for a secret project that had been agreed on with Merck and which was known to the Minister of Defence. When the note landed on Ralston's desk for signature, the minister scribbled in the margin: "Please have Maass put on record any recommendations that he has. I have no recollection of any specific discussion re definite increase. Whatever Mr. Merck said, verbal understandings lead to misunderstandings." Then he approved it. Maass subsequently wrote the memo Ralston requested, but he still didn't mention what the extra money was for.[15]

Murray was now home free and wrote to General Kelser about the "giant autoclaves" and assured him they would be ready to start producing anthrax by mid-February, using methods developed by Reed at Queen's University in Kingston. The Grosse Ile joint committee met in Boston on February 6, approved Murray's plan, and named Dr. J.C. Duthie as the science director.[16]

It fell to Canada to look after the actual operation of the anthrax plant and Murray sent a flurry of memos to Fildes at Porton asking about British protective clothing, methods of conducting field trials with anthrax and decontamination procedures. He also arranged for a contractor to overhaul the autoclaves and for the purchase of bakelite trays on which to grow the bacteria.[17]

In the context of Murray's efforts to mass-produce germ warfare bacteria, an ironically parallel project was under way back in Toronto: an attempt to develop mass-production techniques for the new wonder drug – penicillin. At the centre of it all was the on-again, off-again Dr. Philip Greey, who seems never to have been entirely comfortable working with deadly organisms.

Penicillin most definitely did start with the British. It was discovered in 1929 by Dr. Alexander Fleming of St. Mary's Hospital, London, when he happened to notice that cultures he was working on seemed to have stopped growing where the plates had been contaminated by an airborne mould. The mould appeared to be producing a substance that inhibited bacterial growth and he named it penicillin, suggesting after further study that it might have antiseptic properties.

Other than finding a method of extraction, nothing much was done with this discovery until the war. Then Dr. H.W. Florey and others at Oxford tried it out on a number of patients suffering from various infections. It seemed to work rather well and the significance of that did not escape the British authorities. Something that preserves the lives of your own wounded soldiers has a military value similar to something that kills the enemy's.

At first, though, Florey had trouble getting mass-production organized in Britain and in 1941 came to Canada to ask the help of the Connaught Labs. He received a chilly reception from Connaught's Ronald Hare, a former worker under Fleming, who doubted whether Florey had proved penicillin's merit. Greey, however, was quite interested and he had his own University of Toronto lab in the Banting Institute building.

Florey left Canada disappointed and went on to the United States with Fleming to try to sell the idea there, but his visit to Toronto was not wasted. All the while that Greey was working for Murray's germ warfare committee, he was also developing methods of preparing penicillin and testing it on patients in Toronto General Hospital across the street. By 1943, aided by Dr. Colin Lucas and Dr. S.F. Macdonald of the Banting and Best Department of Medical Research on the floor above him, he had achieved sufficient success for the NRC to agree to finance the building of an experimental production plant.[18]

Nowadays we take antibiotics for granted, but fifty years ago a major cause of death among those with open wounds received on the operating table or otherwise was bacterial infection, chiefly by staphylococci. Gangrene was also a terrible problem as that family of bacteria, to which botulinus belongs, is everywhere in the environment and attacks moribund flesh with deadly efficiency. Before penicillin, all a doctor could do was cut away the infection, taking live tissue as well as dead. On the battlefield, that often meant severing otherwise healthy limbs.

Penicillin dramatically changed all that. Greey's research was a contribution to humanity entirely in keeping with Banting's discovery of insulin and it is a pity there appears to be no archival record of his work. As so often happens, it was left to the jealous Dr. Hare, who viciously criticized Greey behind his back,[19] to write a book, *The Birth of Penicillin*, that minimized

Greey's contribution and maximized his own. Fortunately, Connaught director Dr. Robert Defries set the record straight in his history of the institution.

Murray and Reed, however, were working in quite the opposite direction. For a brief moment, indeed, they nearly succeeded in launching the first systematic bacteriological attack in history. In October 1942 the British Eighth Army under General Bernard Montgomery had hurled Rommel back from the Egyptian frontier at the battle of El Alamein, while in November mainly American forces landed in the Vichy French colonies of Morocco and Algeria and proceeded to push at the Germans from the west. It looked for a while as though the Germans were going to be pinched out in Tunisia until Rommel snapped back, dealing the Americans a devastating defeat in February 1943 at Kasserine Pass. This was the first real test of U.S. troops in the European war and the experienced Germans chopped them to pieces.

The American high command was panic-stricken. The Germans had built up an opposing force in Tunisia far faster than expected and had scored a success that might convince fascist Spain, which had so far been neutral, that theirs was the better side to bet on. The Americans looked at their supply lines and realized that they relied on a single railway line through coastal Spanish Morocco. If fascist saboteurs cut this line, the forces facing Rommel would be in trouble.

The fledgling Office of Strategic Services, the U.S. "dirty tricks" agency that had been set up to fight behind enemy lines, was approached for help. The OSS was asked to devise a method – any method – to guarantee that people in Spanish Morocco could not interfere with the orderly transportation of U.S. supplies to the front. Murray and Reed just happened to be in Washington when OSS scientific adviser Stanley Lovell received this assignment.

Murray and Reed offered an ingenious plan. Certain recipes of bran, soybean and the like were known to be particularly attractive to house flies. If one of these concoctions could be moulded into the shape of goat dung – the goat is the domestic animal of most of North Africa – it could be infected with psittacosis and tularemia bacteria and scattered by aircraft throughout the country. Flies would then spread the diseases to the general population, which would be too preoccupied by the resultant epidemic to worry about interfering with the Americans. Before the plan could be adopted the Germans were on the retreat and the idea was dropped, to the relief of all three scientists. Bizarre though it was, the scheme had promise. Research on fly attractants and infected baits was now begun at Reed's lab under two young men, A.W.A. Brown and A.S. West.[20]

Meanwhile Murray's anthrax factory marched on, but slowly. The isolation of Grosse Ile made it difficult to obtain materials and get work done. Because the island was a top secret establishment, the scientists and U.S. and Canadian soldiers who staffed it were not allowed to bring their families. As spring gave way to summer, the loneliness gnawed on morale. Soldiers and officers on leave in the nearby village of Montmagny behaved abominably, prompting warnings from Murray of disciplinary action.[21]

The unhappiness overflowed in July when the island's medical officer complained about conditions to the army's District Medical Officer, prompting a formal inspection. The subsequent report was scathing. The DMO found the collective hygiene on the base "non-existent," the kitchen "disgustingly dirty" with flies everywhere, the cooks with dirty nails and hands, swill cans uncovered and unwashed and the fridge full of coagulated blood and bottles of beer. Outside, the grounds were "covered with garbage."

The barracks and latrines were even worse, "filthy," although the DMO reserved his most cutting remarks to describe the state of discipline. "Non-existent," he wrote. "Soldiers deride remarks and recommendations of the medical officer. They destroy the written orders posted in the kitchen by the MO. There is no discipline because the officers . . . are afraid if the men are placed in detention they will be shortstaffed."[22]

Murray reacted angrily. He accused the island medical officer of exaggerating in his complaints to the DMO. "Your statement about conditions at the station are ridiculous. I know enough about them to be certain they are luxurious compared to what thousands of men face on the battle fronts and compared to the situation I was in in the last war." He also wrote to Maass and recommended that the medical officer, Captain L.P.E. Demers, who had once worked in Murray's lab, be removed. It was done.[23]

Another of Murray's germ warfare projects, however, was doing rather better. Dr. Lochhead had found an excellent source of peat from the Albert Bog southeast of Ottawa, and with the help of Murray had arranged to have it ground and screened to suitable particle size at the Department of Mines. The material appeared very promising as a carrier for infectious bacteria, like the sawdust Banting had originally proposed, and while Reed undertook to determine which organism would be most suitable, the peat was to be stockpiled at the NRC's Chemical Warfare Lab on Sussex Street where "its use would be hidden."[24]

The Americans were moving right along, too. In late 1942 they had become alarmed by intelligence reports of German biological warfare preparations and resolved that they must quickly achieve the capability to retaliate in kind. In late November, Colonel W.C. Kabrick of the U.S. Chemical Warfare Service convened a meeting of prominent bacteriologists from all across the United States at the National Academy of Sciences. One of those present was Dr. Ira Baldwin, a colleague of E.B. Fred at the University of Wisconsin, and an agricultural bacteriologist and specialist in the commercial production of bacteria. In an interview in 1989, Baldwin remembered:

Kabrick called the meeting to order and said that there had been a committee of eminent bacteriologists studying the problem of the possibility of biological warfare and that they had turned in a report but there were a couple of questions they really hadn't answered. And he was trying to get the opinion of this larger group of bacteriologists:

One. "Could you preserve the virulence of pathogenic micro-organisms if you grew them in ton lots?"

Second. "Could you grow them in ton lots with safety to the people who are growing them and safety to the community and maintain the virulence?"

Well, most of the bacteriologists in the crowd were medical people who had never worked with anything larger than in the test tube. They were quite skeptical whether this could be done. I had had experience in the yeast industry and in butyl alcohol and citric acid fermentation and other types of commercial fermentation working with 10,000-gallon tanks. And when it came my turn, I brashly said, "Well, if you can do it in a test tube and maintain the virulence, you can grow it in a 10,000-gallon tank and maintain the virulence."

And you can have it much safer in a 10,000-gallon tank than you can in a test tube because in a test tube you transfer it into the open air with a wire loop or a bypass, or pipette to a plate, or test tube to test tube and so forth. When you once get it started, in a commercial system, it's a closed system and consequently there's no chance for the micro-organisms to get out in the air. So, on that basis, I said, "I think it would be safer."

With that I sat down and they went all around the room and there were a few other people who expressed comments similar to mine but most of them were very skeptical.

Well, I went home and thought I'd done my bit for the world. I didn't hear from Kabrick again until pretty close to Christmas. I got another telephone call. This time it was General Kabrick – he had got promoted in the meantime – and he wanted to know if I could come down to a meeting just a few days before Christmas. I think it was the 22nd or something like that. He said there were going to be some Canadians and some British people there and we'd like to have you come to the meeting.

I said I thought I could do that. "How long do I need to stay?"

"Oh," he said, "from now on. You told us it could be done. We want you to come down and do it."[25]

Baldwin was appointed science director of the U.S. biological warfare research program and given $6-million – a colossal sum in those days – and *carte blanche* to hire whomever he wanted, and to build laboratories wherever and however he wanted. His choice of location fell on a disused National Guard air base near Frederick, Maryland. Work on Camp Detrick began in April.[26]

In Britain that summer of 1943 Dr. Fildes carried out a second series of field trials on Gruinard, this time with an aircraft actually dropping 30-pound and 4-pound prototype anthrax bombs. The corpses of test animals mounted, and they were buried by piling them at the base of an island cliff and dynamiting the top down. Unfortunately, at least one infected carcass floated out to sea.[27]

Anthrax broke out among sheep on the nearby mainland. This caused near-panic at Porton, and Fildes rushed up by

Beaufort bomber to deal with the crisis. He must have realized now, suddenly, the danger the island posed. He ordered that the heather in which it was deeply cloaked be set on fire, in an attempt to sterilize it. Soon the island was submerged in a pall of black smoke. Flames flickered through the night but it was not enough. Gruinard was sealed off. It was the end of field trials with anthrax in Britain.[28]

Incredibly, on September 27, 1943, some weeks after the Gruinard catastrophe, Fildes sent a message to Murray urging him to carry on with the "large scale" field trials with anthrax Murray had originally proposed for Suffield. He even sent one of Porton's precious (possibly the only) anthrax bomb charging machines and 200 empty 4-pound bombs.[29] There is no evidence in the available documents that the British even hinted to the Canadians about what had happened at Gruinard. Years later, there were rumours among the war scientists that there had been fatalities among the Porton personnel on the island.[30]

Despite pressure to do the anthrax field trials that fall, Murray continued to have production problems. During a visit to the island by him and Reed in October, they found the gaskets around the sterilizing ovens leaked (a dangerous situation) and a contractor had to be brought over from the mainland to make repairs. There must have been other problems, too, for it was not until the following February that Reed was able to send Fildes a sample of "Canadian" anthrax.[31]

To make matters worse, Davies, the British chief superintendent of Suffield, now began a campaign to have a germ warfare lab of his own at the Alberta field station. By late 1943 Suffield was engaged in a wide variety of elaborate field trials using the various toxic gas weapons that had been developed, not to mention flame-throwers, rockets and other weapons. Area E, thirty miles north of the base, had been set aside for BW testing but it would appear that Davies wasn't content merely to provide facilities and staff. He wanted to be in on the research ground floor.[32]

This led to intense awkwardness, particularly for Murray. Suffield was a joint venture of Canada and Britain and Davies was a senior Porton scientist before he came to Canada, with years of experience in weapons research and the dispersal of chemical agents. He undoubtedly felt more comfortable with the expertise and direction of his British colleagues than he did with the Canadians. In any event, he got permission to build the germ warfare lab with construction to begin the following spring. The first resident biological warfare scientist was to be assigned to Suffield at the same time.

Murray and Reed both protested, together tackling Maass. They must have been eloquent because that same day Maass wrote to Davies to remind him that Murray's C1 Committee was in charge and had final say on all questions of safety involving BW trials in Area E. Then Maass added: "I question your field layout and pickup organization where you put Prof. Reed on the laboratory assessment team. Prof. Reed, or whoever may be assigned by C1 to look after the bacterial aspects of the trial (it may be Lord Stamp, for instance) should be treated as a consultant whose advice MUST be taken on the bacteriological aspects of such trials."[33]

The reference to Lord Stamp is interesting. Lord Trevor Stamp was a bacteriologist who started working at Porton in 1941, not long after his parents and older brother were killed in their Anderson shelter by a bomb during the Blitz. In 1943 he toured all the biological warfare establishments in Canada and the United States and stayed on in North America for the rest of the war, serving as a kind of British germ warfare liaison officer. He made Camp Detrick his base because Baldwin had been able to get research moving rapidly, having installed his labs in the former airfield's main hangar and literally getting his pick of the best young scientists in the country. Stamp pursued his own research program, apparently on anthrax, because before long he was joined by Porton's Dr. David Henderson, who had worked on the bacteria with Fildes.[34] Stamp also established direct communication with Davies and that summer conducted his own private experiments at Suffield, quite possibly without Murray's knowledge.[35]

The chief superintendent's ambitions are also revealed in the contractor's specifications and plans for the new Suffield germ warfare lab. It was to be built as a wing on the physiological building where animal autopsies were done and included various individual labs, a "hot room" for growing dangerous organisms and a "cold room" for storing them, a germ-proof glass-walled enclosure for experiments and the ever-present autoclaves. At one end of the building was the office of the lab superintendent, specially sound-proofed to allow him to have "confidential discussions."[36]

Nevertheless, Maass's memo to Davies appeared to put Murray firmly in charge, enabling him to turn his attention to other issues. By the end of 1943, though Europe was still a Nazi fortress, the Russians were grinding the Germans back and the British, Americans and Canadians had gnawed halfway up Italy and were threatening Rome. The Atlantic, thanks mostly to radar, was becoming dangerous for German submarines, while in the Pacific the tenacious Japanese were being systematically pried out of their island strongholds one by one. There was no question now, barring the enemy employing a new and devastating secret weapon, who was going to win the war.

It was to discuss just that subject, that of a new German secret weapon, that brought Murray and Reed to Washington at the end of December. Several months earlier French and Polish spies had reported that the Germans were working on "rocket guns," which fired pilotless, jet- or rocket-propelled bombs later to be known as the V-1s and V-2s. Allied bombers had been able to destroy some of the factories and launching sites but not sufficiently to halt deployment. The question was: How did Hitler intend to use them?

The chief American spokesman at the conference was Colonel M.B. Chittick, the military commander at Camp Detrick. He described what the intelligence services had gleaned about the weapons, their range and payload, and, most revealing of all, their accuracy. It was plus or minus ten miles. It hardly seemed reasonable, the meeting decided, to send a flying bomb all that distance to explode randomly on the countryside. Gas under those circumstances would not be effective either. A biological payload, however, would be perfect. The past year's research had shown that live organisms or their toxins could be used invisibly to contaminate very large areas.[37]

Botulinus toxin seemed a likely candidate. The British, it was said, based that conclusion on the information of the refugee German scientist, Helmuth Simons, whose report Murray had read over a year earlier. The Canadians needed no convincing. The toxin is chemically extracted from the bacteria, and live-animal trials of the past year had satisfyingly demonstrated its deadliness. Ground into a fine dust, it was found that even the smallest particle could be lethal.

There must have been some doubt expressed at the conference about the likelihood of botulinus being used. A few weeks later Murray appears to have taken upon himself to consult with Lovell, the OSS scientific adviser, who told him the U.S. Surgeon General's Office discounted Simons's report, suggesting he was a fraud and had made up the story about the Germans working on botulinus in order to "worm his way" into the United States. Murray disagreed.[38]

Back in Canada, Murray laid the matter before Maass who took it to General Maurice Pope, secretary to the Canadian Chiefs of Staff. He found out that neither British Chiefs of Staff nor the U.S. War Department had come to any real decision. Moreover, Vannevar Bush, of the War Department's scientific advisory committee, had ruled that the use of botulinus toxin by the Germans was possible, but improbable. Such lukewarm reaction should have dampened Murray's enthusiasm. It didn't.[39]

Now began a course of events that must have made Murray rue the day he got involved with biological warfare. Somehow he managed to set Ottawa's alarm bells ringing over the botulinus threat. It may have been because the danger was now linked to the Allied invasion of France, then in its planning stages and set for the late spring of 1944. Colonel Ralston, the Minister of Defence, personally phoned C.D. Howe to ask that the Ministry of Supply urgently procure $25,000 worth of equipment for Reed's lab for a project of a "most secret nature." That project was to manufacture enough toxoid to immunize the thousands of Canadian troops now in England being assembled for the invasion.[40]

Reed's effort was prodigious. He hired extra staff, expanded the lab yet again and by April had produced 25,000 doses of toxoid with 150,000 projected by mid-May. The work was dangerous, because the toxin had to be made before making the toxoid, and both men were exceedingly proud of the accomplishment and the way the scientists, soldiers and technicians at the Kingston lab had all pulled together. It looked certain that they would be able to provide protection for every Canadian soldier who was to put his life on the line on the beaches of France. It was a fine achievement.

The Americans made a parallel effort. At the beginning of January 1944 a special biological warfare subcommittee was formed under the U.S. Joint Chiefs of Staff (the "Barcelona Committee") to assess the rocket threat and devise counter-measures. It made two key recommendations: botulinus toxoid should be made on a large scale so that it would be possible to inoculate troops, and the offensive side to biological warfare should be pursued vigorously.[41] The Joint Chiefs of Staff approved both. Camp Detrick began rushing full production of a suitable toxoid and with the help of private biological supply companies, it hoped to have enough for 650,000 men in six weeks.

As the weeks passed, and the probable time for the invasion neared, the Canadians noticed an unusual silence on plans to immunize the Allied troops. Murray and Reed decided to go to England to confer with their British colleagues and with General Crerar, the commander of the Canadian forces earmarked for the landings, while Maass sent messages to General Porter of the Chemical Warfare Service. He was recommending that U.S. troops be inoculated, Maass asked. Wasn't he?[42]

The blow fell on May 19 when Lieutenant-General Kenneth Stuart, Chief of Staff of Canadian Military Headquarters in London, routinely checked with his British opposite number on what cover story was to be used when the Allied troops were inoculated with the toxoid. To his amazement, he learned that the British War Office and SHAEF, the Allied command organization in charge of the invasion under Dwight D. Eisenhower, had decided against the inoculation program. They said that there were no intelligence reports to indicate that botulinus toxin might be used.

Stuart immediately contacted his boss, General Crerar. What were they to do? Should Canadian troops be inoculated unilaterally? What should they recommend to the War Cabinet back in Ottawa? Crerar said they would just have to go along with the decision of their allies because, should only the Canadians be protected and the Germans attack with the toxin, the survival of the Canadian troops while the Americans and the British were destroyed would have "no general or enduring military significance." The Canadians represented only one-tenth of the invasion forces so they would be promptly overwhelmed anyway.[43]

To the credit of the Canadian War Cabinet, chaired it will be remembered by the generally despised Mackenzie King, it rejected Crerar's logic, cabling back that it couldn't "accept the view that Canada should take responsibility for forgoing potential protection for its own troops just because other Allied troops were not afforded the same protection." It then ordered Stuart to ask the British and Americans to reconsider or at least agree to allow Canada to go ahead with an inoculation program on its own.[44]

In the meantime Murray, Reed and the Director General of Medical Services, General Brock Chisholm, were asked to deal with the crisis and on May 26 they attended a meeting in Davidson Pratt's office in London. To the astonishment of the Canadians, Pratt presented one of his own scientific experts who declared the intelligence on the botulism threat was "worthless" and there was absolutely no need to inoculate anybody. It's easy to imagine the chagrin of the Canadians as they heard themselves told that all their work had been ill-advised and wasted, especially as they had been manufacturing the toxoid for British troops as well, at Britain's request.[45]

Then the messages really flew between London and Ottawa, and between Ottawa and Washington. The Canadians were next astounded to learn that a U.S. expert had proclaimed that the toxoid was poisonous and that deaths had occurred when it was tested on U.S. troops. Moreover, because trials with yellow fever vaccine had resulted in four thousand deaths and had incapacitated "a couple of divisions," the War Department was not prepared take a chance on another experimental inoculation just before operations. Crerar also insisted that Canada should go along with the British and American decision.[46]

The Canadian War Cabinet dug in its heels. Canadian troops would be inoculated no matter what the British and the Americans did. Stuart argued it would cause alarm among the other Allied soldiers if the Canadians got an inoculation and they didn't. Then there was debate about whether a suitable cover story could be concocted. Maass and Chisholm flew down to Washington to try to find out just what was going on.

The sad thing about all this controversy is that the British and the American high commands had definite reason to believe that the Germans were not planning to resist invasion by the use of a bacteriological toxin, or with germs, or even with gas, for that matter. At this point in the war, the decipherment of German radio messages was virtually complete. Thanks to the British code-breakers, and to their intercept stations around the world including in Canada, the Allied high command had access to German military preparations in the most minute detail. Not only did the decrypts show that there were no preparations on the part of the Germans to resist invasion with gas or toxins, they showed the Germans were desperately afraid of inadvertently giving the Allies an excuse for such attacks.[47]

Murray, Maass and apparently the Canadian Chiefs of Staff and the War Cabinet knew none of this. Ultra, the code name for the interception and deciphering of German wireless messages, was one of the most closely guarded secrets of the war. It involved the use of a primitive computer to break the Enigma ciphers – those messages supposedly impossibly scrambled by a machine the Germans possessed. This enabled the British to read almost all the exchanges between the German high command and its various military units. Shortly after the United States came into the war, Roosevelt and the top U.S. military leaders were told about Ultra but apparently not Mackenzie King nor the Canadian military leaders. Had they known, they most certainly would not have pursued the inoculation matter so determinedly.

General Crerar, on the other hand, did know. As Canadian commanders fighting in Italy had been under the overall command of the British, they had remained in the dark. Crerar, however, was to be the operational commander of the Canadian forces in the invasion of France, so it was deemed advisable to let him in on the secret. He received his briefing sometime in February or March of 1944.[48] It was this inside knowledge, and the fact that he would be supported by people far more important than his own superiors, that gave him confidence to reject unilateral inoculation at every turn, turning back reasonable suggestions from Ottawa with a temerity bordering on insubordination.

The U.S. expert, on whose opinion the Americans claimed to have based their decision, appears to have been a red herring intended to quiet the Canadians while withholding the truth. Maass triumphantly returned to Ottawa with the news that he had turned out to be an expert on radar and Maass had been able to demolish his every point in meetings with U.S. Army authorities, including the suggestion four thousand had died during tests with yellow fever vaccine. Apparently the actual number was only about 120.[49]

The Canadian War Cabinet grudgingly deferred ordering unilateral inoculations until the invasion high command and U.S. War Department and the Combined Chiefs of Staff reacted to the latest Canadian arguments in favour. Ralston, for one, was at the limit of his patience and on June 1 told his secretary to make arrangements for Stimson to be telephoned directly (Republic 6700, Ext. 2254) if they didn't hear on the issue soon. Murray was ordered to return to Canada at utmost priority via Canadian Lancaster bomber.[50]

Suddenly it was D-Day – June 6, 1944 – and Canadian troops were on the beaches of Normandy dodging bullets. The issue of inoculating them had become academic. The crates of Canadian toxoid sat at the depots or on the ships unopened. And so they remained.

The final irony about the D-Day inoculation episode is that Canada's defence minister, Colonel Ralston, should have known about Ultra. Direct control of Canada's fledgling radio intercept and cipher-breaking operation had been taken over by the British in January 1942, with the appointment of Oliver Strachey, a veteran member of Britain's Government Code and Cypher School. It was immediately expanded into a number of intercept stations which fed signals to headquarters in Ottawa where they were deciphered and then sent to London and Washington via a powerful transmitter code-named Hydra located at Camp X, the British Secret Service sabotage school near Oshawa, Ontario. Ralston, who had to approve the financing of the operation and its subsequent expansion, seems to have been led to believe that the intercepts dealt only with Occupied France and Axis weather reporting.[51]

What Ralston did not know did not hurt him as much as it appears to have hurt Murray and Maass. They seemed to have been deeply affected by the inoculation contretemps. They must have felt a sense of excruciating embarrassment in having caused such anxiety among members of the War Cabinet and Chiefs of Staff. From here on Maass's grip on Canada's chemical warfare effort falters. His signature, even his name, vanishes from much of the correspondence that still pours out of his office. His secretary takes memos in to him and returns with them suitably initialled but the writing isn't his. She is suspected of signing for him. Many of the more important memos don't even get to him. They're handled entirely by his aides.[52]

Maass is drinking heavily much of the time. Everyone knows it. Sometimes he will sit at lunch conversing with staff, apparently normal in every way, then get up and suddenly collapse. His staff, nearly half a century later, still remember these incidents with pain. Rumour has it that it is not the quantity he drinks, but a violent allergic reaction to alcohol. No one quite believes it. The change in Murray is more subtle, but no less certain. The enthusiasm disappears from his correspondence. He becomes defensive, strident. Other things begin to go wrong. Suffield and Grosse Ile are the problems again.

In April, just before he and Reed went to England, Murray and his full C1 Committee met at Suffield and toured the germ warfare testing facilities of Area E. They were not pleased with all they saw, in particular a pipe from the decontamination centre that simply drained into an open pond which they feared would "contaminate the region and probably drain into the lake." Murray ordered Davies to install a holding tank so the effluvia could be chemically sterilized. Murray's sharply-worded memo must have further abraded relations between them.[53]

The committee then held its formal meeting to discuss the forthcoming field trials with anthrax as proposed by Dr. Fildes at Porton. The minutes of this meeting are among those documents still withheld by Canada's Department of National Defence and that is a pity. It would be interesting to know who on the committee raised the key objection. All we have on the discussion is one paragraph from Murray which slipped through in an related document. It's well worth quoting: "Mr. Davies was not worried about carrying out the entire procedure outlined (by Fildes) but the committee are not satisfied it could be done safely. It would involve permanently contaminating large areas and would infect gophers and antelope and be therefore spread."[54]

The committee apparently reserved decision on the trials, for shortly afterwards Murray wrote to the military commander of Camp Detrick asking whether he thought the new biological warfare proving grounds at Granite Peak, near Dugway, Utah, would be suitable for doing them instead. It was a reasonable request in that the Americans had agreed to a joint experiment with anthrax and botulinus toxin at Horn Island, a sandbar island off the coast of Mississippi. Dr. Lochhead's finely ground peat was to be used as the carrier of the agents and a team from Kingston was to supervise the trial. This, however, would be on a much smaller scale than a bombing exercise.[55] Murray's request was turned down. Perhaps the Americans disliked the idea of the permanent contamination of large tracts of their own territory. In fact, Camp Detrick's liaison scientist at Porton had witnessed the tests at Gruinard.[56]

Sir Frederick Banting (left) and Israel Rabinowitch in November 1939. The two men were about to leave Canada to visit the British chemical warfare research station at Porton Down.

General A.G.L. McNaughton with J.L. Ralston, Canada's Minister of Defence, in Britain in 1942. McNaughton was then assuring Ottawa there was great danger that Germany would attack Britain with poison gas.

Three thousand tons of mustard gas in 45-gallon barrels crowd a field in Cornwall, Ontario, in January 1946. *(George Cooper / DND / National Archives of Canada)*

J.C. Arnell and T.E. King examine barrels full of mustard gas in a field near Cornwall, Ontario, prior to arranging to ship them to Halifax for disposal at sea in January 1946. *(George Cooper / DND / National Archives of Canada)*

Aerial view in May 1945 of the chemical and biological warfare research station of Suffield, Alberta. This was the nucleus of an open-air proving ground of about fifty square miles and was used to test the weapons of the United States and Britain, as well as Canada. *(National Archives of Canada)*

1989 view of western end of Grosse Ile. The buildings in the centre were occupied by the military staff during the war. The buildings at the right are the disinfection sheds which were converted to the mass-production of anthrax.

1989 view of the massive disinfection ovens in which the anthrax was grown at Grosse Ile. After the war they were apparently discarded in the underbrush nearby.
(author's photographs)

Workers supposedly at Porton Down harvest anthrax by "open-tray" method as practised at Grosse Ile. The procedure was dangerous and required elaborate precautions. There is some possibility that this photograph may actually be of work at Grosse Ile rather than Porton. *(UPI)*

Ira Baldwin, the first scientific director of the U.S. biological warfare research program, 1943. *(U.S. Army)*

E. Ll. Davies, the British superintendent of experiments at Porton Down, who was sent to Canada to take charge of operations at Suffield, Alberta, during the war. *(Suffield)*

Painting of E.A. (Alison) Flood, 1941. *(J.R. Dacey)*

Photograph of Don Dewar taken during the Second World War.

G.B. Reed in his office at the secret Kingston Biological Warfare Laboratory on the Queen's University campus, January 1946. *(Frank Royal/NFB/National Archives of Canada)*

Canadian scientists tour Camp Detrick, the U.S. biological warfare research station near Frederick, Maryland, 1944 or 1945. Beginning third from left is G.B. Reed, James Craigie, Charles Mitchell, E.G.D. Murray and the new scientific director at Detrick, Orem Woolpert. The pathogenic bacteria were grown in a connected series of large tanks like the one in the background. *(U.S. Army)*

E.G.D. Murray in his lab at McGill University, January 1946. First as head of the M-1000 Committee and then the C1 Committee, he was directly in charge of Canada's wartime biological warfare research. *(Frank Royal/ NFB/National Archives of Canada)*

Otto Maass in January 1946. He was then still Director of Chemical Warfare and in overall charge of Canada's research into chemical and biological warfare. *(Frank Royal/NFB/ National Archives of Canada)*

There was another incident that spring which must have caused Professor Murray grief. In mid-April a representative of Ducks Unlimited, the hunter-sponsored organization dedicated to the conservation of migratory birds, was called to McLelland Slough, a shallow prairie pond next to the Suffield perimeter wire and adjacent to the section known as the British Military Block. There he found a local farmer, Ole Olsen, and a neighbour pulling the bodies of dead ducks from the water and piling them in heaps on the prairie. They counted over one thousand dead and estimated at least another thousand in another pond less than a mile away.[57]

The local authorities assumed that the ducks died as a result of a gas experiment done too close to the wire, and requested through the Ministry of Mines and Resources that Ottawa be asked to limit such trials to the centre of the proving ground. A polite promise to that effect was duly received. However, the fact that Murray angrily refers to the incident later, connecting it to Suffield's new bacteriological lab, suggests that Davies was now sanctioning germ warfare trials without Murray's knowledge or the C1 Committee's consent. The ducks may even have been killed deliberately.[58]

Whether this incident contributed to Murray's reservations about field trials with anthrax is unclear. The available July 1944 memos deal mostly with obtaining empty British and American-made 4-pound Type F bombs so that both could be filled with anthrax and their merits compared. By the end of the month Murray was able to report to Fildes that Suffield was ready to do the tests. All they needed was delivery of some American-made bombs.

The primary weapon to be tested was the 500-pound "cluster bomb" which had been originally designed for incendiaries but had been adapted for chemical and biological warfare. There were two main types of British or American manufacture. The No.14, Mark I, cluster carried 106 4-pound bomblettes and the No. 4, Mark I, carried 14 30-pound bombs. The American version was billed as an "aimable" cluster designated the M-17. The advantage of the cluster bomb was that it could be set to explode at a predetermined height above the ground, thereby showering the bomblettes over a large area in a more-or-less controllable pattern.[59] In the course of the war cluster bombs were tested with a wide variety of chemical and biological chargings, the latter including poison darts tipped with botulinus toxin and other deadly agents. By the end of the war it had become the principle BW aircraft weapon of the Allies.

In the summer of 1944, however, it was still relatively untried in its anthrax version and a lot was riding on the large-scale tests at Suffield. For the past few months the U.S. Army's Chemical Warfare Service had been lobbying Washington for a special $2.5 million allocation to mass-produce BW cluster bombs on a large scale, proposing to build factories that could produce 275,000 botulinus or one million anthrax bombs a month. To get that kind of money, the military needed solid proof the new weapons would work as intended.[60]

Meanwhile that summer the Grosse Isle anthrax factory was finally up and running, but not without shakedown troubles. "The risks run by you and your staff in the Procedures of the project have been given careful consideration," Murray wrote Duthie, the scientist in charge. In view of concerns expressed, Murray said he had contacted the Chemical Warfare Lab in Ottawa and it would supply some new gas masks, hoses and an air pump which should greatly increase the comfort and safety of the workers. But, Murray added, the hoses had to receive great care when undergoing sterilization "to maintain their efficiency." One wonders how Duthie must have reacted to such a monumental understatement. A worker submerged in an atmosphere of anthrax spores would not last long with an inefficient – that is, leaky – air hose.[61]

Murray may have cut some corners to get anthrax production going. The project was over a year behind schedule and the Americans and British were undoubtedly impatient. Camp Detrick had perfected its own production pilot plant the previous March and flasks of the stuff were being traded across the border so that labs in both countries could try to determine which brand was better, Canadian- or U.S.-made anthrax. Murray had to hurry if he wanted Canada to be a major supplier of anthrax to the Allies.

Duthie, however, was a good scientist and a careful man. He had tests taken of run-off water around the old disinfection building where the anthrax was being produced and found micro-organisms that resembled the deadly bacteria. He suspected they were coming from a sump where waste water was collected and sterilized. He was also having trouble with flies in the building. These were grave matters of safety and he reported them the island commanding officer.

Murray was furious. He accused Duthie of jumping to conclusions based only on the appearance of the wayward bacteria, which might not be anthrax at all. Moreover, he said he was familiar with the sump and it was both heated and filled with disinfectant. Anthrax *couldn't* be escaping from it. "The story does not hang together and it is improper to raise an issue of such moment on such flimsy evidence."

As for the flies, "you state, rightly, there is every possibility that these flies were grossly contaminated," but as Duthie hadn't caught any, Murray ordered him to trap some now, from both within and without the building, and see if he could isolate anthrax from them. Then Murray would decide whether his fears were warranted and what to do about them.[62]

Duthie didn't take this rebuke lying down. His reply to Murray is a classic:

1. Leaking sump: Kindly refer to my second letter to Commander Olive dated Aug. 14th, a copy of which was forwarded to you. Salient facts:
a) We know the sump was leaking.
b) We know N [anthrax] finds its way to the sump through waste water. That's why the sump is there.
c) We have recovered N from the bodies of workers before they pass through the showers. Water from the showers goes to the sump as does water from pits in front of the autoclaves. . . .

Your third paragraph (about raising the alarm without checking with Murray first) will be dealt with the first time we meet. . . .
2. Flies: On at least three occasions it was reported to me that flies were present in the autoclave during inoculation or harvesting, and on one occasion a fly was killed by one of the operators on the surface of a tray. The time, the place and the surroundings were hardly opportune to institute a fly hunt and likely to prove more dangerous to the hunters than the hunted.[63]

It is easy to imagine the consternation of Duthie's workers, clad as they would be in protective suits, hoods and gas masks, and trailing their air hoses, when they caught sight of that fly landing on a culture tray and promenading through the live anthrax. The picture of men dressed like deep-sea divers lumbering around trying to catch a vastly more nimble fly would be comic if it were not for the potentially deadly consequences. Only the month before the District Medical Officer had reported that the station's kitchens positively seethed with flies. There must have been widespread loss of appetite in the mess halls that night.

When guinea pigs tested with suspect bacteria found inside cracks in the sump died, Duthie did not wait for Murray's reaction. He immediately shut down the whole operation, laced the sump with chemical, drained it, and applied a mastic coat that was so thick that it would be "impervious to everything but strong sulphuric acid." Murray had no comment.[64]

Duthie may have prevented a ghastly accident, but in any case it was too late for Murray's anthrax dream. That same last week in August the Americans informed him that they would produce anthrax themselves. Two months earlier Baldwin had successfully started up a pilot plant that was producing anthrax in a 10,000-gallon tank, a technique that was infinitely more efficient – and safer – than Grosse Ile's open-tray method. Duthie wasn't even producing enough anthrax to take advantage of the bomb charging machine the British had sent. On the recommendation of Lord Stamp, who probably had a hand in the American decision to abandon the Canadian project, it was crated up and sent to Camp Detrick. Then Murray, just when Duthie had brought the safety problems under control, had to order the Grosse Ile operation halted.[65]

It wasn't a total failure. Duthie reported that he had completed lots 75 and 76 consisting of 1,280 trays of anthrax each. He then undertook to mothball the operation in such a way that it could be restarted any time.[66]

He also asked Murray if he could "trade off" the twenty-seven barrels of corn steep water he no longer needed, and there is irony here. Corn steep is a byproduct of making corn syrup and until the First World War it had simply been discarded. Then the Americans discovered it was an ideal medium for growing the bacteria that produce acetone, a component in some explosives. In 1941 they established that it was also excellent for culturing penicillin mould, and later germ agents. Perhaps Duthie's surplus corn steep was traded to the Connaught Labs in Toronto which by this time was trying to mass-produce the life-saving substance in the old Knox College building on Spadina Crescent.

Canada's effort to produce penicillin parallels Murray's anthrax experience. The Connaught adopted the British technique of trying to grow the mould in thousands of bottles, separately inoculated by hand. The Americans did it in huge tanks, just as they did with anthrax. By mid-1944 the United States was poised to produce immense quantities of both. War germ or godsend, the techniques of production were much the same. And so were the scientists. Like Greey, the year before being put in charge of biological warfare research, Baldwin had been working on penicillin.[67]

Though the British and the Americans no longer needed the anthrax factory at Grosse Ile, Canada's wideopen spaces still beckoned. On August 14, 1944, Murray at last gave the go-ahead for the anthrax bombing trials at Suffield, citing authorization by Maass whom he said wanted them "to confirm Porton results and partly to develop our own ideas." He suggested they be done soon so that Lord Stamp and David Henderson could be on hand to watch.[68]

The British scientists must have liked what they saw. Britain put in an order for 500,000 anthrax bombs from the United States about a month later.[69]

C·H·A·P·T·E·R
S·I·X

Ships of Ice

It was probably the stupidest project of the whole war, on both sides. C.J. Mackenzie dismissed it out of hand. When told Churchill was pushing the idea, he paid more attention. It was still fantastic – a 2,000-foot slab of ice to serve as a giant airfield?

Churchill was a great man and his flaws were of like proportion. One of these was his belief in his own infallibility, even in areas of which he knew nothing. This was especially the case when it came to science, which was useful when Churchill was convinced something like radar needed support, but disastrous if a hare-brained scheme happened by. For the most part his personal scientific adviser, Lord Cherwell (pronounced Charwell), buffered him. But Geoffrey Pyke got past.

Pyke was a crackpot. He was an eccentric inventor who never encountered any obstacles in his projects because he had no technical knowledge or scientific background. He had had a difficult youth. Born into an affluent London Jewish family in 1893, his father died when he was only seven and he was raised in reduced circumstances – household servants but smaller house – which his mother contended was poverty. She apparently was a strong-minded woman and sent him to Wellington, a public school mostly for the sons of professional soldiers. She also insisted he observe the key rituals of his faith in the matter of clothes and diet. He became the cruel butt of his schoolmates.[1]

He was pulled out of public school, privately tutored, and sent to Cambridge where he soon flunked out. At the outbreak of the First World War he had the bright idea of reporting on Germany as an undercover journalist but was promptly imprisoned as a spy. He escaped in 1915, wrote a book about it, and after the war opened a progressive school at Cambridge which purported to teach children by "the scientific method." He speculated heavily on the stock market and went bankrupt, school and all, with the Crash of 1929. By 1939 he was living alone in real poverty, working for various left-wing organizations and pestering newspapers and politicians with a variety of madcap schemes.

While running his school at Cambridge during the 1920s, Pyke had made contact with some of the university intellectuals. He became a Marxist[2] and one of the key communists he met was the eminent crystallographer, John Desmond Bernal. He, and economist Maurice Dobbs, were the chief proponents of Marxism among the Cambridge dons and did much in the 1930s to tutor impressionable undergraduates on the merits of the Soviet economic and social experiment. Cambridge, indeed, became in that period a kind of intellectual cradle of communism for young people disillusioned by the Great Depression and the apparent failure of capitalism. Kim Philby, Anthony Blunt, Guy Burgess – almost the entire panoply of Britain's postwar traitors were undergraduate acolytes of Bernal and Dobbs before being recruited as spies by Russia's secret services.[3]

The third component to what was to become the most colossal security failure of the Second World War was King George VI's cousin, Lord Louis Mountbatten. Great-grandson of Queen Victoria and nephew of the deposed and assassinated tsar of Russia, he was undoubtedly the most popular member of the royal family's immediate relatives. He was good-looking, wealthy, amiable and in the 1930s a highly visible member of an international set that included movie stars such as Douglas Fairbanks and Mary Pickford. Son of a former First Sea Lord, he had been a career naval officer since the First World War, getting his first destroyer command in 1934. When war with Germany broke out again, it was only natural that much would be expected of this dashing 39-year-old aristocratic naval commander. As captain of a destroyer flotilla, he did not disappoint.

Racing injudiciously for home port in high seas a month after war was declared, Mountbatten's destroyer *Kelly* was damaged when it nearly capsized. One man drowned. A few weeks later the ship hit a mine, and was towed to dry dock. Within days of getting back to sea in March 1940, the *Kelly* rammed another destroyer. Back to dry dock. Six weeks later the ship saw genuine action off Norway and narrowly escaped destruction in an attack by dive-bombers. A week later, Mountbatten indulged in sending silly messages by bright Aldis light to a fellow destroyer off the Dutch coast while they hunted for a submarine. "How are the muskets? Let the battle commence," Mountbatten signalled to the neighbouring captain's consternation and alarm. The joke was cut short when the *Kelly* received a torpedo amidships.

Had Mountbatten not been a royal cousin, he would have been cashiered for this stupidity. As it was, he was also lucky. The *Kelly* did not sink but was towed back to port, a shattered wreck, while the rescue ships were harried by German aircraft and torpedo boat attacks. It took ninety-one hours and people lined the banks of the Tyne cheering as she was pulled up the river. The feat captured the imagination of a nation. Mountbatten was a hero. But twenty-eight men had died.

The report on the incident covered up his folly and Mountbatten got another ship. In November he led an attack on German destroyers off the coast of France and through an error in tactics, received two torpedos, one in the bow and one in the stern. This time forty-six men died and the Germans got off scot-free. The Royal Navy brass conceded that Mountbatten's direction "does not appear to have been up to the required standard" but press reports again painted him a hero. He was awarded the Distinguished Service Cross and invited to dinner with Churchill at Chequers. And he got yet another ship – the *Kelly* again, almost completely rebuilt. The following May German dive-bombers made a thorough job of it. The *Kelly* was sunk off the coast of Crete with the loss of over half her officers and crew of 260.[4]

What he lacked in brains Mountbatten made up for in courage, literally going down with his ship. Incredibly, he survived, and on a raft waiting for rescue with a remnant of his crew kept up their spirits in the finest tradition of the Royal Navy. Whether he was at fault for the loss of his ship this time is unknown, but afterwards his chief, Admiral Sir Andrew Cunningham, observed privately that the flotilla he was in charge of was "thoroughly badly led."

Despite doubts in the navy as to his competence, Mountbatten was a hero again. Churchill offered him command of the aircraft carrier *Illustrious* and he was sent to the United States on a public relations tour which included meeting the U.S. Navy top brass and dinner at the White House. Mountbatten could do no wrong because the prime minister had decided he was a fighting sailor.

Instead of sending him back to sea, Churchill changed his mind and put Mountbatten in charge of Combined Operations, the group responsible for planning attacks on the German-held European coastline. Before long the prime minister vaulted him three steps in rank and made him an acting vice-admiral and a Chief of Staff against the express objection of the First Sea Lord, Sir (Alfred) Dudley Pound. Mountbatten had done nothing to merit this gross favouritism and it scandalized the top leaders of both the army and navy. It was equivalent to a bank appointing a junior branch manager with a record of financial recklessness to its board of directors. Pound was one of the few with the courage to tell Churchill so and it cost him dearly. Churchill hinted that he was grooming Mountbatten for First Sea Lord, and for the next fifteen months Pound lived in terror – for the safety of the nation – that he might actually make good this threat.[5]

And so, after two years and losing three ships, Mountbatten had soared from a captain of destroyers to vice-admiral, and sat at the very centre of British military power and authority, an equal voice to the three senior admirals and generals who headed the British Army, Royal Navy and Royal Air Force. While all doubted his suitability, he had the ear of Churchill and that's all that mattered. His biographer, Philip Ziegler, suggests that he was one of the few who could stand up to the prime minister. Documents from Canadian archives suggest otherwise. People who accept undeserved favours do not usually bite the hand that feeds them.

On arrival at Combined Operations headquarters, Mountbatten immediately started filling key posts with friends. Then he cast around for scientific advisers like those attached to the army and navy. One of Churchill's friends of public school days, Leo Amery, then a cabinet minister, sent along a letter he had received from Pyke outlining a scheme he had for sending raiding parties into Occupied Europe. Amery suggested that Pyke might be the kind of man Combined Operations was looking for. Any suggestion from a friend of Churchill's received eager attention from Mountbatten. He hired Pyke immediately.[6]

It is difficult to over-state the stupidity of making Pyke a scientific adviser to Combined Operations. He was just one of thousands of crackpots who deluged the authorities in Canada, the United States and Britain with wild ideas on how to win the war. Some of the suggestions from actual scientists were often far-fetched, but the 48-year-old Pyke was a university dropout, had never had anything to do with science or engineering and had never held a steady job. One of the first ideas he submitted to his new boss was to sink the German battleship *Tirpitz* by blowing compressed air through perforated pipes secretly laid underneath it so that the ship would fall into the bubble thus created. For this kind of puerile nonsense Mountbatten paid him £1,500 a year, a salary then equivalent to that of a senior scientist or administrator.

Pyke's big plan to win the war was to develop machines that could travel on snow and parachute them with parties of commandos onto the glaciers of Norway from where they would harass the Germans on the coast with "snow torpedoes" – bombs tied to logs which would be slid down hills at the enemy. This would tie up thousands of troops, Pyke reasoned. Mountbatten took the idea to Churchill who liked it but thought the Americans, now newly in the war, should be given the job of designing the vehicle. Pyke was immediately sent to the United States to get American help. No one gave any thought to how such raiding parties could be supplied, hidden from aircraft or what kind of terrain they would encounter.[7]

Churchill, it should be said, was suspicious of scientists. They forever seemed to pour cold water on his ideas for aerial mines, rocket barrages and the like. He could little grasp their practical objections and invariably concluded they were deliberately foot-dragging, or were unimaginative in their thinking. He came to rely only on his personal scientific adviser, Lord Cherwell, who was flippantly known as Lord Barrage of Balloons for having pushed through the deployment of the familar tethered balloons which were flown over London to discourage bombers but did nothing of the kind – enemy aircraft simply flew over them. Cherwell, a raw-egg eating health faddist, was intensely disliked by most of the senior scientific community, but he had been a friend of the prime minister before the war and he was about the only scientist Churchill would listen to. He was given a large experimental facility of his own called MD1 (Ministry of Defence No. 1) where he could independently test out the prime minister's pet theories, as well as his own.[8]

Dr. O.M. Solandt, who later headed Canada's Defence Research Board, was in charge of the Army Operational Research Group in Britain during the war and remembers the situation well.

It was one of the terrible tragedies of the war that Churchill took up with Cherwell who was not very suitable. He was the typical academic physicist who thought because he knew academic physics he knew everything. And he would back his own views on new weapons and things ahead of anybody else's.

He never represented the scientific community to Churchill – just the exact opposite of Van Bush in the States who had the entire confidence of the (U.S.) scientific community. When Van Bush was asked something by the President, he went to the right people and said, "Here's the question and you boys tell me what I should say." Cherwell never did that. In fact, none of British scientists would speak to him. There just was no real communication.[9]

Cherwell, of course, could not develop on his own any really big projects for Churchill, so when the United States came into the war the prime minister regularly used his influence to get the Americans to undertake large-scale schemes he knew he couldn't get done in Britain. One of these, typically, was a Most Secret project code-named Canal Defence Lights. The file on it in the British War Office archives has been emptied of all details but Dr. Solandt was one of those involved in assessing its worth.

It seems a Greek stockbroker who was a friend of the royal family was introduced to the "right" people and convinced them that gunners could not aim if a light was shone in their eyes. This led the Americans to be asked, undoubtedly through Churchill, to design and produce tanks with two-inch slots in their turrets through which a powerful light mounted in a parabolic mirror could be shone to dazzle enemy gunners during night attacks. Hundreds of these tanks were built in the United States and Canada and held in reserve at Fort Knox, even though tanks were desperately needed by British and American forces battling the Germans in the Middle East.

Eventually, someone in the War Office decided the idea should at least be tested, and Solandt was asked, unofficially, to run some field trials. He calculated the number of machine gun hits that would be registered on a tank without the light, and then tried it with the tank advancing against a machine gun with its light on. Slightly more hits were scored.

"The gunner said he could see with no difficulty at all. It didn't upset him a bit. It was a damned easy target.

"So we said let's do some firing trials with the 2-pounder (anti-tank) gun and again we predicted the accuracy of the gun and the accuracy of the gunner, which we knew pretty well. He did exactly as predicted. He even got a shot through the slot. Completely wrecked the mirror."[10]

With that kind of attitude to science at 10 Downing Street, it isn't any wonder that Pyke was immediately dispatched to the United States with his idea. Mountbatten, however, still needed more science advisers and Sir Henry Tizard, likely at the prompting of Professor P.M.S. Blackett, a Cambridge Marxist who had worked with Tizard in the Air Ministry, suggested J.D. Bernal, who was then working for the Ministry of Home Security on the effects of bomb damage. He was hired forthwith, along with South African Solly Zuckerman, and they arrived at Mountbatten's headquarters in April 1942.

Bernal was a well-known security risk. Sir John Anderson, who had originally hired him for the bomb damage study, had said he did not care whether he was "as red as the flames of hell" as long as he could do his job[11] and Bernal had, and well. Where Pyke was a rambling fool, the 41-year-old Bernal was an accomplished and well-published scientist. They shared in common only their dedication to Marxism and their inclination to slovenly dress. Both were exceedingly unkempt, wore their hair long, and rarely wore ties in an age when propriety of apparel was important. With Pyke it was a matter of poverty; with the affluent Bernal, affectation.[12]

Whether Mountbatten knew Bernal was a practising, outspoken and dedicated communist is unknown. Certainly, everyone else did. Bernal and Blackett had both been experimental physicists at Cambridge in the 1920s, although Bernal had been much more public about his Soviet sympathies. Even Solandt was warned that Bernal wasn't someone with whom to discuss sensitive matters.[13] Mountbatten was probably too important to be told, and too much of a gentleman to ask. In any event, by this time Mountbatten was preoccupied with planning the attack on Dieppe. On August 19, 1942, approximately four thousand Canadians landed on the coast of France in a frontal attack against an alert enemy in fortified positions. It was the *Kelly* all over again: 3,367 were killed, wounded or captured.[14]

Canada's official history of the Second World War, three volumes published between 1955 and 1960, spends several pages examining claims of survivors who said the Germans had told them they had been forewarned of the raid. It concludes no, but official histories must meet the approbation of governments which might still be sensitive of the feelings of allies. Moreover, in 1955 the historian would not have had access to all secret sources. In a 1963 book on his wartime experiences in the Office of Strategic Services, the U.S. sabotage agency and forerunner of the CIA, Stanley Lovell reports that his colleagues in British Intelligence told him there had been a major foul-up on the day of Dieppe. The raid had originally been scheduled for August 18 but had to be delayed one day because Mountbatten failed to show at the appointed time. Unfortunately, Britain's Security Intelligence Service had arranged for a captured German radio operator to notify Berlin of the attack one day after it occurred to convince his superiors he was supplying accurate intelligence that happened to be "just too late." It was Mountbatten who was too late. On Monday the SIS operator radioed: "A great commando raid is laid on, destination Dieppe. . . . Time: Tuesday at dawn." The Canadians were right on time.[15]

At a dinner gathering shortly afterwards, Canadian-born press baron Lord Beaverbrook lit into Mountbatten and accused him of "faulty planning leading to the needless sacrifice of human lives." As late as 1958 Beaverbrook wrote his son, Max Aiken: "Don't Trust Mountbatten in Any Public Capacity . . . he took full responsibility for Dieppe. Four thousand set forth and three thousand did not return."[16] Because Mountbatten throughout his life was an amiable, approachable, likeable man, as well as a royal cousin, most writers have tended to attribute the muddle of planning prior to Dieppe to a kind of collective incompetence, rather than give him primary blame. Yet the fact remains, not only was the Dieppe raid planned by Combined Operations to the exclusion of the regular British military intelligence services,[17] after it had been postponed several times and finally cancelled – to the relief of just about everyone – it was Mountbatten alone who suddenly thought it should go ahead regardless. It was he who convinced Churchill. Without Mountbatten, there would have been no Dieppe.

While this Combined Operations débâcle was in progress, Pyke was in the United States promoting his snow machine scheme. The Americans were intrigued by the idea and suggested various tracked vehicle designs. These Pyke imperiously rejected. The machines he had in mind had to run on the Archimedian screw principle – a kind of auger underneath the vehicle which would provide propulsion by boring its way through the top layers of snow. Even a person with marginal mechanical aptitude could see that the auger would be smashed on the first bit of hard ground or ice it encountered and the Americans told him so. Pyke, who knew nothing about mechanics and nothing about sub-Arctic winters, stuck to his guns. The Americans responded by cutting him out of all discussion on the project.[18]

As the Americans would now only talk with the uniformed officer from Combined Operations who had come over as his aide, Pyke had nothing to do. Aside from peppering all and sundry with complaints about American lack of "scientific integrity" – earning himself the eternal loathing of Vannevar Bush – Pyke had months of well-paid idleness in which to dream up another scheme. This manifested itself as a bulky package that arrived on Mountbatten's desk five weeks after Dieppe via diplomatic pouch from New York.

What he found inside was 232 typed foolscap pages of the most incredible twaddle. Pyke had ingratiated himself into the labs of the Brooklyn Polytechnic Institute where he learned that Professor Herman Mark had discovered that ice mixed with from 4 to 10 per cent sawdust became remarkably tough and slow to melt. That, combined with some academic papers he read on super-cooled water, led Pyke to conceive of a grand scheme to build a fleet of giant aircraft carriers, freighters and assault ships of the ice/sawdust combination, which he labelled "pykrete" even though it was someone else's discovery. This ice fleet would sail down from the Arctic and assault the coasts of Europe and

Japan, immobilizing the Axis battle fleets by pulling alongside their ships and spraying them with super-cooled water, which would immediately freeze and immobilize the gun turrets.

Probably no one at the time read Pyke's monster memo in its entirety. Mountbatten certainly didn't, sloughing it off to an aide for assessment with the comment that he should keep an open mind. Because the scale of Pyke's idiocy is relevant to this story, it is necessary to quote at some length from his biographer's precis of Pyke's proposal and from the memo itself:

> A berg ship fleet would first launch waves of bombers against the enemy port to be attacked. Cruising into the bomb-softened port, the ships would next capture the enemy's vessels in the harbour by ramming or drawing alongside them, catapulting canvas troughs with grapnels on their ends at the vessels, and flooding these troughs with super-cooled water which would freeze instantly on contact, creating eighteen-inch bridging. Boarding parties from the berg ships . . . would then go on the enemy ships to spray their superstructures with more super-cooled water, sealing up guns and companionways, imprisoning the crews below decks. The enemy sailors would have the choice of freezing to death or surrendering. . . .

For some reason, Pyke thought the first attack by the berg fleet should be through the Straits of Gibraltar and against Italy, preferably Naples or Genoa.

> After the bombers had finished their pummelling and the enemy's ships in harbour had been captured, the first berg ships to reach the docks would disgorge special tanks either to tow containers of crushed ice or to push ready-made blocks of pykrete into the city. "Across the streets at a prearranged perimeter," the memo explained, "short of the outskirts of town, the blocks, the crushed ice and the super-cooled water which is pumped through hoses – and some of which, to make quite sure, is brought ashore in armoured containers – are combined to form a barricade which stretches around the part of the town it has been arranged to hold."

This perimeter wall would have a gross length of about six miles, would be twenty feet high and thirty feet thick.

Nothing could blast through it. Ice fortresses would, at the same time, be constructed hastily for the necessary shore fighting installations, and wherever rooftop fighting seemed imminent, the buildings of Genoa would be sprayed with super-cooled water to cave them in. While this ice was forming, the roofs would be too slippery for snipers to run across them.

A berg ship would enter the Kiel Canal to ram shipping . . . berg ships that attacked Hamburg would make it perfectly clear they had no intention of killing women and children . . . ice shelters should be set up as quickly as possible in Hamburg to be used as court rooms for war criminals . . . German soldiers must not be allowed to surrender – "If they are starving, we must throw them sausages . . ."

There was much, much more in the same vein. Central to the idea was an aircraft carrier of pykrete, 2,000 feet long and with a hull of ice 30 feet thick. A beautiful drawing of this behemoth was produced minus, of course, any actual engineering or architectural detail. In fact, there appears to have been precious little practical detail of any kind in the memo, save for specifications Pyke pulled out of the air and then charged with mystical immutability. It had to be Italy first attacked, the perimeter ice wall had to be six miles, the ships had to be propelled by electric motors mounted on its sides, and so forth. Pyke named his grand plan Habbakuk.[19]

Anyone familiar with the English boys' magazines of the inter-war period, especially the popular Chums magazine, will recognize the similarity of Pyke's plan to the kind of science fiction stories these publications then carried. One strongly suspects that its main elements came from just such a source, at least indirectly. In any event, it was not a plan at all but a fantasy, and a pretty juvenile one at that.

Mountbatten's aide passed Pyke's memo along to Combined Operations' real scientific advisers, Zuckerman and Bernal. Zuckerman rejected it immediately but Bernal, perhaps out of sympathy for a fellow Marxist, suggested there could be some merit in the concept of reinforced ice.[20] On the strength of that, Mountbatten sent a memo of his own to Churchill in which he enthused about gigantic aircraft carriers of pykrete, and frozen freighters "immune to bombs, mines and torpedoes." If it was too costly to freeze the ice artificially, he suggested the Arctic cold of Canada or Russia could be utilized to build Habbakuks. The prime minister, predictably, bit.[21]

Two days later Churchill ordered the Chiefs of Staff to give Mountbatten every assistance in developing the Habbakuk idea and appended to his memo a few thoughts of his own:

> Something like the following procedure suggests itself to me. Go to an ice field in the north which is six or seven feet thick but capable of being approached by ice breakers: cut out the pattern of the ice ship on the surface; bring the right number of pumping appliances to the different sides of the ice-deck, spray salt water on continuously so as to increase the thickness and smooth the surface. . . .[22]

Churchill was of the opinion that the success of the project really rested on being able to make a Habbakuk in the Arctic out of a great "lozenge of ice, 5,000 feet by 2,000 feet by 100 feet" which could be floated down to the coast of France or Norway and serve as a base from which to hurl tornados of fighters and bombers at the startled Germans. Work was to proceed urgently, and with maximum secrecy.

C.J. Mackenzie was tipped off on the scheme on January 2, 1943, when he was startled by a note from the National Research Council's scientific liaison officer in London, Archie Laidlaw. Combined Operations headquarters had told him that the British cabinet was shortly to ask the Canadian government to undertake research into the building of huge "bergships" which were to serve as "unsinkable aircraft carriers." The president of NRC, an engineer by profession, was astonished. It seemed ridiculous.[23]

Meanwhile Mountbatten had abandoned Pyke's original idea of using reinforced ice and had ordered the Combined Operations planners try to work it out with natural ice. "The solution they are working on is substantially along the lines you suggested," he wrote Churchill on January 8. "Namely, letting nature do the work and building the ship on ice from blocks of the same material which would slide into place by gravity." He "purposely" did not want to trouble the prime minister with technical details, but the time had come to talk to the Canadian government.[24] Thus it was basically Churchill's plan for Habbakuks, not Pyke's, that was in the large brown envelope marked "Top Secret, By Safe Hand" and bearing heavy seals which arrived a week later at 100 Sussex Street in Ottawa.

Years later W.H. Cook remembered Mackenzie outlining the scheme at a meeting in his office with a half-dozen other NRC scientists. There was considerable incredulity. Mackenzie invited them to scan the 100-page report from Britain. "It was quite verbose," Cook recalled, "and described the value of this floating airfield in much more detail than how it was going to be constructed, protected, or operated. The structure was to be covered with an 'insulating skin' and maintained by refrigeration, but no details were given. . . . The whole thing sounded fantastic."[25]

This plan, drawn up by Bernal to fit in with Churchill's ideas rather than Pyke's,[26] called for a "floating air field" at least 2,000 feet long made out of ice. The Canadians, however, were only required to do theoretical studies, Mackenzie was told by London. The design of the first Habbakuk was to be done in Britain and Canada was "not to be consulted until construction had commenced."[27] British naval architects soon pointed out that such a structure would have to be at least 50 feet above the water if was not going to be swamped by waves. Allowing for the buoyancy of ice, that meant it had to be about 500 feet thick if it was solid. The alternative was to make it hollow but that required refrigeration or the hull would melt.[28]

Orders were orders. Mackenzie started the NRC staff specialists on some of the immediate and obvious problems and over the next few weeks sought the assistance of the engineering faculties of the three Prairie universities. It is clear from his diary that he never had much faith in the idea, although the scientific problems intrigued him. Very little was known about the physical properties of ice. However, one suspects that he took direct charge of the project because if he had delegated it, it would not have been treated seriously. As it was, for the next four months it consumed an enormous amount of his time when he could ill afford it.

Mackenzie had another very major concern on his mind. A year earlier, in the spring of 1942, the British had come to realize that if they were going to make any real progress in developing nuclear fission and an atomic bomb, the work was going to have to take place outside the country. British scientists and industrial resources were too tightly stretched to devote much effort to what was still a long shot and so Mackenzie was approached and asked if Britain's nuclear team could be established in Canada under the National Research Council. The British also realized that the Americans were surging ahead in their nuclear research and it seemed sensible to establish the parallel project in Canada where information could freely and quickly be exchanged between the two groups.

It was an exciting prospect for Mackenzie. George Laurence's attempt to produce a sustained chain reaction in a primitive apparatus at the NRC had seemed far-fetched and was just petering out when the delegations from Britain arrived to disclose that the idea was theoretically sound. Refugee scientists from France and Austria working in Britain had determined that if a reactor could be built using heavy water to control the fission of uranium, a rare radioactive element called plutonium could be produced. Plutonium, in turn, could likely be made into a bomb of unimaginable explosive power.

The negotiations dragged on through the summer. The spokesman for the American project, Vannevar Bush, was at first warm to the idea, particularly as Canada's Supply Minister, C.D. Howe, undertook to get government control of Canada's supply of uranium ore, which was being mined in the Northwest Territories and processed for its radium content in Port Hope, Ontario. This was vitally important because Canada was one of the few countries in the world that mined uranium and while the Americans had considerable stocks that had come from the Belgian Congo, this could not be considered a guaranteed source while German submarines were at large in the Atlantic.

The scientists from Britain began arriving in December 1942, just as the Americans achieved the first sustained chain reaction in an experimental atomic pile at the University of Chicago. They were more European than British, consisting of two from France, one from Switzerland, one from Czechoslovakia, two from Austria and only two from Britain. Mackenzie cast a wide net to pull in Canadian scientists to augment the team, settling them all in temporary quarters in Montreal. It was a frantic time for the president of the National Research Council, and the need also to pursue the Habbakuk project was most unwelcome.

In Britain, of course, all in the know except Mountbatten and Bernal thought the ice-ship scheme madness. Lord Cherwell and Charles Goodeve, a Canadian in charge of the Admiralty's research and development department which produced many novel devices during the war, were forced to sit on the Habbakuk steering committee. It was one of the few times the two men agreed about anything. Both were outspoken in their negative comments, and Goodeve in particular angered Mountbatten considerably.[29]

The puzzle is Bernal. He was the only scientist or technical person who ever showed any faith in the concept. He even championed it. Churchill's version of Habbakuk was even more harebrained than Pyke's and it is difficult to see how a scientist of proven ability could put his signature to such an impossible idea and persistently assure Mountbatten that the principles were sound. One possible explanation – and there is the evidence of Bernal's background and character to support it – is that Bernal may have simply been trying to see how much of a fool he could make out of Mountbatten.

Bernal was born in Ireland, 96 miles from Dublin, and raised a Catholic. He would have been 15 when British troops bloodily put down the so-called Easter Rebellion. When an adult, he became a dedicated Marxist, philosophically opposed to everything Mountbatten represented – wealth, class, privilege and power undeservedly acquired. In 1932 Bernal had written that science outside Russia was only for the benefit of the privileged, and it could be made to serve the people only by "the complete overthrow of capitalism."[30] Habbakuk was evolving as a sweeping parody of this view. As Bernal was known for his quixotic sense of humour, it looks suspiciously as if he was "taking the mickey" out of Mountbatten and, through him, the whole British establishment.

The Habbakuk story sometimes approaches high farce. When Mountbatten was finally forced to concede that natural ice was not going to work, he had to convince Churchill of the merits of pykrete. As Mountbatten himself described it: "I went to Chequers to see the Prime Minister and was told he was in his bath. I said, 'Good, that's exactly where I want him to be.' I nipped up the stairs and called out to him, 'I have a block of a new material which I would like to put in your bath.' He plopped the block of pykrete into the bath and the two men expostulated over its slowness in melting.[31]

Zuckerman also tells a much-quoted story of how Pyke came down with jaundice and insisted that a Habbakuk conference be held in his bedroom. Mountbatten, Bernal, Zuckerman and Sir Harold Wernher sat around the foot of the bed where Pyke sat up like "some kind of jaundiced Christ. Mountbatten tried to assure him that work was proceeding as fast as it possibly could. Pyke was not satisfied. 'Without faith,' he kept protesting, 'nothing will come of this project.' 'But I have faith,' replied Mountbatten. 'Yes,' said Pyke, 'but have others got faith?' and turning to Harold Wernher he asked solemnly, 'Have you got faith, Brigadier?' Poor Wernher did not know what to say, but before he could utter a word, CCO [Mountbatten] had chipped in with the remark, 'Wernher's on my staff to see that I'm not over-lavish with my own faith.'"[32]

The Canadians were soon informed that the line of inquiry had been changed to include reinforced ice, while Mackenzie was warned in a "Most Secret" memo that Churchill was taking "a violent and personal interest" in the project.[33] Canada was now also expected to build the thing. To Cook, it all seemed even crazier. "To my mind Habbakuk had again entered the realm of the fantastic: Pykerite was not a natural material and would have to be produced by mechanical refrigeration equipment of mammoth capacity requiring large amounts of power." Nevertheless, work continued in centres across the Prairies and in the Rockies NRC scientists undertook to build a scale model of the ice platform on Lake Patricia near Jasper.[34]

In March Pyke and Bernal came over to Canada to see how work was progressing. They made a lasting impression on Mackenzie:

They were the strangest characters. Bernal had come right out of Africa. He didn't have a hat. He didn't have a coat. He didn't have any footwear. He didn't have a watch. And Pyke came over. Pyke didn't have a watch. He didn't have a coat but he had spats and a felt hat on. And they came over with letters from Churchill to see Mackenzie King. . . .

They wanted to go out West. So I went with them. I went over on the train and I never had such an experience in my life. . . . Well, first Pyke left, about one minute before the train was to leave, to go look for the luggage. And then Bernal went in another two minutes to get Pyke. They both came back just as the train was about to pull out ten or fifteen minutes late. As for the luggage, it was in their compartment all the time.

We were stopping at Winnipeg and then going on to Saskatoon. And Pyke lost his tickets. So I had to go into the CPR and explain. These were very great men. They were sent over by Churchill. They were geniuses. They were going to win the war . . . you couldn't think of a man like this bothering about the tickets, you see.

Then, we got to Saskatoon and I kept telling them, "You know, this is going to be pretty cold and. . . ." Oh, well, they were from England and Englishmen didn't mind the cold very much. You know, that type of thing.

So, we got off at Saskatoon at two o'clock in the morning. It was about twenty below zero. And they had all this luggage with them and there were no taxis. So I walked from the CNR station to First Avenue, down to the Bessborough [hotel]. And I just let them perish. . . .[35]

The next morning Mackenzie's wayward charges bought fur hats, winter coats, gloves – the works. Pyke may even have bought socks because the reason he wore spats was so that he didn't have to wear them, thereby saving on their wear and tear and having to wash them.[36] He must have had pretty cold toes as he walked up a Saskatoon street in ordinary shoes with no socks at 20 below.

When they got to Jasper, the deans of engineering from the universities of Alberta, Saskatchewan and Manitoba accompanied them on a tour of the work in progress. They saw the model ice platform under construction on Lake Patricia, and examined experimental beams which had been made out of the pulp and water composite, 50 feet long and 6 feet high. They were huge and Bernal, who had become an expert on explosives, tried firing a pistol at the things. The bullets just bounced off. Everyone was impressed.

When it came time to leave for the east, Bernal and Pyke again gave Mackenzie problems. They had been staying at the hotel at Lake Louise and a few hours before their train was to leave, they decided to go skiing. They were warned that snow conditions were dangerous but went anyway, Pyke only wearing his hat, jacket, spats and shoes. Shortly before train time, Bernal came back alone. Pyke had decided to climb a mountain, he said. Mackenzie figured he was probably already dead and buried in an avalanche but, no, with just five minutes to spare a little figure "like Charlie Chaplin" came striding down the lake. When Mackenzie got the pair on the train to Calgary, he took no chances. Once they settled into their compartment, he closed the door. And locked it.[37]

Later Pyke and Bernal had their audience with the Canadian prime minister. Pyke had been persuaded to buy a new suit for the occasion and the trousers had been fitted with a zipper, a Canadian invention only just then replacing buttons on flies. As a precaution, Pyke slipped into the lavatory just before being presented and found he could not get the zipper up. With great presence of mind, when he appeared before the old-ladyish and prim Mackenzie King, he drew attention to his open flies and declared: "Prime Minister, I would not have to present myself to you in this state were it not for the fact that Canadian engineers are totally inefficient."[38]

The antics of Habbakuk's loony inventor did not reassure Mackenzie of the project's practicality. He made it very clear in his progress reports that it would have to be made, not cut from some Arctic ice shelf, and that the work had to be done in southern Canada because of the cost of delivering supplies and maintaining crews in the far north. Nevertheless, Canada now had the job of designing the beast and Mackenzie contracted the problem out to the Montreal Engineering Company, which likened it to building the Hoover Dam in the United States.

It would have been the biggest ship ever. The largest vessel then afloat was the giant Japanese battleship, *Yamato*, which weighed in at 70,000 tons and was three city blocks long. The first Habbakuk would have weighed 2.2 million tons and would have been ten city blocks long. It would have been a quarter longer than Toronto's 1,500-foot CN tower is high, and would have needed water at least 150 feet deep to float. It would have gone aground long before it could enter most of the ports of Europe. The Montreal engineers noted that the 6 per cent wood pulp required by even one Habbakuk would use up a substantial portion of Canada's total annual output.[39] Vincent Massey, Canada's High Commissioner in Britain, even pleaded with Mountbatten that "the many hundred thousand tons of pulp" required would be in direct competition to the newsprint required by Canada's newspapers.[40] The concern appears not to have registered.

By early spring Mackenzie had had enough. So had C.D. Howe, who had been continually pestered through channels about the status of the project. In June Mackenzie was to go over to Britain to discuss problems that had developed over atomic research. The Americans had decided that the international makeup of the "British" group in Montreal posed a security risk and were refusing to exchange information. Mackenzie was to attempt to explain the American point of view but Howe also asked him to make it clear to the British that Canada was not prepared to commit itself on the building of a Habbakuk. After four months of intensive research, this was telling the British that the Canadians wanted out.[41]

When he got to London Mackenzie was immediately asked to dinner with Mountbatten and two of his top advisers, Admiral Sir Charles Kennedy-Purvis and Sir Harold Wernher. Over a meal consisting of poor soup, poor coffee, a cold bit of salmon and a "greasy" sweet, Mackenzie broke the news. "It won't work," he told them. "You could do it cheaper in a refrigerator plant in the Tropics than you could do it in the North." Mountbatten was crestfallen. When he left the table for a few minutes, the other two quickly told Mackenzie that his remarks were the first sense they had heard talked about Habbakuk since it first arose. "This was the fantastic part," Mackenzie later said. "They were first-class people and they really didn't dare oppose Mountbatten and Churchill out loud."[42]

It looked as though Mackenzie had torpedoed the scheme, but no such luck. In a few days he was summoned before a committee especially convened to consider the Canadian position. It included some of Britain's most distinguished scientists and engineers, the director of naval construction, and a young designer named Barnaby from Thorneycroft, Britain's big shipbuilding firm. Mackenzie had invited him to Canada to study the feasibility of building a Habbakuk and he had confirmed in a separate report to the Admiralty Mackenzie's judgment that it was impractical.

"And Bernal and Pyke put this problem again and it was the most ridiculous thing. Here were these distinguished, competent people, sitting around this room, and these two nitwits, crazy as Hell, talking about something they didn't know anything about." Finally, one of the scientists "just blew his top and said that all the facts that they had presented were just partial facts – the same thing I had been saying to them – and that they didn't have the problem solved. The problems were construction and economic, and a few little problems (solved) in a lab at Oxford did not amount to a hill of beans."[43]

Next they went over to Combined Operations headquarters to confront Mountbatten. He refused to accept the consensus. Moreover, he did not like the fact that Barnaby had given Habbakuk an unfavourable report. Mackenzie was scandalized to see Mountbatten put pressure on the young engineer. "He actually threatened Barnaby in quite an obvious way. This was done very eloquently – 'It would be a great mistake for a young man starting out creatively to put in a report which was obviously wrong,' and that the consequences to Barnaby 'would be very great.' They tried to make him withdraw his report, but he didn't."[44]

Mountbatten then asked Mackenzie to head up another committee to try to resolve the conflict, but when the Canadian listened yet again to Bernal arguing against Barnaby's conclusions, he finally got fed up. "This is ridiculous," he told Bernal. "I'm not going to have anything more to do with it if you are going to keep on stating opinions as if they were facts." This stand earned Mackenzie the silent applause of everyone involved – except Bernal, Pyke and Mountbatten.

Finally, when Mackenzie was ready to return to Canada, he laid it right on the line for Mountbatten: Canada was not going to do it, it could not be done, and all it was doing was draining resources from work that was more worthwhile. "Then we must see Churchill," Mountbatten said.

"I'm leaving," Mackenzie replied. "I'm leaving tomorrow night."

"Oh, you can't leave. You can't go because the Prime Minister wants to see you."

"Well, I'm not engaged by the Prime Minister. I'm engaged by C.D. Howe in Canada, and I have told him that I'll be back and I must be back."[45]

The next day, June 10, 1943, Mackenzie saw Churchill.

We went in at 12 noon, at 10 Downing Street. It was a very interesting, memorable occasion. In our party were Lord Louis Mountbatten, Sir Stafford Cripps, Sir Charles

Kennedy-Purvis, (the) First Sea Lord, Freeman who was the chief engineer, Bernal, Rivett and myself. We met at Mountbatten's office and then went across to 10 Downing Street. We were met by a bank of butlers in the outside anteroom, went through the library and then into the Cabinet Chamber. It was like going into church – people did not talk out loud.

Lord Cherwell ushered us in and sat at Churchill's right . . . Churchill was sitting at the table – a little old man in a zippered suit with a big cigar in his mouth. . . . We sat down and for seconds, which seemed like minutes, no one said anything. Churchill kept reading from his papers and finally said, "Well, Lord Louis, what is the situation?"[46]

Mountbatten meekly explained that Habbakuk did not look quite as favourable as first supposed and Canada did not appear to have the manpower to undertake it. Churchill interrupted, peevishly accusing Mountbatten of leading him to think it was practical and then going on to quote word for word from the original memo he wrote on cutting a "lozenge of ice" from the Arctic ice pack.

He accused Lord Louis of having told him the thing was possible and Mountbatten, who is an excellent fencer, danced around, figuratively speaking. Churchill did eighty per cent of the talking and it was very obvious that he is a dictator who does not take objections very kindly. Even Cripps, Kennedy-Purvis and Cherwell, who I know are very much against the project, found it difficult to oppose. . . .[47]

At length, Mountbatten asked Churchill if he would listen to what Mackenzie from Canada had to say.

Churchill couldn't have cared less but he grunted. So I talked. I said that we had really taken it seriously, but we had found that it wasn't practical, and it could be done cheaper with other materials. And I mentioned the difficulty of freezing; that you could do this cheaper at the Equator than at the North Pole. . . .

The idea which he had suggested of going up north, while it was a very brilliant idea, it just wouldn't work because of the crews and the fact that you would have to feed all the camps, and anyway men froze as well as water up there. And I sat down.[48]

Churchill paid no attention. He set up another committee to pursue the matter, completely ignoring the fact, "if he ever knew it, that he had asked Mackenzie King if Canada would undertake the construction of one of these units." Nevertheless, Canada was officially off the hook. Mackenzie went straight from 10 Downing Street to the Athenaeum Club – likely for a stiff drink.[49]

Mackenzie might have thought he had seen the last of Habbakuk, but not quite. Two months later Churchill and Roosevelt met at Quebec City to discuss the projected invasion of Europe, and to discuss problems surrounding atomic energy research. Again, as with the Tizard mission three years earlier, Mackenzie invited himself along. He had no status, no position, and here he was again, in the thick of the top secret deliberations of the Allies. And who should he encounter there as well? Bernal!

Lord Cherwell had become sick so Churchill had named Bernal his acting scientific adviser. The contrast between the two, Mackenzie observed, could not have been more profound. Cherwell was a nattily dressed aristocrat and vegetarian; Bernal was the radical left-winger, unshaved, in old clothes, his hair sticking out in a frizzy mop. But, likely unknown to Mackenzie, it was Bernal's communist connections that made the situation really bizarre. One of the subjects to be discussed by Roosevelt and Churchill was the resumed sharing of atomic secrets which the American scientific leaders had steadfastly opposed. And the security leaks they feared did not just involve the Germans.

About a year earlier, even before they got their first atomic pile going, the Americans scientists realized that they stood a good chance of producing an atomic bomb before the end of the war. The theoretical had become practical, the possible probable. Scientists like Vannevar Bush and James Conant glimpsed over the horizon the world's most spectacular weapon. It suddenly became the war's most important secret. Why share its development with the British when their contribution was less than a tenth the total effort? Why hazard security by making room for people who did not need to know?

The Americans were worried the refugee scientists might be subject to Nazi pressure on their families in Occupied Europe. Moreover, the French scientists were known to have links with the communists. Bush and Conant wrote innumerable memos in 1942 and early 1943 pressing Roosevelt to impose only a very restricted exchange of atomic secrets with the British group in

Canada – some pure science stuff but nothing at all on the processes being developed to obtain fissionable uranium or the
actual design of the bomb. They almost had him convinced.

The British authorities had fought back and had appealed to
Churchill. In the run-up to the Quebec Conference he had
badgered Roosevelt incessantly about the way they had been
freely exchanging secrets since 1940 and how wounding it was
for the Americans to change their position now. In a weak
moment, before Bush and Conant had presented all their arguments, the president had agreed to the resumption of free interchange, realizing after talking with Bush that he had made a
mistake. Still, he would not go back on his word. Bush then
proceeded to work out the details of the arrangement the two
leaders would discuss at Quebec.[50]

Churchill arrived in Canada first, to be entertained by Mackenzie King with a visit to the Quebec Legislature and tours of the
Old Town. The two leaders talked about the progress of the war
and the invasion proposals. Churchill also reported his discussions with Roosevelt on the need to move as quickly as possible
on developing an atomic weapon (code-named Tube Alloys)
because he "did not want the Russians in particular to get ahead
with the process."[51]

A few days later, in the limestone bastion of Quebec's Citadel
overlooking the St. Lawrence, Roosevelt and Churchill signed
the "Articles of Agreement Governing collaboration between the
authorities of the U.S.A. and the U.K. in the matter of Tube
Alloys." Right at their elbows, figuratively at least, was Bernal,
dedicated communist, admirer of all things Soviet and close
friend of Britain's notorious traitors-to-be, Anthony Blunt, Guy
Burgess and Kim Philby, who were already busily burrowing
into their country's secrets on behalf of Stalin.

The three spies had learned at least some of their Marxism
from Bernal at Cambridge in the 1930s and Bernal, conscien-
tious tutor that he was, had maintained regular contact with
them. Malcolm Muggeridge remembered encountering him in
late 1941 in the flat that Burgess and Blunt shared. "John Strachey, J.D. Bernal, Anthony Blunt, Guy Burgess, a whole revolu-
tionary Who's Who . . . Cabinet Minister-to-be, honoured Guru
of the Extreme Left-to-be, Connoisseur Extraordinary-to-be, and
other notables, all in a sense grouped round Burgess. . . ." As
various historians of the Russian penetration of Britain's intelli-

gence services have noted, both Blunt and Burgess were actively feeding information to the Soviets at this time.[52]

Even if Bernal did not know his communist colleagues were spies, it is impossible to believe he did not tell them of what he learned at Quebec. While at Cambridge Bernal had been an outspoken champion of all things Russian; he was a first-generation communist in Britain's intellectual community. He took the view in the 1930s that "under capitalism, cultural decay everywhere; in the Soviet Union mighty cultural progress. Under capitalism, the inescapable impoverishment of the masses; in the Soviet Union, joyous work in the clearly outlined road to a classless society."[53] He believed that war between the capitalist powers and the communists was inevitable, and he made no secret about which side he was on. This was certainly the kind of man who would pass secrets to the Russians if he had the chance. Bernal's presence as Churchill's scientific adviser at the Quebec Conference was a breach of security that you could have sailed a battleship through. And all because of Habbakuk.

After Mackenzie left the June meeting with Churchill, the other members of the War Cabinet took advantage of his pessimism to persuade the prime minister that it would be impossible to build a Habbakuk in time for the war against Germany. To mollify him, they said the idea should be reserved as a long-term venture for possible use against Japan.[54] That should have been the end of it.

Bernal did not let the matter drop. He suggested to Mountbatten that they try selling Habbakuk to the Americans at the upcoming Quebec Conference. He then personally and apparently without Mackenzie's knowledge pressured the Montreal Engineering Company for a full feasibility study. The company worked frantically for the next two months, and on August 17 produced an elaborate report which came out eloquently and firmly against the project. It appears Bernal discarded the negative comments and extrapolated only the alternative designs the report discussed. He then managed to get Mountbatten to include him on the trip to Quebec as an "expert" on Habbakuk and he set sail on the *Queen Mary* with Churchill and the service chiefs. When Cherwell got sick he was appointed to take over for him.[55]

At Quebec, Bernal was almost too successful. Despite American misgivings, the Combined Chiefs of Staff agreed it was worth working on a Habbakuk built entirely out of pykrete, having rejected ice and steel or ice and timber alternatives.[56] The American Chiefs remained skeptical, so Bernal helped them draw up their objections, obligingly pointing out all the flaws in the concept as well as any merits. This annoyed Churchill and he told Mountbatten that the next time he came to a high-level conference, "you come without your scientific advisers."[57] Mackenzie, indeed, remembered Bernal being "quite the humorist" about the whole affair. He certainly had reason to laugh. Habbakuk may have already served his purpose.

The Quebec Conference would have paid big dividends in terms of information of value to the Russians. Details of the proposed invasion of France, which had been withheld from Stalin, were discussed. More importantly, Roosevelt and Churchill hammered out agreement on how the two countries would work toward the atomic bomb. If Stalin did not know it before, he could have learned through Bernal that the Americans reasonably expected to make an atomic bomb before the end of the war, that there would be a full exchange of nuclear secrets between the United States and Britain, that British atomic research was to be concentrated in Canada at Montreal and there would be a Combined Policy Committee set up in Washington to co-ordinate atomic research between the United States, Britain and Canada.

The more one considers Bernal's presence at the Quebec Conference, the more the coincidences pile up. How else did the Russians learn enough about Allied atomic bomb research to know that it was worth opening a spy network in Canada? None of the spies now known to have been operating in Britain in 1943 was in a position to tap the details of the Tube Alloy secret. The actual number of British scientists in the know was very small. Even the Germans never guessed the progress the Allies were making, and some of their scientists had been in on the first key discoveries.

Mountbatten was fond of telling a particular story about Bernal. The almost universally observed principle of wartime secrecy was the idea of "need to know." Those involved in military planning or war research were only to confide in colleagues working on the same project. When a young naval officer involved in invasion planning approached Bernal and asked him if it were possible to make a small echo-sounder to measure shallow depths, Bernal would not help him until he explained why he was asking. Reluctantly, the officer said it was to measure beach gradients surreptitiously along the coast of France to determine which were best for assault craft. To Mountbatten, this incident showed "the importance of the stand taken by Desmond [Bernal] in insisting on participating in the formulation of questions." It was also a gross breach of security discipline which Bernal, apparently, regularly practised and Mountbatten blithely ignored.[58]

Spy or not, how did a known communist like Bernal get to Quebec in the first place? Even allowing for Mountbatten's woolliness, why was Bernal not bounced by Britain's counter-intelligence agency, MI5? Today's historians are increasingly inclined to the view that MI5 had been penetrated by the Soviets before the war, and right at the top because of a lengthy list of suspicious intelligence failures before spies such as Blunt and Philby had had a chance to get to work. Bernal at Quebec is the most glaring failure of all, especially as MI5's central registry had been keeping track of the Cambridge communists throughout the 1930s and Bernal must have been noticed. And the man most responsible for setting up the agency's prewar watch on communists was also a frequent wartime visitor to the flat shared by Blunt and Burgess – MI5 counter-intelligence chief, Guy Liddell.[59]

It has been argued that while Liddell must have known that Blunt and Burgess were left wing in their views, this is not reason to conclude that he knew they were confirmed communists as he socialized with them. Bernal is a different case altogether. Liddell had specialized in tracking prewar communists and he would have known Bernal's sympathies and previous activities in detail. If he also knew he was attached to Combined Operations and everything that implied, then the only conclusion is that he deliberately failed to act on the knowledge. On the other hand, he was also excellently placed to make sure that MI5's security division did not find or act on the file it must have had on Bernal.

Churchill certainly was unaware of Bernal's political stripe. It would have enraged him. The prime minister hated communists, whether Russia was an ally or not. The following April he learned that there was some thought of inviting French exiles of communist leanings to Britain to help in invasion planning and he reacted characteristically: "I suppose you realize we are weeding remorselessly every single known Communist from our secret organizations," he wrote one of his advisers. "We did this after having to sentence two quite high-grade people to long terms of penal servitude for their betrayal, in accordance with the Communist faith, of important military secrets." And to another: "You will remember that we are purging all our secret establishments of Communists because we know they owe no allegiance to us or to our cause and will always betray secrets to the Soviets, even while we are working together."[60]

In talking to Mackenzie, Bernal delighted in recounting his duties as the prime minister's temporary scientific adviser. "Bernal would report to Churchill at 9 or 10 o'clock. Churchill didn't get up but he worked. He said he sat in bed with all these papers in front of him and he would say, 'Give me that paper. Give me this.' And he would kick the right foot out. 'This one down here.' Then the left foot out."[61] Churchill's private papers must have been engaging reading for a communist like Bernal.

Pykrete received its last public display when Mountbatten insisted that a block of it be wheeled into a conference room in the Chateau Frontenac before the assembled Allied Chiefs of Staff. To demonstrate its toughness, Mountbatten pulled out his service revolver and fired two shots into it. The second ricocheted across the room and the spent bullet lightly nicked Admiral Ernest J. King, the U.S. Chief of Naval Operations. The Americans were impressed, sort of.[62] They rejected the British proposal for a United States-Canada-Britain joint board to work on Habbakuk and agreed only to study it independently and arrive at their own conclusions. They soon found it could be made more cheaply and better out of reinforced concrete. The Habbakuk idea was officially killed on March 1, 1944.[63]

No one, it seems, ever thought to ask Mountbatten during or after the war whether he knew Bernal was a communist. He was always willing to talk about his so-called scientific advisers, and did much to create the myth that Pyke and Bernal had made lasting contributions to Combined Operations. This is not true. They were the objects of almost universal ridicule – Mountbatten's "circus" – and there is no evidence other than Mountbatten's empty say-so that they did anything of practical worth.[64] He might have eventually figured out the truth, however. After Quebec, Bernal lobbied Mountbatten to appoint a prewar crony to Combined Operations and when his chief asked through channels why the transfer he had approved was being held up, he was told it was because before the war the man had been "associated with a notorious Communist, one J.D. Bernal."[65]

Mountbatten went on to become Supreme Commander of the Allied forces in the Far East[66] and after the war, Viceroy of India, leaving a legacy of controversy over his competence in both positions. Afterwards, he assumed various senior roles in Britain's military hierarchy and on retirement was an active supporter of many worthy causes. In 1979 a bomb planted by IRA terrorists blew his pleasure boat to pieces. It was the *Kelly* one last time – he was even wearing a *Kelly* commemorative T-shirt as he steered his boat to sea. He died a hero.

Bernal subsequently made many trips to the Soviet Union and China, even at the height of the Cold War, and declaimed publicly and often against the evils of capitalist society while praising Stalin unreservedly. He received one of the Soviet Union's highest decorations, the Stalin Prize, and eventually the censure of much of the British scientific community. After a series of strokes he died in 1971, his faith in communism – and Stalin – apparently unshaken.

No one in Combined Operations would listen much to Pyke's ideas after Mountbatten left in late 1943. A year later he was dropped entirely, and soon returned to poverty and obscurity. For a few years he worked furiously on an elaborate monograph entitled *The Origin of Thought*, and pestered newspapers with a grand scheme to replace Europe's transportation system with vehicles powered by human muscle. He was treated as a crank. On February 21, 1948, he took an overdose of sleeping pills.

The establishment British newspapers, *The Times* and the *Manchester Guardian*, ran lengthy obituaries which claimed he had been some sort of original genius. This was nonsense. The obituaries demonstrated the only real accomplishment of his lifetime. He had been noticed by people in high places.

It was the end of Habbakuk.

C·H·A·P·T·E·R
S·E·V·E·N

Guinea Pigs

The raid began at 7:30 p.m. and was over in twenty minutes. Four ships were damaged, including one loaded with gasoline. The JU 88s – slow, clumsy things like flying grasshoppers – quickly fled into the darkness of the Adriatic. When they had gone, the first ship blew up.

Bari is a seaport town on the eastern heel of Italy and on December 2, 1943, it had been in Allied hands for a little more than two months. It was a vital possession. From it flowed the tons of supplies needed for the British Eighth Army battling the determined Germans further north. It was crowded with shipping – vessels loaded with food, fuel and munitions tied bow or stern to the harbour mole and side by side like sardines – an incredibly tempting target even for a Luftwaffe supposedly driven from the skies by the Allies.

As they looked back as they sped away, the crews of the raiding aircraft would have been only moderately satisfied at the result of their daring: a ship on fire, three others damaged. But the gasoline ship was like a delayed action bomb. When it exploded the fireball sent rivers of flame racing between the docked ships, including one called the *John Harvey* tied up at berth 29. Then an ammunition ship exploded.

In the next couple of minutes one thousand men died and sixteen cargo ships were sunk. It was more spectacular than the Japanese sinking of the Pacific Fleet at Pearl Harbor for the anchorage became an inferno. Smoke and fire billowed across the water and sailors, blown from their ships by explosions, struggled to stay afloat in a slurry of fuel oil, bodies and debris. Rescue boats were soon darting in and out of the curtains of smoke and, later, both rescuers and rescued would remember a garlicky odour mixed with the acrid smell of burning fuel.

As well as other munitions, the *John Harvey* had been loaded with 100 tons of mustard gas in 100-pound bombs. Allied planners always had to allow for the possibility the Germans might resort to gas, so provision had been made for stocks of chemical weapons to be near the fighting. The *John Harvey* had been a little too close. Its toxic cargo now lay at the bottom of Bari harbour or scattered as discharged bomb casings along the mole.

In the investigation afterwards, it was said that the *John Harvey* had been ordered to scuttle herself as the flames approached. Who gave the order and whether she received it remained unknown because all aboard were killed. The who was important because in the maelstrom of fire and destruction, no one thought to warn of gas, no one remembered that one vessel had a particularly deadly cargo. The biggest, and ugliest, "field trial" with mustard gas had begun.

All the resources of army and navy, ashore and afloat, pitched into the rescue. About one thousand men, most of them uninjured, were pulled from the oily water and rushed to shore. As Bari was a casualty clearing centre for frontline troops, plenty of medical help was at hand, although the sheer numbers taxed the doctors and their assistants. Those that were severely hurt were looked after first, the majority with minor injuries or none were wrapped in blankets and given hot tea – the standard treatment for exposure. Some didn't even bother to strip and sat in the hospitals for hours, in their water- and oil-soaked clothes, waiting to be released.

The first hint that something unusual was happening came as the doctors started checking through the uninjured. Many had been brought in supposedly suffering from shock, with pulse rates that were barely perceptible and low blood pressure. But instead of being restless and agitated, they exhibited a strange lassitude. Other typical symptoms were missing and when asked, the men even said they felt rather well. Then they would lapse again into apathy. The doctors were puzzled. They put as many to bed as they could.

At midnight, some of the men began to complain of eye irritation; through the early morning hours and with dawn, more men complained of eye problems and others of irritation to their skin. At about noon the first man died.

Death spread like contagion. Men who sat up in bed and told their doctors they felt fine, and who had no obvious signs of physical distress, would be dead ten minutes later. Thirteen more died the next day. It was always the same: "Individuals that appeared in rather good condition ... would in a matter of minutes become moribund and die." By the end of two weeks, the toll would be 69.

In one way, the dead were lucky. They were spared the agonies of the 559 who survived. First it was eyes. Men woke up screaming that they were blind. Their eyelids had swollen shut. Then they broke out in blisters, great red or brown bubbles, six, eight, ten inches long all over their bodies but particularly in their armpits and groins. Their genitalia swelled grotesquely, causing intense "mental anguish" even though there was usually little pain. Sometimes great patches of skin sloughed off. Despite all the research that had been done, there was no effective treatment. The doctors were helpless.

In his official report, 29-year-old Lieutenant-Colonel Stewart Alexander of the U.S. Army Medical Corps noted that the disaster had taught the Allies something new about an "old" gas. Not only did mustard cause incapacitating blisters, it also was a potent systemic poison. It could cause the body to completely shut down even before blisters appeared. It had been mixed with the oil that had soaked the survivors' clothing and as the men sat wrapped in wet blankets sipping their tea, it had had plenty of time to do its deadly work. Those most affected just stopped living.[1]

The Allied high command clamped tight secrecy over the catastrophe. Churchill expressed astonishment that such a thing could have been allowed to happen, while the commander in Italy, General Dwight D. Eisenhower, proposed various euphemisms to conceal the nature of the injuries and deaths from next of kin. Two months later the Combined Chiefs of Staff issued a statement vaguely admitting the accident while reiterating that Allied policy was only to use gas in retaliation, in case the Germans thought the gas stocks were there because an attack had been planned.[2] The horror of the 628 who suffered or died was hidden from the public. In his 1948 war memoirs, four years before becoming president of the United States, Eisenhower briefly mentioned the raid and the release of the mustard gas, and then said: "Fortunately the wind was offshore and the escaping gas caused no casualties."[3]

Eisenhower's statement is curious. American author Glenn B. Infield, the former USAF major who in 1971 wrote *Disaster at Bari*, chose to ignore it even though he cited Eisenhower's *Crusade in Europe* in his bibliography. He also blamed Churchill for the cover-up while claiming that one thousand Italian civilians died from a cloud of mustard vapour that swept over the city. The more recent *A Higher Form of Killing*, first published in Britain, blames Eisenhower for the cover-up, quoting an actual telegram he sent the Combined Chiefs of Staff on January 2 which the authors found in the Public Record Office archives.[4]

Do American presidents lie? Historians are certainly known to reflect national biases, but as this is a Canadian book, the reader is invited to decide for himself. Infield cites no actual documents for his claim about Churchill, although there is absolute proof that both Churchill and Eisenhower knew about the mustard deaths and injuries to the soldiers and seamen and that the latter wanted it kept secret.[5] On the other hand, despite what Infield says, there is no evidence that there were more than a few incidental civilian casualties. Moreover, eyewitness interviews and documents Infield reproduced (but misinterpreted) prove conclusively that there was no toxic cloud over Bari that night because the wind was indeed offshore.[6] Eisenhower must have been expressing relief that the disaster had not involved civilians, although it does seem odd that he should ignore the hundreds of military casualties.

Colonel Alexander's report, in all its graphic detail, was sent to the U.S. Chemical Warfare Service at Edgewood and widely circulated among the Allied commands. Don Dewar, then in Canada's Directorate of Chemical Warfare and Smoke, remembered reading it, and the British at Porton were sent a copy. They immediately dusted off a report of their own on sea trials done with oil and mustard gas mixtures the year before at Tipnor and Lyme Bay, and bombing trials at Saunton Sands. They had concluded that the oil spread so rapidly on the water that the mustard became too diluted to penetrate clothing well enough to cause significantly severe burns. They initially stuck by their findings, although a whole new line of research was begun on foams that would keep mustard gas afloat.[7]

In Canada's Department of National Defence there was also discussion, although it was recognized that there was little danger in Canada of such a catastrophe from enemy action. The concern became mostly focused on what would happen if a train loaded with mustard was wrecked. Hundreds of tons of all kinds of poison gas were regularly rumbling between Halifax, Cornwall, Toronto, Windsor, Winnipeg and Medicine Hat, usually looked after by crews ignorant of what was being carried. After much debate, it was concluded that civilian casualties were an inevitable risk of transporting toxic stores but they could be "reasonably controlled" in the event of an accident.[8]

The Canadian authorities had reason to be blasé. They had more experience with the devastating effects of mustard gas than either Britain or the United States – a lot more. By the beginning of 1944 the medical staffs at Suffield had seen hundreds of mustard burns, many of them severe. They had seen men blinded in the same way as those at Bari. The difference was that at Suffield Canadian soldiers were not injured by the King's enemies. It happened in the name of research.

To understand how Canada came to lead the Allies in human experiments with toxic substances one must go right back to the beginning of the war. In the spring of 1940, in his own lab while his staff under Dr. Dudley Irwin experimented with ways to treat mustard burns, Banting tested some on his own leg. He later regretted that he put as much on as he did – a 6½ × 1½-inch strip – for it gave him a painful injury which took over a month to heal. Nevertheless, he kept careful notes on the progress of the burn and there is even a photograph of his leg, fiery welt and all, in the Banting archives.[9]

Parallel studies on the physiological effects of mustard were also being done at the NRC labs in Ottawa under biologist J. Gordon Malloch, who complained in November to Otto Maass that he could no longer use volunteers from the staff at the laboratories. Sensitivity to mustard increases dramatically with each exposure until soon minuscule amounts cause severe burns and eye problems. Even more distressing, the sensitized individual's testicles swell grotesquely. Malloch asked Maass if it would be possible to get volunteers from the military.[10]

The trickle of soldiers that followed was not enough for Malloch and he complained bitterly that essential experiments involving the treatment of mustard, its penetrating power through clothing and so forth, were being held up. Finally, that summer the Canadian Chiefs of Staff approved a program for doing "arm" tests on soldier volunteers. The formalized rules provided every reasonable safeguard, right down to the amount of mustard that was to be used and the kind of medical supervision. So far so good.[11]

Like Banting, Malloch also deliberately gave himself mustard injuries in his search for an effective treatment. In wartime, in a more idealistic era, such risks were often taken by scientists as their patriotic duty and they assumed there would be similar dedication from a reasonable portion of the country's military personnel. Interestingly though, Malloch wrote Maass that "women volunteers are not acceptable for scientific reasons."[12] One wonders what these were, considering that females must have otherwise been ideal since they could not suffer from the distressing difficulties that sometimes afflicted male volunteers.

The nature of toxic weapon research also involves the killing of a lot of animals. The number of goats, cattle, sheep, horses and mice killed at Suffield runs into the many thousands. On a smaller scale, it was the same at the Banting Institute and the Chemical Warfare Labs in Ottawa. The trouble with experimental animals, however, was that they could rarely be deployed in ways that effectively imitated combat conditions. When put into trenches or vehicles and pillboxes at Suffield and drenched in the whole spectrum of poison gases, they could do no more than passively await their fate. Human beings, on the other hand, could be trained to take evasive measures. The temptation to test weapons on humans was overwhelming, and the precedent, particularly with mustard gas weapons, had already been set at Porton.

Porton Report 2377, still tightly secret in Britain, describes the deliberate drenching of unprotected British soldiers in clouds of mustard vapour produced by combining mustard in a smoke bomb. With only gas masks and wearing ordinary clothing, on two occasions in 1942 three British soldiers stood like sheep in the mustard cloud. All were subsequently hospitalized as "severe casualties" with mustard burns and blisters over their entire bodies proving, the report noted, that the weapon had "behaved to design expectations." It identified the victims only as "Sapper A, Sapper B" and so forth.[13]

The severity of this test in terms of the injuries it inflicted represented a relatively new departure for Porton. Two years earlier, the approved procedure for human trials with mustard gas was for the troops to be entirely covered in protective clothing except for a small patch cut out at the shoulder where a burn could register. But with the Nazis dominating Europe, better experimental procedures were urgently needed.

Suffield, with its vast open areas, offered excellent possibilities for testing mustard gas under combat conditions. Undoubtedly at the request of the British, or at the suggestion of Davies, the British chief superintendent at Suffield, the Canadians rewrote their regulations on using troops in war gas experiments, expanding them far beyond the restrained arm tests Malloch had originally sought. The new rules were drawn up at a meeting of the administrative committee of the Chemical Warfare Inter-Service Board on June 12, 1942. They called for a hundred volunteers to be provided each month for Suffield, and sixteen per week for the Ottawa lab, to be drawn from the military districts in western and central Canada. Each man would be paid $1 at the time of exposure to a war agent, and up to $20 at the discretion of the medical officer in charge for "any single severe lesion" that might result.

Medical officers at Suffield and Ottawa were also required to "examine all subjects who have undergone tests, at least once a day until any lesions that are produced are healed and . . . to order hospitalization if necessary." Clearly, the program was expected to produce a certain number of injuries, but the candidate soldiers were not to be told that. The meeting agreed they were to be informed only in a "general way" of the purpose and nature of the tests, and were to be assured in the notices to be posted on unit bulletin boards that "the actual tests are carried out under scientific control, so that no personal injury is likely to result."[14] This last statement was a falsehood. Causing injury was what the program was all about.

In a taped interview shortly before his death in 1976, Dr. Alison Flood, the former chief of the Chemical Warfare Labs, said that the new regulations on using Canadian soldiers for war gas experiments were drafted by Malloch and approved by Colonel Ralston, the Minister of Defence, who went through them line by line. He also mentioned that the concept made many army medical officers uneasy but they were warned that they had to "toe to line" or face dismissal.[15] In a kind of indirect acknowledgment of the deception they were perpetrating, the Canadians now adopted from Porton the misleading term "observers" to describe the human subjects of experiments.

In any event, those in charge at Suffield did not wait for formal authorization to expand the mustard tests. Long before the chemical warfare board approved the new rules, Canadian soldiers were being seriously injured in trials similar to the one described at Porton. The push had come with the realization in the year after Dunkirk that British ideas on how to use mustard as a weapon were not all that sound. When invasion from across the Channel was expected, it was thought that pure mustard could be sprayed from low flying aircraft directly on the Germans as they hit the beaches. A year's fighting, particularly in North Africa where the British had tasted at first hand the efficiency of German anti-aircraft fire, had made it evident that low-flying aircraft stood little chance of survival. The answer was to develop better methods of spraying from higher up.

The search was stepped up to find suitable additives that would thicken the mustard and allow it to make the descent from several thousand feet as discreet droplets rather than simply evaporating. The next problem was to develop techniques for hitting ground targets with the droplets, given variables in wind speed, air speed and altitude. The final problem – and the most important – was to determine whether these high-altitude sprays would actually cause casualties. In the spring of 1942, as a direct result of urgent requests from Porton and Britain's Ministry of Supply, the high spraying of troops was given "highest priority" at Suffield.[16]

Suffield field trial reports on mustard gas do exist but are among those documents still unavailable. It is doubtful this is because they contain experimental information that is still a military secret; modern anti-aircraft weapons generally preclude the use of aircraft flying at the low speeds necessary for spraying, no matter what the altitude. It is more likely it is because they contain descriptions of experiments the average person would find horrific.

On May 2, 1942, Private L.V. Devitte and Private R.H. Caldicutt, among others, stood at attention on the prairie in helmet and ordinary battle dress facing downwind. The air temperature hovered at the freezing mark so they wore winter underwear. An airplane droned in the distance. They were ordered to put on their gas masks and the plane passed overhead at 1,000 feet. They waited. After a suitable interval, the men dusted one another off with decontamination powder (ordinary bleach) and marched three miles back to camp where they changed clothes. The results were duly tabulated and photographed.

> Pte. Devitte: Mild burn on shoulders, sharp burn on lower back, two medium-sized blisters on left buttock, large intense burn 17 × 10 cms. on back of right knee, medium-sized sharp burns on thighs. Disabled 14 days. Casualty Class I.
>
> Pte. Caldicutt: Sharp burn on entire back plus right side and flank. Sharp burn between buttocks developing into opposing ("kissing") blisters in fold. Burns and blisters over legs and forearms. Disabled 14 days. Casualty Class I.[17]

Similar trials were held in the summer of 1942. One was held to be particularly "successful from the offensive point of view." The minutes of a meeting in Ottawa described it:

> Eight people were hospital cases, six of whom were really bad. One of these men had a blister 9″ × 12″ × 2″, but was fit to be released from hospital in 6 days time. If mustard burns can be kept clean, they are quite easily healed. However, once they become dirty it is a very difficult problem. The results from aircraft spray were not as good as was hoped for. Mr. Davies said that the only other hopeful way was the 50-lb. bomb.[18]

Field Experiment 68, "The Casualty Producing Power of Mustard Spray on Troops," was a recurring field experiment with variations. The following spring twenty-nine received eye injuries from experiment 68 and were hospitalized from five to twenty-one days, their eyes inflammed and eyelids tightly stuck together. They were kept in darkened rooms and the doctor looking after them noted that they "were usually silent, depressed and introspective at the height of the eye effects." These were the same symptoms noticed later at Bari among those who died suddenly.[19]

Although there had been scarring of the eyeballs, it was believed that none of the men had suffered permanent damage. To be sure, they were to be brought back from their units a few months later for re-examination on the assurance they would not be used for further tests. This was done in July. The medical officer's findings are missing from the file.

The Canadian mustard gas experiments were popular with the British and American chemical warfare services. The Americans were particularly fascinated by the quality of data produced. While the British and the Canadians permitted field tests on humans, this was denied the U.S. Chemical Warfare Service for much of the war. In May 1943 a direct request came from General Porter's office to Suffield requesting photographs of the mustard gas injuries mentioned in Suffield reports 33, 39 and 47 so that they could be incorporated in a training film. The Americans were especially anxious to have them because they were better than anything they had, and the "contamination was accomplished under simulated battle conditions."[20]

The Canadian trials were even more useful to the British. They enabled Porton to do the majority of its human subject experiments on Canadian rather than British troops. And because Britain had a 50 per cent share in the operation of Suffield, plus the fact that Davies, the superintendent, was the former head of experiments at Porton, the trials could be tailored to exactly what the British deemed necessary. The definition of a mustard casualty – a man unable to perform his duties even if willing – was even originally supplied by Porton. It was later refined by Suffield to a man unable to do his duty "under all circumstances."[21]

It was an ideal situation, with the Canadian authorities always ready to co-operate when consultation was necessary. Usually it was not, for Suffield was run essentially as a British establishment with Davies receiving direction as much from London as from Ottawa, often dealing directly with his colleagues at Porton or with Davidson Pratt in the British Ministry of Supply. As a result, the British were free to do whatever human trials in Canada they liked short of causing death. By the time the war ended, more than one thousand Canadian soldiers at Suffield had been injured in mustard gas experiments.[22]

It was an entirely different situation with bacteriological trials. Although these (as far as we know) were never done deliberately on humans at Suffield until after the war, they always posed an indirect risk because usually much less was understood about the agents involved, and personnel had to be protected where possible by vaccination. In 1946, for example, and presumably in 1944 and 1945 when the experiments first began, the field staff at Suffield were inoculated against Rocky Mountain spotted fever for fear this novel and highly infectious disease would somehow get free.[23] Consequently, at Professor Murray's insistence, all BW field experiments had to be cleared for safety by Murray's C1 Committee, regardless whether they originated with the British, the Americans or the Canadians themselves. This was the source of much friction between Murray and Davies.

The severity of the early mustard gas experiments on Canadian soldiers should also be seen in the context of the perceived threat to Britain. While in Canada in February 1942 to confer with the Cabinet War Committee, General McNaughton, then commanding Canada's First Division in Britain, held a special meeting on chemical warfare. He warned that a cross-Channel invasion of Britain was still considered a danger and that intelligence had reported that the Germans had massed substantial stocks of poison gas along the coast of Europe. That summer, when Maass and Ralston visited Britain, McNaughton again warned he considered it a "serious possibility" that chemical warfare could break out at any moment.[24] With that kind of pressure coming from Canada's top soldier, Maass, Ralston and others in authority in Ottawa inevitably wanted to help as best they could.

Canada, it should be said, had no monopoly in the Commonwealth for experimenting with poison gas on its own soldiers. The British set up a co-operative chemical warfare proving grounds similar to Suffield in Australia, at Innisfail, Queensland. After doing various jungle trials with mustard gas, in December 1943 the station began experiments with humans in a stainless steel chamber where soldiers were required to perform heavy physical tasks until they succumbed to the agents being tested. The tests elicited a certain admiration from the U.S. liaison officer observing them. "It is important to keep in mind," he reported back to the United States, "the keen individual pride in physical prowess inbred in each Australian when comparing casualties obtained here and in other countries. The men who are classed as casualties here, are truly casualties." Tests with mustard gas on Australian troops began in the new year.[25]

As self-governing dominions, Canada and Australia could at least share with Britain the costs, responsibility (or blame) and the scientific spin-offs of operating chemical warfare stations. Not so India. The Chemical Warfare Research Establishment at Rawalpindi in Britain's largest colony was an "off-shoot of Porton" but conducted no pure research. Its sole purpose was to do physiological – that is, human – and veterinary experiments with chemical weapons under tropical conditions. India was perceived to be too remote and under-developed to support a real scientific effort. But it had lots of people.[26]

For two weeks beginning August 12, 1943, dozens of "British" troops were paraded around in the mid-day heat on mustard-soaked ground on the experimental field at Maurypur, near Karachi (in modern-day Pakistan). The men wore various degrees of protection and from their injuries it was deduced that a man's scrotum appeared to be particularly vulnerable to mustard effects under conditions of high heat and humidity. Five men were then selected to receive especially long exposures with no protection whatever. The results were horrific.

This report exists in full detail, complete with pictures, in the U.S. Chemical Warfare Service archives. The injuries to the genital areas of the five men were grotesque and they suffered "intense and crippling pain." They were in such agony that the doctors administered a quarter gram of morphia for the first four nights, followed by Nembutal and chloral hydrate. After a month two were diagnosed as having developed neuroses, "a slightly morbid genital consciousness." The report concluded that troops must be protected in their genital areas in the event of gas warfare in the tropics. The pictures show that all five men were Indian soldiers.[27]

At the same time as this was going on in India, Suffield had progressed to almost identical experiments involving unprotected troops in long exposures to mustard-contaminated ground, the difference being that the Canadian volunteers were provided with gas-proof shorts under their battle dress to cover the genitals. Nevertheless, in a July 1943 trial designed to simulate the likely battle experience of unprotected troops under gas attack, all the volunteers became "severe casualties" requiring hospitalization for up to a month,[28] although the special protection likely spared them the grief of the Indian troops.

The tests on soldiers at Suffield continued throughout 1943. In both May and August more men received unspecified "severe" mustard burns while Maass received high praise from the U.S. Chemical Warfare Service for the quality of reports being received.[29] But as the year wore on, it became increasingly difficult to maintain the pace of experiments. As men recovered from their injuries and returned to their units, fewer soldiers were willing to volunteer. Word was getting around.

As early as January 1944 Davies was sending strident pleas to Maass to put pressure on the army to supply more men. The four western military districts, 10, 12, 13 and Pacific Command, were supposed to provide 200 volunteers every six months but the last time had come up with only 154. The shortage was making it difficult to carry out the full program of experiments, Davies said.

New incentive for mustard gas experiments was coming from the U.S. Chemical Warfare Service, which had recognized gas as the ideal means of prying the Japanese out of their island fortresses. In early 1944 the CWS opened tropical field stations at Bushnell in Florida (about sixty miles from modern-day Disney World) and on the island of San José off the coast of Panama. The Canadians were invited to co-operate and, aware that the Americans had little freedom in running casualty tests on their own troops, offered one hundred Canadian soldiers.[30] As this had rather delicate international implications, the proposal went all the way up to Roosevelt, who is reported to have said: "What the hell is wrong with American volunteers?" Told that Canada had regulations for using its own troops for experiments and the United States didn't, Roosevelt ordered similar rules drawn up. Nevertheless, U.S. soldiers continued to be exposed only if fully protected except for test patches.[31]

Suffield was still the only place in North America where really useful gas warfare data could be obtained, but by May 1944 the shortage of volunteers had become critical. Davies wanted twice the number of volunteers for an expanded program of experiments, while the military districts were having difficulty in producing even half their quotas. The consequent prodding by Army headquarters in Ottawa brought the frank admission from Military District 12 (Regina) that "previous volunteers have been advising other personnel not to volunteer for duty at Suffield." This reply was duly relayed for comment to Suffield by H.W. Bishop, an aide to Maass. After a month's silence, Bishop rather snarkily asked Suffield to "favour" the Directorate of Chemical Warfare and Smoke with a reply.

That reply, when it came, was snarky in its turn. The fact that some volunteers leave Suffield with an unfavourable impression was "no news to us," it said, but these were soldiers who turned out to be laggards and had to be sent back because they refused to carry out their duties. The fault was with the officers of the military districts for sending poor quality volunteers. They should be reminded that it was their duty to provide suitable troops in adequate numbers because the experiments were essential; otherwise, the Canadian Army would not be prepared should chemical warfare break out.

Suffield won its point. Army HQ sent copies of its letter to all the military district commanding officers, along with a stiffly worded note which insisted they not only meet their quotas but make sure the troops did not get the wrong impression about Suffield: "The observers are not to be given the impression that they are 'guinea pigs' to some weird scheme. They are not called upon to make sacrifices. Their job is merely to render co-operative understanding to those who conduct the trials."

This hard bunt from Army HQ did the trick. There was an immediate surge of volunteers. It didn't last. By spring of 1945 the supply of troops for gas experiments had dried to the barest trickle. Everyone could see the end of the war in sight. There was some thought of using new recruits, but Suffield held that volunteers should have at least four weeks basic training. Suffield's casualty-causing mustard experiments gradually withered away.[32]

Ironically, for all their sophisticated research into gas warfare, the Germans apparently did not run the risks with human subjects that the Allies did. In touring the big chemical warfare station at Raubkammer, near Münster, shortly after Germany surrendered, an American CWS expert commented that "the Germans seemed to have been afraid of using human observers directly. The method used was to expose the portion of the uniform to be tested and then have a man put it on and observe his reactions." He found no equivalent to the casualty-causing experiments being done in Canada, Australia and India.[33]

The full extent and severity of the injuries inflicted by Suffield field experiments with mustard gas is unknown. None of the Canadian files pertaining to human experiments have been released. Indeed, the description in this chapter of Experiment 68 was not obtained from a Suffield report. It was found in a 1946 memo from Suffield replying to a request from the U.S. Chemical Warfare Service for background information on the mustard burns shown in a series of "lantern slides" it had been sent.[34] Had it not been for this fragment of mislaid information, the true nature and extent of Experiment 68 might have remained forever unknown.

It would be a mistake, and unfair, to think of the men who conducted these trials as irresponsible monsters. As Flood remembered, the medical officers certainly felt torn between their duties as doctors and their duties as soldiers. And Flood himself, like many of the other chemical warfare scientists, was a serving Army officer who took the view that risking a few soldiers for the welfare of the many was what war was all about. In wartime men were expected to take risks, whether in battle, during training, or for research. Almost every scientist interviewed for this book had been injured by gas during the war, in two instances quite seriously. Maass himself set a tough-to-match example of disregard for personal safety. As Flood recalled: "There was something very appealing but somewhat incongruous in seeing this gentle professorial type of man wearing a tin helmet, eye shields, etc., and exposing himself as a 'human guinea pig' to mustard gas spray, to be with him in a tank during firing trials, to see him dashing about rough terrain in jeeps, bren carriers, operating flame throwers, etc. He wanted very much to be as near the 'battlefield' as he could get."[35]

Even in medicine, risks were taken in wartime with human subjects which would not be otherwise acceptable. In their search for a cure for seasickness, which was very costly in terms of a ship's battle readiness, scientists from Collip's Institute of Endocrinology at McGill tested a wide variety of barbituates and amphetamines – including sodium pentothal and the familiar benzadrine – on six hundred soldiers at Camp Borden in mid-1943. While these drugs were a far more pleasant experience than a war gas, such tests were hazardous in other ways.[36]

J.G. Malloch, after being posted to Washington as scientific liaison officer, reflected the attitude to casualty-producing experiments – be they in Canada, India, Australia or the United States – in a diary entry for September 24, 1944. He had been visiting chemical warfare scientists at the University of Chicago, and in commenting on the field trials then being done by the Americans in Panama, they complained that "they were still working under great handicaps through not being able to take risks with observers."[37]

A press release prepared for Maass shortly after the war to describe Suffield's activities, but apparently never distributed, explains the rationale behind the experiments with humans even better:

> During the war of 1914-18 many men suffering from minor mustard gas burns were evacuated to rear areas unnecessarily, clogging hospitals and throwing a tremendous strain on the supply of reinforcements. In order that such a situation should not occur again, over a thousand Canadian soldier volunteers were exposed to mustard gas in field trials at Suffield, and blistered. As the result of their courage the medical services were able to determine scientifically when a man should be sent to a rear echelon for treatment, and when it was a legitimate risk of war to keep him fighting. At the same time new treatments were developed which insured rapid healing of mustard burns and greatly reduced the danger of secondary infection.[38]

The reference to the courage of the soldiers is deserved, but specious. If the physiological staff at Suffield followed the rules as drawn up for the Chemical Warfare Inter-Service Board, then the men were brave after the fact, not before, because the true nature of the experiments would have been deliberately concealed from them. Similarly, the insistence on using only volunteers rings hollow because a man is no volunteer who steps forward for what appears to be an easy and safe thing, and then finds it to be both painful and dangerous. He really is a guinea pig. How many were told that their severe burns were an unusual and exceptional event, whereas in reality they were commonplace, even desired? No wonder volunteers became scarce.

The tests on humans were approved at the highest level. Chances are, however, that the Minister of Defence never saw a report that described severe injuries. Ralston certainly recognized that the practice was political dynamite. As Flood recalled: "Sometimes we'd get an instruction from the minister to let a certain man come and look over our operation. Normally anyone that was a politician was issued a little pass with a pink slip and that meant, 'This fellow is not a German spy but don't talk to him unnecessarily. Soft-pedal everything and by no means let him know what kind of experiments you carry out with animals, for example. And especially don't let him know anything about the Canadian troops who are exposed.'"[39]

There appears never to have been a problem obtaining volunteers for experiments at the Chemical Warfare Labs. These were done on a much more restrained scale, focusing mainly on treating mustard burns rather than seeing how they can be caused. A typical procedure would be to apply a tiny drop of mustard to a person's arm and then attempt to neutralize it with an experimental ointment.

Suffield was where the elaborate experiments were carried out. As late as November 8, 1944, the authorities there were entertaining the possibility of a field trial dubbed "Exercise Hedgehog" in which a company of soldiers – one hundred men – would dress in standard anti-gas gear and take up hidden positions, which would then be soaked by mustard bombs and shells to determine how long it took to create how many casualties. It was acknowledged that the information to be gained would no longer be useful for the war in Europe, where Germany's surrender seemed imminent, but it was argued it might still have application to the war with Japan.[40] It is difficult to see how, especially as the Japanese were known to be without adequate anti-gas equipment. The casualty-producing program had acquired a life of its own.

One can also guess where the inspiration for this exercise came from. Hedgehogs are unknown in North America. They are small, spiny, insect-eating mammals a little like porcupines. They are native to Britain.

C·H·A·P·T·E·R
E·I·G·H·T

Poised to Strike

The visitor wanted to see him in secret. By late 1942 C.J. Mackenzie had seen a hundred such people. He probably sighed as he got up from a desk heaped with paper, put on his suit jacket and walked next door into the president's office. This room was four times larger than the cubby-hole where he usually worked, and boasted walnut panelling, marble fireplace, arm chairs, chandelier, the works. It was too opulent for a man used to working in his shirtsleeves, but perfect for impressing people.

When Mackenzie was comfortably settled in his official chair, behind his bare-topped official desk, the man was shown in. He got straight to the point. He was employed by one of the overseas subsidiaries of I.G. Farbenindustrie, the great German chemical conglomerate. He had important information. Germany had discovered a new poison gas that was many times more deadly than anything the Allies had. He had the formula.

It is to Mackenzie's credit that he listened. As president of the National Research Council he had long endured a constant procession of well-meaning visitors with new inventions and war-winning ideas. He had only just recently turned down a physicist's suggestion that radio transmissions be investigated to see if they could be focused and made into a death ray. Mackenzie noted there had been reports of people suffering from unusual fatigue after being exposed to the radio beams in radar research, but he considered the idea too far-fetched to pursue.

We know now, in the age of the microwave oven, that high-intensity microwaves can kill.[1]

A new German poison gas was more plausible. Mackenzie didn't need to be a chemist to know that if the McGill scientists could discover a deadly gas like Compound Z, so could the enemy. He took the man's formula down, thanked him, promised he would keep the visit secret, and showed him out. Then he took the piece of paper down the hallway to the Chemical Warfare Labs and gave it to Alison Flood.

Flood by this time was Canada's leading expert in poison gases. He was on top of all the research being done in Canada, the United States and Britain. He immediately recognized that the formula called for a chemical combination that was impossible – no such substance could be made. But he didn't reject it. After the war started it was found that for some years previously the German chemical and pharmaceutical industries had been deliberately scrambling the published or patented formulas of new compounds. This might be the same kind of thing. Flood immediately began intensive work on the formula, a compound of phosphorus, and sent it to colleagues in Britain and the United States to see what they could do with it.[2]

One of the biggest failures of the Allied chemical warfare effort during the Second World War was the decision not to develop the nerve gases, even though as early as 1943, and likely before, the Allies had a nerve gas of their own and knew that the Germans had been developing others. The error could have cost hundreds of thousands of casualties, and possibly the war. The German gases were ten to fifty times more poisonous than phosgene and infinitely more efficient than mustard.

"The existence of the G-agents (nerve gases) was unknown to Great Britain and the United States until German chemical shells were captured and analyzed in 1945, although vague hints about them appeared occasionally in intelligence reports from 1943 onward," a U.S. Army official history said in 1959.[3] Recently declassified documents show that this statement is simply not true.

A German scientist with I.G. Farbenindustrie, Dr. Gerhard Schrader, stumbled upon the first nerve gas in 1936 while trying to develop insecticides from organic fluorine-phosphorus compounds. The possibility that pesticides might be quite toxic to humans was well recognized by Allied chemists, and they also examined many such substances during the war, although not with quite the dramatic result that accompanied the German discovery.

Nerve gases work by interfering with a body chemical called acetylcholinesterase. When a muscle is flexed and then released, this chemical messenger enables it to relax. Without it, muscles lock into place and when these involve the heart or the lungs, death is swift, usually from one to ten minutes. Moreover, some nerve gases easily enter the body through the skin as well as the lungs. Exposure to even trace amounts can have instant effect, showing up first as the inability of the pupils to dilate. Eyes with pupils reduced to pinpoints is a classic symptom of nerve gas poisoning.[4]

Schrader realized he was onto something unusual when he found he had difficulty breathing as he worked with the new substance. His vision also became impaired, even though only the tiniest amount was exposed to the air in the lab. Test animals died immediately. Schrader notified the military authorities and intensive study began. The first nerve gas was called tabun, an acronym of the names of those involved in its production, the second, sarin, and the third, soman, each more deadly than the one before. A factory producing tabun began operation in April 1942 and by June 1944, had produced an estimated 12,000 tons, more than enough to bring the Allied invasion of Normandy to a dead halt – literally.[5]

C.J. Mackenzie did not receive the only tip-off. Allied military intelligence had repeatedly tasted rumours of new German gases. As early as the fall of 1940, following the Tizard mission to Washington, Porton queried the U.S. Chemical Warfare Service about "German stories of Nerve gases." The Americans replied that it was "judged that the Germans do have some gas which can be used in this manner" and speculated that it might be finely divided arsine,[6] prompting a flurry of research into this gas.

By mid-1943 the Allies knew the Germans had several nerve gases; that they were code-named Trilon (after a popular German detergent) and that they were principally organic compounds of fluorine and phosphorous. They had also come up with a promising candidate to match the new gases – diisopropylfluorophosphate, code-named PF-3 – which showed the same toxic effects as attributed to the German discoveries. The pupils in the eyes of test animals exposed to it shrank dramatically before they died. The Allied scientists even established that atropine sulphate was an effective antidote. PF-3 was a nerve gas.[7]

It is both puzzling and amazing that it doesn't seem to have occurred to British and American scientists that PF-3 might only be one of a whole family of toxic gases. It was not remarkably lethal but the fact that the Germans, with their world-class reputation for chemistry, obviously set a lot of store by the nerve gases should have suggested that they must have found related compounds which were much more deadly. The indications were certainly plain. In May 1943 a German chemist captured in Tunisia told his interrogators of a German super gas which "cannot be classed with any of the other war gases as it is a nerve poison." The prisoner described how it affected the eyes and of plans to use it in shells against towns and fortified positions where "panic will be caused by its blinding effect without its being necessarily in fatal concentrations."[8]

Two months later, General Porter of the U.S. Chemical Warfare Service received a summary of research to date into the fluorophospate gases which had been under way at Edgewood Arsenal, the University of Illinois and the Monsanto Chemical Company in Anniston, Alabama. The report described eight fluorophosphate compounds that had been developed and tested – some very close in formula to the German nerve gases – and then observed:

> The agents referred to by the Germans as "Trilon" have been known to the British and our forces for some time. The British have not felt that these compounds were satisfactory war agents because of the warning which they give by constriction of the lungs in very low concentrations.[9]

This was a classic example of seeing only what one wants to see. Nerve gases kill by restricting breathing; the British rejected them for the very reason that the Germans developed them in the first place.

The Americans came very close to hitting one of the actual German nerve gases. They tested dimethylfluorophosphate, while the formula for sarin is isopropyl methylphosphonofluoridate.[10] "Nobody had the brains to investigate the significance of the isopropyl group," Dr. Flood recalled after the war. "A report came back from England – 'Oh, we've investigated these compounds.' But nobody thought of taking one of the compounds we already had and taking out an ethyl group and putting in an isopropyl group. And then try it. If they had, they'd have got an awful shock."[11]

In February 1944 the U.S. Chemical Warfare Service announced it was dropping work on PF-3 because of "poor performance" in field tests. It was also decided that the new poison gas developed by the Canadians – Compound Z – was "not practical for this war" because of the high cost of the initial equipment to produce it.[12] The Allies had their chance to match a major new chemical weapon developed by the enemy, and they let it slip away.

A plethora of documents in the Canadian archives suggests that British chemists turned their backs on the potential of nerve gas, despite knowing that the Germans had it, because they were preoccupied with mustard gas. Porton and the British Ministry of Supply pressed for casualty-causing mustard gas experiments at Suffield long after there was any new information to be gained. They hung stubbornly to the idea of aircraft spraying mustard gas even when it was obvious many would not survive the new anti-aircraft technology. By 1944 it would have been suicide for the pilots.

The U.S. Chemical Warfare Service seems to have fallen into the same trap. Its chief, General Porter, also had his sights firmly fixed on mustard gas. Vast stocks had been accumulated in a wide variety of bombs and shells and he and his deputies were certain that by using it, they could end the war against Germany and Japan virtually overnight.

By the beginning of 1944 the strategic picture with respect to gas warfare had significantly changed. The Germans were on the run on all fronts so it was no longer likely Britain would have to defend herself with gas. The advantage to Germany of initiating gas warfare was diminishing as well. The tropical trials with mustard in India and Australia, however, suggested an intriguing new possibility.

Dr. Richard Tomlinson was a green lieutenant when he was posted to the office of the Director of Chemical Warfare and Smoke in the large three-storey wooden army building (since demolished) opposite Canada's Parliament Buildings: "I worked with Don Dewar from September /43 in the army building in Ottawa and Donny Dewar was in chemical warfare and, as such, every (secret) publication on CW or BW, released in Canada, Britain or the U.S. used to cross his desk. . . . "

> We had no idea at the beginning of the war that mustard gas would be as effective as it was in the jungles. It turns out that if you drop some mustard gas into (a jungle) it wouldn't really evaporate immediately. It would sit there. With high temperature, and high humidity in particular, it's really nasty.

> And one of the things I did with Don Dewer was . . . we sat down and we calculated we could take some of the Japanese islands at an incredible saving of life – it's odd I should put it this way. Well, we did the calculations. I think it was for the island of Truk. If you dropped a relatively small number of (mustard) bombs on the island the Japs would have had to come out onto the beaches and either fight or surrender. There'd have been no alternative. They just couldn't have stayed in the woods.

> It gets onto the ground and evaporates slowly and you just couldn't stay in there. And I understand that some of those islands, like Guadalcanal, there was terrible fighting.[13]

Tomlinson and Dewar concluded that if mustard gas was used on the Pacific islands held by the Japanese, they could be taken with virtually no loss of American lives. It was an attractive alternative, on paper.

The U.S. Chemical Warfare Service was also doing its sums. By late 1943 it had grown into a huge organization, dwarfing the efforts of Britain and Canada. In the first year of war it spent $1 billion and was producing thousands of tons of mustard gas along with the whole array of other toxic chemicals in army factories across the country. It had opened the Dugway proving grounds in Utah where it tested its chemical rockets and shells on captured enemy vehicles and replicas of German and Japanese houses. But it was still not doing human trials, so news that mustard was especially effective in the tropics was a bit of a surprise. Reports that the jungle canopy kept mustard vapour from dispersing created a lot of interest.

The American service was keen to use gas. After all, the United States was one of the few major nations not to have ratified the 1925 Geneva Protocol banning chemical warfare, so there was no hindrance under international law. In 1942, when

Germany had the power to strike back if gas were used, the Combined Chiefs of Staff, at the direction of Churchill and Roosevelt, ruled that no allied nation would use it except in retaliation. By late 1943, having lost the air war and apparently the ability to retaliate, Germany was a tempting target for a first strike. Nevertheless, the retaliation-only policy stood.

Fighting in the Far East, however, posed a special problem. Guadalcanal had fallen to the Americans in February 1943, after six months of tough slugging in the jungle. It was the first island the Americans attacked and it taught them that Japanese soldiers had particularly high morale and fought with impressive determination even when their resources were meagre. The attack against New Georgia Island in the summer met with resistance that was even fiercer. The island-hopping war was not going to be easy using conventional weapons.

In September, at the suggestion of the Americans, a meeting of the Canadian and U.S. chemical warfare services was held in Washington. Otto Maass arrived with his two most important deputies, Davies, the superintendent of Suffield, and Flood, in charge of the Chemical Warfare Labs. General William F. Porter, chief of the U.S. Chemical Warfare Service, came with his key staff. The purpose was to set up a high-level, U.S.–Canada advisory committee which would meet regularly to co-ordinate the chemical warfare efforts of the two countries.[14]

The Canadians must have been gratified that the Americans thought such a body necessary, considering that CW information was already freely flowing across the border. The U.S. service was also overwhelmingly bigger than the Canadian. Quite apart from the vast disparity in budget and resources, where Maass was classified as the equivalent of a brigadier, Porter had the rank of major-general. Where Flood was a lieutenant-colonel, Porter's deputies were generals. In terms of military hierarchies, the Americans were major league and the Canadians bush.

The first working meeting of the U.S.–Canada CW Advisory Committee convened on November 2 at the Dugway chemical warfare proving grounds. Maass, Flood and Davies were again present, along with Porter and his staff. Most of the discussion was about mustard. It was decided to assess the amount of mustard gas in production, including that from the Cornwall plant in Canada, and to do new field trials establishing the casualty-causing power of both mustard and other gases in all manner of conditions – jungle, built-up areas, against fixed emplacements and in sub-zero temperatures. It was also decided to set up a sub-committee to assess the relative efficiency of chemical weapons versus high explosive in producing casualties.[15]

A few weeks later, on November 20, 1943, following a saturation bombardment, U.S. marines landed at Tarawa – a 540-acre group of islands in the Gilbert chain defended by less than 5,000 Japanese. In three days of desperate fighting about 3,000 marines were dead and 1,000 wounded against 4,690 Japanese dead and 17 captured. The American high command was shocked. Guadalcanal was a picnic compared to Tarawa. In the long fight for the former, the Japanese soldiers had never been without hope and when the island fell, some were even evacuated. At Tarawa there was no chance of help or escape. The garrison fought to the final suicide charge, killing an unacceptable number of marines in the process.

If there was any doubt about the direction of thinking in the U.S. Chemical Warfare Service at year-end, it was dispelled with the visit to Ottawa in January 1944 by Brigadier-General Alden H. Waitt, Porter's second-in-command. He told the Canadian chemical warfare committee that both CW services should be prepared for "G-Day" – the all-out gas attack against Germany and Japan. All they needed was the go-ahead from the Allied political leaders because "there has been sufficient use of gas by the Japs to justify retaliation when, and if we wish to do so." In fact, other than a few clumsy glass grenades filled with hydrogen cyanide in 1942, military intelligence had turned up little to support this statement.

General Waitt continued: "You are familiar with our analysis of the type of operation at Tarawa if we were in a gas phase of the war. Consider the vapour effect of mustard and the state of Japanese protection. We figure about 900 tons of mustard at Tarawa would have completely saturated the place and almost certainly eliminated the resistance of the garrison. That is, 900 tons against 3,000 tons of HE [high explosive]."[16]

Waitt went on to say that the U.S. Chemical Warfare Service believed in "overwhelming attack" with the main gas weapons on hand – the 100-pound mustard bomb and 500- and 1,000-pound bombs filled with phosgene, cyanogen chloride and hydrogen cyanide. "I do not believe in harassing the enemy. I want their resistance eliminated completely." By May 1, he said, the United States would have a plant capable of producing 4,500 tons of cyanogen chloride a year. Canada's projected production of 1,800 tons of HT mustard a year must have seemed piddling by comparison to the tens of thousands of tons the Americans already had, but General Waitt assured his listeners that the Americans considered the stockpile from the Canadian effort as contributing to "the common pool."[17]

The 100-pound mustard bomb the general referred to was the one which had caused all the trouble at Bari. The M47A1 was a cylinder 8 inches in diameter by about 4 feet long containing about 70 pounds of liquid mustard and a bursting charge. It could splash an area 50 yards in diameter. It was a significant advance over the British 65-pound LC (for light case) bomb which was nothing more than a 5-gallon thin metal container with fins which simply broke on impact. This bomb was so simple it was made in the United States and Canada by American Can and Continental Can, companies which specialized in making tin cans for food. It was dangerous in long storage because its corrosive content soon seeped through.[18]

Waitt was simply parroting the ten-page proposal to attack Japan with gas which his boss, General Porter, had put before the U.S. Joint Chiefs of Staff the month before. His memo also cited the 4,000 U.S. casualties at Tarawa, the "ferocious" resistance of the Japanese, and claimed that 900 tons of mustard would have "prostrated the entire garrison." Ironically, Porter backed up his argument by citing Suffield Field Experiment 141 done the previous July. This involved exposing a group of normally clothed men, protected only by masks and gas-proof shorts, to mustard vapour in battle conditions for a half hour. All became severe casualties, Porter reported, some requiring hospitalization for twenty-seven days. "It can be stated that exposure of the men in the target area for somewhat longer than the 30-minute period would have undoubtedly proved fatal."[19] This, obviously, was what he had in mind for the Japanese.

None of the Canadians in General Waitt's audience would have been aware his remarks masked political manoeuvring at the highest levels of U.S. military planning, but most would have recently read Lieutenant-Colonel Alexander's description of the mustard gas catastrophe at Bari. At about the same time another disturbing document crossed their desks – a report from a Major

A.R. Gordon, Royal Canadian Army Medical Corps, on the death of a Canadian soldier during a mustard gas training exercise.

The report began by describing how, six months earlier, Lieutenant "A" had undertaken to illustrate to his platoon the action of a 6-pound mustard gas mine which he had obtained from the local depot. In accordance with the gas training manual's advice on demonstrations, no one wore any protection "to avoid instilling too much fear in troops." The lieutenant ignited the device and everyone stood clear. When nothing happened, he went over and kicked it. It went off and drenched him in liquid.

The thoroughly frightened young man called for water, washed off his face and covered it with anti-gas ointment. He stripped off his clothes and was rushed to the nearest casualty clearing station where his whole body was covered with ointment and he was put to bed. All this was done according to the field instructions for treating mustard gas exposure.

He died, horribly, a week later. Blisters burst out everywhere, some of them the size of a fist, particularly around the groin area. His eyes became inflamed, his temperature soared to 106.2, he coughed up gunk, his skin came off at the touch, and finally his lungs collapsed. The autopsy found complete chaos in his vital organs. So much for the regulation techniques for prompt treatment, and so much for all that anti-gas ointment sold by Canada to South Africa.[20]

Whether in 1944, or 1989, a reader of that report cannot fail to be appalled by what the mustard did to that human being. There had been no experience quite like it, for the mustard gas used during the First World War was poorly refined, consisting only of about 60 per cent of the actual liquid, and dispersal techniques were primitive. By 1944 production had been perfected so that it could be made nearly 100 per cent pure. This superior product had never been tested to the ultimate extreme. The young officer's death showed what it was capable of.

It was in the context of that report, and the suffering at Bari, that Otto Maass assigned his principal aide, Major Donald Dewar, to serve on a joint U.S.– Canada – U.K. sub-committee to study the relative merits of chemical weapons versus high explosive in causing casualties.

Dewar had been working for Maass almost from the beginning of the war. A chemistry student of E.W.R. Steacie at McGill, after finishing his doctorate he was invited up to the NRC in 1940 to work on some of the early war projects Maass had got under way. On joining the army, he was attached to the NRC and was the first scientist/soldier in the fledgling Canadian chemical warfare service to be sent to Porton after Banting's return. Instead of doing research, however, Dewar became Maass's principal aide when chemical warfare was reorganized under the Department of National Defence.

"I always thought Maass pushed me into this," Dewar recalled in a 1988 interview. "I think you might be interested in that report if they've ever declassified it. For me it was obvious. This was a loaded thing. But they were very careful they didn't put any CWS people on the committee."[21]

The group consisted of Dewar and two other Canadians, two scientists from the U.S. National Defense Research Council, and a British chemical warfare liaison officer who later dropped out. They were assembled at Edgewood Arsenal in June and for several weeks ploughed through Chemical Warfare Service data, air force pin-point bombing results and various studies on the effects of high explosive bombs and shells. They were given access to all Allied chemical warfare reports and every facility to produce a reasoned, well-documented assessment of the merits of using gas to crush resistance on Japanese-held islands.

Forty-four years later, retired and living alone in a trailer park in southern Ontario where his tiny patch of lawn is clipped to billiard table perfection, Dr. Dewar smiled at the memory: "There was a lad from Suffield, Brian Griffith, who had been a professor of mathematics at Toronto, and this one lad from Kelowna, B.C., and we said, 'We're not going to be used this way.' There was one British lad but he very carefully stayed away. The two Americans were also worried. We felt we were being pushed into something we didn't like. . . ."[22]

That something was a three-nation scientific agreement to use gas on the Japanese. If their report came down strongly in favour of gas over high explosive, it would be a powerful 'expert' argument to present to the U.S. Joint Chiefs of Staff – and from there to Roosevelt himself. Dewar and his colleagues were afraid their support might tip the scales of opinion and result in a U.S. first strike against Japan.

Then an amazing thing happened.

The report was presented on July 20, 1944. It is available in the Canadian and American archives and it is a marvel to read –

sixty-five pages of technical language, formulas and learned analyses leading to the deeply considered conclusion that CW is "difficult if not impossible to assess until it has actually been used in a combat theatre." High explosives, flame-throwers and white phosphorus also had their merits, so it was a toss-up which was better. The report is a model of technical mumbo-jumbo and scientific obfuscation raised to high art.[23]

"I think I can even quote our conclusion," Dewar chuckled. "If troops are in the open HE would be better because it was more available, but if the enemy is in bunkers, CW would be better." This was not kind of statement calculated to launch phalanxes of bombers raining mustard on Okinawa or Truk.

"Maass never said anything to me. When the report was discussed, I remember I was present when the head of CWS came into camp, General Porter. He never made any comment at all but I think he twigged pretty well to what we were doing. If you read the report you'll see that in effect we said ... (whispers) it doesn't matter a damn! (laughs) I think that is about the sum total of that report. We were rather proud of what we did on that thing."[24]

They also recommended that no further casualty-causing experiments be done comparing CW and HE weapons, but that suggestion was rejected when the full U.S.– Canada CW Committee considered their findings. The disappointed committee had no option but to call for more experiments. When Porton sent in its assessment six months later, its comments were condescending but devastating. Dewar and the others had handled the data in ways that were "doubtful" and had made "debatable" assumptions based on highly irregular interpretations of mustard casualty experiments. Quite the opposite to their conclusion was indicated, the British said. They must have privately despaired of the quality of specialist being turned out by North American universities.[25]

The charade of Dewar and the others may not have changed the course of history, but it was no mere pebble in the Mississippi either. It had dealt the U.S. Chemical Warfare Service's campaign to use gas a serious setback, and it was months before General Porter could again advance it seriously. This time, however, he singled out a specific target – Iwo Jima, the volcanic island in the Pacific south of Japan that was a key stepping-stone for the U.S. bombing campaign on the Japanese homeland.

Ignoring the unreliable Canadians, Porter sought support directly from the British. They, presumably Porton, secretly produced an analysis that recommended that the U.S. fleet stand off from Iwo Jima and soak it in gas, simultaneously jamming the island's radio transmitter so that the garrison could not tell Tokyo the nature of the assault. Moreover, it even suggested that the yellow identification bands be removed from the gas shells so that the gunners wouldn't know they were firing anything but high explosive. The American public, and the world, need never know.

OSS scientific adviser Stanley Lovell was assigned the task of convincing the U.S. Navy man in charge, Admiral Chester Nimitz. He argued that intelligence reported that Iwo Jima was "stronger than Gibraltar," a veritable maze of concrete tunnels and strong points. Nimitz could expect enormous casualties. The admiral wavered. Lovell drove home the OSS embellishment to the plan. Obviously Tokyo would be suspicious if the radio was jammed so Nimitz should receive a message in a code known to have been broken by the Japanese to the effect that the Americans planned to use a new death ray. The ray would be blamed for the blocked transmissions and, obviously, for a Japanese garrison dead without a fight.[26]

Nimitz finally agreed. The plan then went to the president, approved on all sides. It was returned with the note, "All prior endorsements denied – Franklin D. Roosevelt, Commander-in-Chief." On February 19, 1945, Iwo Jima was attacked in the conventional manner and 7,000 Americans were killed and 13,000 wounded. About 22,000 Japanese died. Lovell wasn't convinced the president's sense of propriety in war was worth the price of grief to the thousands of American families who lost loved ones. On the other hand, the photograph of American marines raising the flag on Mount Suribachi became one of the most celebrated images of combat heroism in American history.

From a strictly military point of view, one can sympathize with the U.S. Chemical Warfare Service's desire to use gas on Japan. Its leaders were unaware of the work on the atomic bomb, which was still months away from completion. Bacteriological warfare had possibilities, but a large arsenal of practical weapons, chiefly bombs filled with anthrax, was still well into the future. Chemical weapons, however, were in ample supply and Japan was in no position adequately to defend herself from them. Neither was Germany.

Bomber Command Operational Instruction No. 74 was issued in Britain on June 5, 1944, the day before Allied troops landed in France along the coast of Normandy. While on the beaches, the U.S., British and Canadian troops would be particularly vulnerable to gas warfare, so Bomber Command alerted its units to be ready for operation "Knockabout" or "Infusion," code words for large-scale retaliatory gas attacks on German cities. The first involved saturation bombing with mustard only; the second with a mixture of 65-pound mustard bombs, 500-pound phosgene bombs and high explosive. The idea of including high explosive was to break windows to allow the gas easily to enter buildings.[27]

Porton Report 1230/2, entitled "Attacks on Cities with Gas," calculated that 650 65-pound mustard bombs would be sufficient per square mile of a city, with the following result:

1. People in the area or entering the area would risk blistered skin up to 24 hours after attack;
2. gas masks would have to be worn for 24 hours because of risk to eyes and lungs;
3. anyone "who removed his respirator, even for brief periods (e.g., to eat) would be in danger of later becoming blinded for some days;"
4. the 65-pound bomb would go through the roofs of some buildings and make them uninhabitable for months;
5. decontamination would be impossible;
6. casualties would be high but the number of deaths comparatively low.

The report calculated that 10,000 bombs filled with HT mustard would paralyse Hamburg and 30,000 would do for Berlin. If the aim was to kill the one and a half million people of Hamburg outright, 2,700 of the 500-pound phosgene bombs would suffice while 8,000 would do for the three million people of central Berlin. Both cities could easily be dealt with on the same night, and others in the days that followed.[28]

There seemed little doubt among British planners that such an attack would shorten the war with Germany, if not stop it in its tracks. It was known that the Nazi government had invested little in civilian gas masks and the Luftwaffe was already powerless against massive bomber assaults. The Porton report's suggestion that the number of deaths would be comparatively low was not allowing for the Bari experience. People would have been exposed to the gas for days and many thousands would have died from systemic poisoning. Even not allowing for the deaths, the prospect of the three million people of Berlin – men, women, children and infants – going painfully blind simultaneously while suffering lung damage and blisters, is a nightmare that may well have surpassed the A-bomb tragedies of Hiroshima and Nagasaki.

Ironically, while in the United States the generals wanted to use gas but Roosevelt didn't, in Britain Churchill wanted to use gas but his generals didn't. The Porton report cited above was the basis of a secret assessment on the advantages of initiating a gas attack which the prime minister had demanded a month after the Normandy invasion. He strongly felt that Britain should launch a gas attack unilaterally. On July 6, 1944, he wrote the British Chiefs of Staff:

> I want you to think very seriously over this question of using poison gas. I would not use it unless it could be shown that (a) it was life or death for us, or (b) that it would shorten the war by a year.
>
> It is absurd to consider morality on this topic when everybody used it in the last war without a word of complaint from the moralists or the Church. On the other hand the bombing of open cities was regarded as forbidden.
>
> Now everyone does it as a matter of course. It is simply a question of fashion changing as she does between long and short skirts for women.
>
> I want a cold-blooded calculation made as to how it would pay us to use poison gas, by which I mean principally mustard. We will want to gain more ground in Normandy so as not to be cooped up in a small area. We could probably deliver twenty tons to their one and for the sake of their one they would bring their bomber aircraft into the area against our superiority, thus paying a heavy toll. . . .
>
> I quite agree it may be several weeks or even months before I shall ask you to drench Germany with poison gas, and if we do it, let's do it 100 per cent. In the meanwhile, I want the matter studied in cold blood by sensible people and not by that particular set of psalm-singing uniformed defeatists which one runs across now here now there. Pray address

yourself to this. It is a big thing and can only be discarded for a big reason. I shall of course have to square Uncle Joe and the President, but you need not bring this into your calculations at the present time. Just try to find out what it is like on its own merits.[29]

It is significant that Churchill requested the above review just after receiving reports from British intelligence that German radio traffic confirmed earlier assessments that the Nazis had no intention of trying to repel the Allied armies with gas and, if anything, were afraid of it being used by the Allies. In his reply to Churchill the Chief of Staff concluded:

It is true we could drench the big German cities with an immeasurably greater weight of gas than the Germans could put down in this country. Other things being equal this could lead to the conclusion that it would be to our advantage to use the gas weapon. But other things are not equal. . . .

The "not equal" was the fact that whatever German retaliation there was, it would be aimed at British civilians whose morale, the service chiefs said, might suffer adversely.[30]

The position taken by the British Chiefs of Staff is not borne out by the facts as they knew them. They were unaware of the extent to which the Germans had developed the vastly more deadly nerve gases, so they could not have helped but privately agree with the judgment that German retaliation – with standard gas weapons like mustard and phosgene – would have been feeble. Allied air superiority certainly would have prevented most German bombers reaching their targets while the Allies could rain mustard on Germany with impunity. Nevertheless, the British generals preferred to fight the war out with conventional weapons, and rejected Churchill's proposal. "I am not all convinced by this negative report," a disappointed prime minister complained. "But clearly I cannot make head against the parsons and the warriors at the same time."[31]

Britain's military leaders appear to have anticipated the prime minister's bid to launch gas warfare. A few months earlier they had proposed to the Combined Chiefs of Staff that the allied policy be revised to the effect that no allied nation could initiate chemical warfare without prior approval of the Combined

Chiefs, whether they were acting in retaliation or not.[32] That effectively blocked any chance for Churchill or the U.S. generals unilaterally to order a chemical warfare attack under the pretext the enemy had done it first. Gas had lost its chance.

It's just as well. What Churchill did not realize was that if the Allies struck first, killing and blinding tens of thousands of German civilians, Hitler had ample capability for revenge. He had at least 12,000 tons of nerve gas in bombs and shells, against which the Allies were virtually defenceless.[33] Even with severe losses in aircraft, Hitler could have killed every living creature in the Normandy beachhead and a good portion of the civilians in Britain's southern cities. And he could have kept up the killing by loading nerve gas into Germany's new flying bombs.

It didn't happen. The threat of overwhelming retaliation had stayed Hitler's hand. The common sense of British military leaders had stayed Churchill's. Both Germans and Britons escaped mutual massacre. The prime minister, however, wasn't one to give up easily.

In October 1944 Maass received a lengthy message from Washington from a Colonel H. Paget who identified himself as the British liaison officer in the United States for the new British Inter-Service Sub-Committee for Biological Warfare.[34] This group had been set up in June by the British Chiefs of Staff and, although Paget said he had received no instructions to deal with Canada, he assumed it was appropriate to inform Maass of the content of various papers that had been issued by the Combined Chiefs pertaining to biological warfare.

Paget then went on to say that anthrax and botulinus toxin had been deemed the most promising weapons, production of both was to be in the United States, and the British hoped for 500,000 anthrax bombs as soon as possible. It is not known whether this information took the Canadians by surprise, although there was certainly much less candour between Britain and Canada at this point in the war, the United States being much the more important ally. Murray and Maass might have guessed, seeing that the Americans dropped all interest in anthrax from Grosse Ile just two months before. "Work is proceeding at high priority" in Britain and the United States on anthrax, Paget reported. The Canadian effort was no longer a factor.[35]

Britain's sudden enthusiasm for germ warfare appears to have been sparked by a February 1944 memo to Churchill from his personal scientific adviser, Lord Cherwell, who wrote that anthrax had "appalling potentiality" almost equal to what was expected from an atomic bomb. He added that Britain couldn't afford not to have anthrax bombs on hand. After reading Cherwell's memo to his Chiefs of Staff, Churchill asked his Bacteriological Warfare Committee to obtain 500,000 bombs from the United States.[36]

Cherwell, as described in an earlier chapter, had no standing with the scientific community and little with the military. As for the Bacteriological Warfare Committee, it had only a watching brief as a sub-committee of the War Cabinet. Porton, and consequently Britain's entire biological warfare program, was actually administered through the Ministry of Supply on the advice of the Inter-Service Committee on Chemical Warfare.[37] In other words, Churchill's information had come from an unreliable source, and he had demanded action from a body that was not directly in charge of the program.

Between championing iceberg aircraft carriers and wanting to carpet Germany with poison gas and deadly germs, one really must wonder whether Churchill's behaviour was rational at this stage of the war. His repeated advancements of Mountbatten to high command were appalling lapses of judgment. His desire to kill Germans en masse was not justified by the military situation, which clearly had turned in favour of the Allies. But by setting up the Biological Warfare Inter-Service Sub-Committee, the military chiefs strengthened their hold on biological warfare by making it the sole charge of an inter-service committee parallel to the one for chemical warfare. If the United States was going to supply anthrax bombs to Britain, the military chiefs were going to have a substantial say in the matter. Churchill appears to have been out-manoeuvred again.[38]

Cherwell's lack of grasp of the germ warfare situation is further illustrated in that he had told Churchill there was no cure for anthrax infection. This was no longer strictly true. Research and production of penicillin, particularly in the United States, had made enormous strides and sufficiently large quantities were available in the spring of 1944 to meet the needs of the Allied armed forces. It had also been found that the new antibiotic worked excellently against cutaneous anthrax. Because the Axis powers didn't have penicillin, this enhanced rather than diminished the potential of anthrax as a weapon.

Anthrax spores, however, even forty-five years after the war, remain a formidable biological weapon when inhaled as a mist. Then they overwhelm the body's defences and death is almost certain. Indeed, one of the major discoveries made since the days of the old WBC Committee was that most of the animal diseases were effective against humans when delivered in this way in large doses. Moreover, Camp Detrick had perfected the air dispersal of biological agents to such a degree that it now appeared to be a practical and effective new way to wage war. The military now got involved in earnest.

In June 1944, amid controversy and resentment at Camp Detrick, the U.S. Chemical Warfare Service took over the entire biological warfare program, including its scientific direction. Up until then the mandate of the military had been mainly confined to running the bases, liaison with various technical branches, and consultation, with over-all direction theoretically coming from the War Research Service. The scientists at Camp Detrick had been left to their own devices.

It is not easy to determine what politics lay behind the takeover. The roots of it may be in the Barcelona Committee's recommendation in early 1944 that the offensive ability of the United States be stepped up to counter the threat from Germany perceived by the OSS. By May, however, much more reliable Ultra intelligence made it clear that Germany was almost certain not to resort to germ warfare. Nevertheless, Stimson sought and obtained that month approval from Roosevelt to turn the whole program over to the Chemical Warfare Service.

The key to the mystery is probably in still-secret records of the Chemical Warfare Service and the Joint Chiefs of Staff. What is known is that General Porter, the CWS chief, kept Ira Baldwin, the scientific head of biological warfare research, in the dark about his earlier arrangement with Canada to mass-produce anthrax at Grosse Ile. Baldwin also was never told about the deal to supply Britain with half a million anthrax bombs. It therefore came as a surprise to him, just after Camp Detrick got its pilot plant running in the spring, to be asked to help build a full-scale anthrax factory capable of turning out immense quantities of spores.

"It was up to me to design it. I protested. 'Our research isn't far enough along. We aren't ready to design a plant that is both safe and effective.' 'Well, we must have it.' After all, it was somebody else's decision. It wasn't mine. So I said we will do the best we can."

As work got under way at Terre Haute, Indiana, Baldwin assigned his most trusted safety officer, Walter Nevius, to oversee it. Inclined to be fussy, he also was thorough and demanding, which was why Baldwin chose him.

He was very well aware of the heavy responsibility he had in designing a plant that would not only be effective, but would be safe. This was for anthrax. You have to be sure that you didn't let a cloud loose in the atmosphere. So he was super-cautious. And I found out later that the people in construction were getting disappointed with this.

I was asked to go into Washington one day to meet General (Rollo) Ditto, who was in over-all charge of this whole program. Nobody told me why he wanted me to come in and see him. He just asked me to come. So, fair enough, I went in.

And he opened the meeting by saying that the Corps of Engineers was very much dissatisfied by the way in which my engineer was operating and he was going to substitute another gentleman. I inquired what background this other man had in biological engineering. General Ditto replied, "As far as I know, none. But he has a very fine reputation as a chemical engineer."

I said, "Well, in some respects a biological engineer thinks exactly opposite from the way a chemical engineer does. A chemical engineer is interested in what happens in the tank, and if there's a little spilling, so long as it isn't too much, you don't worry much about it. But the biological engineer has to think at both ends. For example, the principal way to avoid contamination at a chemical engineering plant is to keep it under pressure. That means your tank doesn't collapse and you don't get anything in from the outside . . . " And so forth and so on.

Well, in biological engineering we don't want these things to escape into the atmosphere around us. We have to do something different. I said, "Now, that means that this man who's just been in chemical engineering may, at some crucial date, make a mistake that would be very serious." And I said, "Of course, General Ditto, you must do what you feel is right and proper. I only ask that you relieve me of any responsibility for this potential (danger) of the thing."

He said, "I'll not do that."

I said, "I guess I'll have to leave then."

"You can't."

"Oh," I said, "yes, I can. I'm under contract here. I'm not an officer."

And that's the way I left the program.

I never knew why they were so insistent that they must get an (anthrax) plant built immediately. It was probably because the British wanted us to supply them with some and they felt they had a responsibility to do it.

But nobody ever told me that. I didn't know that.[39]

Baldwin was replaced by Dr. Orem Woolpert, who had gone into uniform. The War Research Service was disbanded and George Merck was made special consultant on biological warfare to the Secretary of War. The head of the Chemical Warfare Service's medical division, General Cornelius Rhoads, was put in charge of biological warfare in his place but withdrew after being bitterly challenged by the scientific staff at Detrick. General Ditto took over instead.[40]

The U.S. Chemical Warfare Service was now entirely and firmly in control of all aspects of the U.S. biological warfare program. By the end of 1944 General Porter led a formidable organization. Camp Detrick had perfected techniques – actual pilot plants – for the mass production of anthrax and botulinus toxin and was branching out into the study of the offensive potential of glanders, brucellosis, cholera, dysentery, plague, typhus, coccidioides (a lethal fungus for which there is still no treatment), foot and mouth, rinderpest, fowl plague and various plant pathogens. Research was later undertaken on psittacosis, encephalitis, Rift Valley fever, typhoid, and yellow fever.[41]

Under Baldwin, Detrick had remained closely focused on the development of bacterial agents for use in tactical weapons. The tasks of the scientists were to choose the most suitable germs, increase their virulence by selective breeding, develop methods of mass production and storage, and perfect means of airborne delivery. One of the thorniest problems was trying to make the bacteria resistant to the sterilizing effect of ultra-violet radiation from the sun. An attractive aspect to anthrax was that in its spore form this was not such a problem. Its longevity was, however, and this spurred the search for other less-persistent agents.

Detrick's effort was not confined to anti-personnel weapons. It worked vigorously with animal diseases and anti-crop agents. It kept its own gardens for experiments and even had a plot of rice in Florida where it tested out rice diseases which could conceivably be used against the rice crop of Japan. Florida was chosen for these trials because the state had no domestic rice industry of its own which could be accidentally infected.

Also in early 1944 Detrick became home of the first biological warfare school. In February the first sixty students arrived to be trained in what to watch out for in the event of germ warfare by the enemy, and what to do about it. They soon invented their own class yell:

> Brucellosis, Psittacosis
> Vee! You! Bah!
> Antibodies, Antitoxin
> Rah! Rah! Rah![42]

Anthrax, however, was still centre stage. The Vigo Ordnance Plant at Terre Haute was expected to start production of anthrax in 20,000-gallon tanks on May 1, with the capability of producing four tons of agent in a single run. The Granite Peak installation at Dugway would be ready for field trials by then as well. At year-end a design and procurement order was put out for a 4-pound aerosol bomb to be used with the 500-pound cluster bomb.[43]

General Porter could take satisfaction in knowing that by mid-1945 he would have at hand a weapon of mass-killing power the likes the world had never known.

He was unaware that other scientists, other soldiers, were pushing to completion an even more spectacular weapon. They called it the atomic bomb.

C·H·A·P·T·E·R
N·I·N·E

Deadly Intentions

It was the middle of the night, middle of the winter, middle of the prairie. The steam stood back from the train's engine like a spool of carnival floss. Lieutenant Dick Tomlinson stepped from the coach's warmth onto a white platform, his breath puffing into the frigid air. Hoar frost transformed the CPR station into a Hansel and Gretel cottage and veins of frost spread rapidly on his greatcoat. The train wheezed away. It was the end of January 1944. Suffield, Alberta.

"I thought this was going to be the worst time of my life," Dr. Tomlinson recalled, many years later. "I'd never seen anything so cold in all my life."

A car awaited him and soon it was creaking into the night, taking him to the Suffield military base, by then the jewel of Canada's wartime scientific effort. Under E. Ll. Davies, it had become the finest experimental station of the Allies. There every conceivable land or air weapon underwent firing trials – tanks, rockets, flame-throwers, 2,000-pound bombs and a vast array of smaller missiles filled with high explosive, chemicals or biological agents. There was an airfield, large-calibre naval gun, machine shops and medical and chemical research sections. There was a Chemical Warfare School. If a new weapon was designed in Canada, the United States or Britain, it almost invariably wound up at Suffield for testing.

"I was a gas officer for the field and again a gas officer for the divisional level," Tomlinson recalled. "In other words, I was prepared to lay a gas attack for a whole division, or smoke. You may not realize this but we had rockets at that time. I became an expert at rocketry."

We had these racks. They were V-shaped pipes – I've forgotten how many rockets you put on these things but it was over 100 of them. And you had one of these things like for dynamite you shove it down and suddenly all hell would break loose. A 100 or so rockets would take off in the air and you could see them in flight.

We had pillboxes several miles ahead that we were trying to hit. They'd put observers in there and they would try and tell me how well I was doing.

It was really good fun. They were called five-inch unrotating rockets and they carried phosgene and if you were on target the fellow in the pillbox was really ducking down with his respirator on. These weapons weren't experimental. They were ready for use.[1]

Dr. Murray Sutton was a 22-year-old army private with a university background in chemistry and bacteriology when he was posted to Professor G.B. Reed's bacterial warfare lab on the Queen's University campus at Kingston. Because Suffield's "Area E" was where various bacterial weapons and toxins were tested, he visited the station several times during the war.

The "Queer" section was where the chemical warfare guys produced gases, experimental gases and filled cylinders and things like that. You had chemistry, microbiology, physiology. You had sections. It was almost like a small university in there. It was staffed by civilians and military personnel who had been picked for their knowledge in certain fields. Some of them lived on the base and some of them lived in Medicine Hat and commuted back and forth.

Area E from the main camp was about 30 miles – you had to go 30 miles north. They used to have rations for about 22 people there in case they wanted to do a bomb test when things were at their prime – say when the wind was blowing the right way and everything else was coincidental. Then they would bring in the high-price help – some ranks of major but mostly colonels and whatnot.

Dr. Sutton sat on the balcony of his cottage overlooking a lake in northern Ontario as he remembered his wartime past. He took a piece of paper and sketched rapidly.

> Say this was your tower. You would put your bomb here and you would set an impinger series around it at certain distances to see how far the wind would go. And there was a met officer, a meteorological officer. And he would say the wind was blowing 12 knots or something like that, north by northeast. And when you thought it was in your pattern, you'd let your bomb go.
>
> This would be ground zero, right? (indicating a point within concentric circles) A test tower. Let her go. Blow. And you would have trenches dug out here, impingers with drums which would be automatically set off when the bomb went, and they would suck in so much air through a fluid so that you could sample the air.
>
> There would be animals staked out at each one of these posts. If it was an explosive type of thing, there would be trenches and the animals would be lowered into them so they would have the protection of the trench and there would be no blast. But they would get the toxic products.
>
> Like, I can remember taking two large engineering platoons – which is about 30-odd men per platoon – and we had to dig 278 ditches big enough to hold a cow. Or a horse.
>
> There was a Dr. [James] Patterson and I think he was the pathologist at the Ottawa Civic Hospital at the time. Now he was out there then and he was a colonel. A full colonel. He would do the sections. . . .
>
> When they did animal tests, then we had to autopsy all the animals and bring the bits and pieces in, the spleen, brain and so forth. Like, have you ever done an autopsy on a horse? They used to use horses, cows, sheep, goats, chickens, rabbits, mice, pigs – and they all had to be autopsied. And they were done at 100 yards, 300 yards, 500 yards from the burst site.[2]

Davies could look out on his empire with genuine pride. Not only was the scientific and experimental side of the station topnotch, but it was Canada's central arsenal for chemical weapons. Huge tanks had been built for bulk storage of the most important poison gases, and there were stockpiles of bombs and shells of all types, both full and empty, plus the equipment for filling them with chemical agent.[3]

Professor Murray's achievements in bacteriological warfare were less obvious. He owed much to Reed, who was a brilliant innovator, as well as to others such as Lochhead and Mitchell. By early fall of 1944 he could rightly claim that the Canadians had explored more areas of biological warfare than their counterparts in the United States and Britain. Even though he had faltered on the mass-production of anthrax, and the botulism threat on D-Day had not materialized, Murray could rightly feel a pioneer in a novel form of warfare of vast potential.

With the Americans pulling out of anthrax production at Grosse Ile, Murray considered his options. The island biological station had already demonstrated it could mass-produce tulare-mia – the rabbit fever bacteria – but that disease wasn't nearly as deadly as botulinus toxin. In the spring, when he had been convinced the Germans were going to use it in Normandy, Murray had arranged for the expansion of Reed's lab to produce the toxin in large amounts so that they could make the toxoid. Now Murray ordered Reed to step up production because, he said, neither Britain or the U.S. had significant stocks of X.[14]

Botulinus toxin, code letter X, is at least 5,000 times more efficient than nerve gas in killing ability, and 160,000 times more deadly than phosgene.[5] One micron under the fingernail, in the eye, or inhaled, is sufficient to cause death. That's a particle considerably smaller than the sharp end of a pin. It was estimated that there were 32 million lethal doses in one gram. It had been field tested at Suffield in a Canadian-designed bomb in August 1944 and Murray's enthusiasm shows it must have performed well.[6]

Reed's lab at Queen's University in Kingston thus became the second major facility for the mass production of a bacteriological agent in Canada. As the technicians and much of the military staff at the lab wore civilian clothes and appeared to be students, the rest of the campus little suspected that the grey limestone building in their midst housed one of Canada's most top-secret wartime installations. Workers in the labs on the ground floor innocently studied problems in physiology. Above them Reed ruled a world of deadly poisons and lethal microorganisms.[7]

Botulinus toxin is made by chemically separating it from the slurry produced by growing the appropriate bacteria (clostridium botulinum) in ground meat. "The stink and stench of this process is not pleasant," Dr. Sutton recalled. "I've seen some people come in [the lab] and regurgitate on command almost. The odour could be very upsetting to some people. And your clothes – when you took them home you turfed them right away. Nobody could stand you. Don't forget, you're working with clostridia – gas gangrene organisms. Anaerobes. And they all decompose protein. And when you get decomposed protein [i.e., rotten meat] it's highly odoriferous."[8]

After the separated toxin is dried, the most difficult and dangerous part of the operation is grinding the resulting solid into very tiny particles. This was also done at Reed's lab and by July 31, 1944, ten pounds of raw toxin was available for processing.[9] Much more was to come.

"We did that. My chum and I," said Sutton. "A ball-mill. Carefully. Very carefully. You would also do it in a glove box. And then you would decontaminate everything you'd touched, because if you missed anything. . . . Don't forget, it just takes one little bit. You wore two sets of latex gloves plus a heavy pair. You taped them on. You always wore [the] gloves inside your [glove box] gloves."[10]

Reed's lab at Queen's wasn't necessarily the best place in the country to do this kind of work. The Connaught Labs would have been better. Closely linked to the University of Toronto, even before the war the Connaught specialized in making a wide variety of vaccines and other biological products and had a large research and production facility called "The Farm" in the northern part of the city. In late 1941 Connaught associate professor Donald Fraser had promised the first meeting of the M-1000 Committee that he would look into the possibility of the Connaught mass-producing botulinus bacteria. Because most of its wartime records have been destroyed, there is no evidence that the Connaught accepted or rejected the assignment although Reed was a frequent wartime visitor.[11]

When Sutton arrived at Kingston in mid-1944, Reed's lab was at its peak with forty scientists and soldier-technicians. It was impressed upon the 22-year-old that this was a Most Top Secret operation and he was to keep his mouth shut and his eyes and ears open. He was to serve as a lab technician, but as one of the military personnel he also shared responsibility for security. That included keeping an eye on the civilian scientists and even

Reed himself. The professor had apparently belonged to suspect organizations in his youth. Sutton was to make sure he stayed as loyal as he was supposed to be. Ultimately he came to admire him immensely:

Well, G.B. was a clever man. He could churn out [academic] papers in 24 hours if he wanted to.

I can remember helping him build a dollhouse at 2 o'clock in the morning in the basement of the new medical building, the two of us there pumping away with a saw because he promised a kid on his street, this little girl, that she would have a dollhouse for Christmas. So he came in and he was crawling around the building and I heard a noise – it's a good thing he didn't get shot but he didn't. He said, "Oh, oh, I'm building a dollhouse." So the next thing you know till 2 o'clock in the morning we were building a dollhouse.

The next day he wouldn't even know who you were, because when he would get something on his mind, he would concentrate so strongly that he would be completely out of it. You would say, "Good morning, sir." You wouldn't even get a grunt out of him let alone anything else. He'd just pass you in the hall.

He'd get into his office and go in and sit down and he'd take his coat off – sometimes he didn't take his coat all the way off. He'd only get the one arm off and then he'd start writing. No, this is true. This is no joke.

And when he was writing he was always smoking. His secretary always lived in the fear of burning to death because you had to go through his office into a little cubicle where her office was. She was always afraid that such a conflagration would start in his office from his smoking that she would never get out of it into the main hall.

Anyway, we used to park fire extinguishers on either side of his door because he would smoke as he wrote. And he would write a sentence that was important (on scraps of newspaper) and then another on another sheet of paper. And if he didn't like it he just take it and turf it – just crumple it like that and throw it on the floor. Towards the basket but not necessarily in the basket.

After a while the floor would be just a mass of crumpled up newsprint and the cigarette would get down where it would burn his lips and he'd just take it and throw it [gestures] toward the basket. Then it would go on fire. Everybody would rush out. Put the fire out. He would not stop writing.

I remember one time he left us and went to Toronto for a meeting and when he got there he parked on College Street. He drove up in the morning and went to his meeting, and went to his hotel and three days later took the train and came home. Monday morning he went out to take his car – which was a big Packard, a '38 Packard, the big diamond hub caps and whatnot – and his car wasn't in the garage. And his wife says, "It must have got stolen." So he notified the police that his car was stolen.

A nice man. He used to get his hair and his moustache all bleached white. He was a handsome looking man and during the First World War he had been in the Royal Air Force. He pranged up a couple of planes so they took him off and made him a medical officer of health. He was not an M.D. He was a physiologist, a plant physiologist by profession. But he was a nice guy. A great guy to work with.

Sutton explained that Reed's lab was divided into a medical unit and a biological warfare unit. The latter handled a wide variety of pathogenic organisms – psittacosis, tularemia, anthrax and so on. There was also a "special media" section for infecting insects – particularly house flies and fruit flies. The main emphasis, however, was on producing toxins from botulinus and gas gangrene bacteria and in trying to increase the virulence of various types of germs.

We were engaged in genetic engineering but we called it "selection" in those days. We were looking for mutants that were more virulent, more toxic. And trying to upgrade them all the time so that we could get a better (more deadly) product. There are some that can be enhanced by irradiation, by certain adjuncts. Then you'd pick and select. You'd keep on doing that in a process of selection like you do for the breeding of animals.

The Brits and the Americans were working at this. We were all working for the ultimate culture. Which strain? If one guy had a strain that was better than the other guy's, it would be immediately exchanged and we would start working with it. The trick was to improve those strains at all times and have better means of extraction. That all had to be done by hand.

And the man who was the genius behind Guilford, who actually did processing, was Major James Stevenson, who was a medical pathologist. He taught pathology at McGill after the war. And this guy, he could play hunches like you wouldn't believe. You've got a thousand choices and he'd say, "These are the ten best ones and we should do this one." And he was usually right.

He was very good. He was a small man and we nick-named him Mickey Mouse because the lab coats in those days used to have a belt with two buttons on the back. Well, he was so slim he used to move the buttons together and he ended up with the two buttons close together. And you know how Mickey Mouse had the two little buttons on the back of his pants? Well, this guy had ears that were slightly protrud-ing and . . . but he was a real great guy.

Another key associate of G.B. Reed was his nephew, Roger Reed. One day he and Stevenson told Sutton and another soldier-technician that they had to be immunized against a certain dis-ease. The two men arrived in Stevenson's office and were promptly jabbed in their upper arms.

Normally he would sit and talk, sit on his desk and talk and swing his legs back and forth, just like a kid. But this time he said, "That's it fellows. Sorry, I've got lots to do." So you can take a hint, you know. You depart. We were going down the hallway and there was a long corridor where we were, with no doors on it. Just a four-foot wide corridor with terrazzo floor with the rolled curb and we were walking down and saying, "I guess Jimmy's busy today, eh?"

"Yeah."

"Jeeezus Christ!" We both grabbed our shoulders almost simultaneously. You could feel the tears coming to your eyes. You'd think somebody had a hot poker and was poking it into you. We ended up with our feet braced against the one wall and our shoulders against the other to put pressure on it, to stop it from diffusing so fast. It was that hot. And he came out and apologized after and he says, "We got ours on the week-end. We knew what it was like. That's why I didn't want you in there."

But you know what it was? It was Rocky Mountain spot-ted fever. And you know what they used to do then? They used to grind the ticks up in 6 per cent formaldehyde and inject it straight into you. The formaldehyde would fix the virus. You would have a chemically killed virus but it was in the tissues of the tick. The tick and everything are in the injection. The whole works. Ohhhhhh! Brutal. [Laughs] But it was a way of culturing it. Just take the live ticks with the infection in them. They let the ticks feed on an infected animal, you see.

Murray and Charles Mitchell were frequent visitors to the Kingston lab but it was off-limits to almost all army personnel, regardless of rank. The rule was strictly enforced.

We didn't need too much security. There was only one way in. If you wanted to get in, you had to pass through one door. And a man's sitting there with sidearm and a bayonet. They were part of our unit. A working part of our unit and faithful. They had a simplistic outlook on life.

One man – he was a Private Moses and he was a Brantford Indian. He was a child of nature. But he was the most powerful man. He could lift over 300 pounds. He could lift a keg of what we called corn steep, which was the stuff that was the by-product of making corn syrup but which we used to use for nutritional purposes. It would take two of us young strong guys to do it. I mean I weighed 190-some-odd pounds then and [so did] my chum.

Moses was so powerful he could take a man and grip him like that and pull in and crush his ribs right into his heart. Without even getting red in the face. He was quite a bit older than I was. I never knew his first name. Just Private Moses.

The work at the Kingston lab was risky. Military personnel like Sutton was eligible for danger pay, although precautions were stringent. All effluent was collected in a special holding tank which was sterilized before being released into the sewers. There were no serious accidents, although there was at least one near-miss.

There was a Helen Brown. She was a red-headed girl, tall, very nice and we all loved her. She was a real peach. But she was working on some slurry for anthrax and they delivered it late on a Friday afternoon from the States. Two Marines, sidearms, the whole works, brought this case in and it was packed in ice. Somebody said, "Well, just place it on her bench." Nobody told them they should keep it refrigerated so it sat on the bench until Monday.

When she came in she opened up the box. There was a canister. She lifted the canister out. And it was all taped up. She untaped it, took it out. There was the big bottle, about a four-litre bottle, still full of what we call soup, a slurry. And it had like a champagne cork on top of it, taped, wrapped, wired, everything. But it been refrigerated when they bottled it. Imagine what it had been doing sitting on a bench at room temperature? This was in summer.

So, she went to loosen the thing and it exploded and went up and hit the ceiling. It went out and just came down and cascaded all through her hair, and over her body.

Well, you know, if you have a small cut, and you get one of those spores in there. . . . It forms an exospore which is so big that it plugs up your blood vessels. It just goes in there and multiplies and blocks all your capillaries. It grows as a filament or, actually, just divides. You get more and more – two, four, eight, sixteen, thirty-two. It doesn't take long for a couple of generations. Some organisms, you know, multiply in as little as seven minutes.

She had to get all that soup wiped off of her and showered and all that. She was a redhead. Which means they have no pigmentation and they have thin skin. The whole works. But it was a life full of excitement. . . . [12]

The section of Reed's lab devoted to infecting insects with various diseases for the so-called insect-vector weapons was a Canadian innovation. Up to late 1944 only Canada was working on this aspect of biological warfare, with house flies being bred at the Dominion Parasite Laboratory at Belleville and shipped out from Kingston to Suffield for field trials. [13] Most of the documents dealing with this activity are still unavailable but those that are indicate that the research included work on fleas (for plague), fruit flies, chiggers and ticks. The ticks were excellent vectors for tularemia and Rocky Mountain spotted fever – the latter first developed in Canada as a germ agent. [14]

Glass containers also were procured for dropping disease-inoculated fly bait on enemy territory to infect insects in the wild. Apparently they weren't of very robust construction. "Neither of the present munitions," Murray complained in a memo, "are safe against handling accidents. The Mark II doesn't even stand up to railway travel." He proposed making new containers, the "Mark III munition," out of ureaformaldehyde cardboard. This became Suffield BW project MS-8.[15]

Of more practical significance was the development of peat as a medium for spraying organisms from aircraft, perfected by Dr. Lochhead. This was Banting's "sinker" idea. One couldn't just spray bacteria into the atmosphere because they are so light that they might not reach the ground before being destroyed by drying or sunlight. Camp Detrick's solution was to "coat" them whereas Lochhead's was to stick them to particles.[16] Either way, they could then be made to fall from an aircraft in a controlled plume. Again, available documents are scattered and incomplete, but the program was coded LP, probably standing for lignite peat, and was aimed at developing mechanisms for the mass delivery of contagious organisms selected for their ability to cause epidemics.[17] Field trials were conducted with organisms of the code letters A, P, HL and U.[18] The first of these was *brucella abortus*, the second *serratia marcescens*, the third probably hog cholera, and the last *B. subtilis*. All were believed harmless to humans.

Nevertheless, for Murray and Reed the halcyon days of biological warfare research were nearly over. Reed probably did not care. He had tackled, usually successfully, every problem that had come his way completely dispassionately. The fun, for him, was in the doing. Not so Professor Murray. In terms of biological warfare, he had wanted to lead the world and, preferably, to save it. He was now being denied both. He had been eclipsed by Camp Detrick and its 10,000-gallon mentality on the former, and the enemy had not co-operated on the latter. To make matters worse, his British rival at Suffield was again showing signs of wanting to run his own show.

Davies opened his own germ warfare lab in the spring of 1944. The justification had been to provide a facility for doing field trials on Britain's behalf[19] and it seems to have almost immediately become a sort of Porton branch plant. The first series of experiments directly ordered by Dr. Fildes at Porton and carried out by Davies's staff began that summer. They involved raining showers of poison darts on test animals, mainly goats and sheep, that had been dressed in three layers of heavy serge to simulate a soldier's battledress. Davies was able to report penetrations of up to six inches into the flesh of the animals provided "no bone was hit."[20]

It is worth describing this series of experiments in some detail for it reflects the state of Porton's thinking on biological warfare at this point in the war. A standard 500-pound cluster bomb was loaded with poison darts and, when set to explode from 500 to 3,000 feet above the ground, it could pepper 10,000 square yards to a density of one to five darts per square yard. A typical test scored six hits on twenty-three animals.

These trials went on all through the fall of 1944 and into the spring, with Fildes cabling Davies in February 1945: "Very impressed with the Canadian results. New appreciation being prepared by Porton in favourable terms." That same month Davies alerted Maass that the British were contemplating mass production of the poison darts and asked that forty more cluster bombs be prepared for a really big trial. In April, with Germany in the final stages of collapse, Maass asked Davidson Pratt, of the British Ministry of Supply, if he should go ahead with the order considering it would cost about $50,000 and would take three months for delivery. On May 5, as the German armies were surrendering in Holland, Pratt told him to go ahead so that "we may have adequate information on which to make a final decision."[21]

A cluster bomb loaded with 30,000 darts, while it sounds impressive, was a weapon concept in the same category as Churchill's aerial mines, barrage balloons and iceberg aircraft carriers. It is truly hard to see its tactical value. Combat troops, or anybody for that matter, don't normally stand around like sheep when hostile bombers fly over, or when bombs burst above them. The most elementary cover would stop the darts and the area affected – 10,000 square yards – was pitifully small in comparison to what could be done with a shrapnel-laced high explosive of the same weight. The idea seems to be a relic of the First World War when clumps of steel darts were thrown from aircraft before bombs were developed. In comparison to the aerosol clouds of deadly germs that Camp Detrick was working on, or the insect-vector weapons of the Canadians, the idea was in the Stone Age.

It took until January 1946 for British Air Staff to rule that there was really no need for deadly darts and the program was killed. But thirty years later the weapon was actually used – in fiction. In the movie *Black Sunday* (1977) Arab terrorists plot to kill most of the 100,000 spectators at the Super Bowl football game by detonating a darts-filled bomb from a blimp hovering above the stadium. The author of the best-selling suspense story, Thomas Harris, apparently had hit upon about the only circumstance in which such a weapon would work.

British experiments were not all such folly, although it is a pity official secrecy in Britain prevents historians from trolling through Porton records for other gems. Far more serious work was being done by British scientists such as Lord Stamp and David Henderson who were stationed at Camp Detrick and allowed to do their own research with American facilities. Both concentrated for a long time on anthrax and Detrick's scientific chief, Dr. Baldwin, remembers Henderson complaining about what he considered were the "excessive" safety regulations that were interfering with his work. Baldwin's reply to Henderson became a much-repeated story in biological warfare circles:

"Well, David, you know really I'm not worried about whether you get killed or not. If you do, we'll feel sorry and go to the funeral, and we'll come home and go to work again. But if we get organisms out into the air and Farmer Jones's cows over here get anthrax and they die, we'll have a congressional investigation and that will shut up the whole post. So, I really am not as much interested in you as I am in this question of protecting the community."[22]

The British, however, had Suffield. Here, but for Professor Murray's intransigence, they could set their own rules, and Stamp was a frequent visitor for field trials. It is clear from the documents that Davies was separately serving two masters on germ warfare experiments, even though Murray insisted that his C1 Committee should have a say on the structure on all tests and safety precautions. Whether Stamp knew of the acrimony is unknown, but as the fall of 1944 gave way to winter, relations between Davies and Murray steadily deteriorated. They hit bottom in December.

"I think Mr. Davies feels that the C1 Committee (perhaps me in particular) interferes with work that is wholly his concern," Murray wrote Maass on December 13. He then listed his complaints, citing trials by Stamp and the methodology of Suffield's new staff researchers, Dr. A.J. Wood and Capt. A.W.A. Brown. He reminded Maass of the similar conflict a year ago, and enclosed all that correspondence. He claimed Brown was "sloppy" in his handling of botulinus toxin and argued that "Dr. Wood has very limited experience in pathogenic bacteriology" and that Suffield could not be independent because it relied on Reed's lab in Kingston for its supply of germs and toxins. He asked Maass to give him and Davies a "written brief" so they both knew where they stood.[23]

Unfortunately, Maass's reply is missing. It is probably among those documents still withheld by the national archives. Whatever he said, it at least led to a truce, though an uneasy one.

All was not bleak for Professor Murray that winter of 1944-45. Now that the military was solidly in control of the U.S. biological warfare program, the Americans were more receptive to off-the-wall ideas. At a November meeting with the U.S. Chemical Warfare Service's Special Projects Division (General Ditto commanding), Murray told the Americans that Suffield field trials with houseflies (*musca*) had demonstrated their potential as weapons, but fruit flies (*drosophila*) had not been as successful because of the dry prairie climate. Perhaps the wetter conditions of the U.S. BW proving ground of Horn Island, off the coast of Mississippi near Pascagoula, would be more suitable? The Americans agreed it was worth trying.

Code-named Project ONE by selecting the second letter of first three words of the actual title, Joint Insect Vector Project, it was to be supervised by the U.S. Navy. Four Canadians were to participate and the initial house and fruit flies were to be supplied by Reed until breeding facilities could be established on the island. A biting fly (*stomoxys*) was also to be tried, likely as a carrier of tularemia. Later, with an eye to the war with Japan, experiments were to be done with insects native to the South Pacific. The bacteria initially used were to be strains of salmonella and shigella ("*alka lesiens*") that didn't affect humans. Infected baits would be put out and studied for pick-up, spread and the range and survivability of the insects. The project began on December 15 and ran for many months, later also including botulinus toxin, which, if successful, would have made the ordinary house fly deadly.[24]

By winter, though, the war in Europe was clearly ending. The previous July the Allies had broken out of Normandy and in the autumn swept to the very frontiers of Germany as the Russians hammered into Poland and from the east. There was going to be no need in Europe for the thousands of tons of mustard gas stockpiled by the Allies, nor for the anthrax bombs requested by Britain. That spring the U.S. plan to mass-produce anthrax at Terre Haute was shelved.[25]

In Canada, Mackenzie King resolved his conscription crisis by forcing Ralston to resign as Minister of Defence and replacing him with General McNaughton. There is real irony here, for it was Ralston who in 1943 engineered McNaughton's resignation as commander of the Canadian army in Europe, thereby depriving him of the long-awaited opportunity of leading the Canadian forces in battle. With the end of the war in sight, it was Ralston's turn to be dumped, with the result that neither man ever received much glory or credit for his contribution to the war effort. There were to be no heroes among Canada's top leaders when peace came.

A word should be said about the conscription crisis. Fearing the mood of Canada's French-speaking population, early in the war King had resolved not to impose overseas service on soldiers conscripted into the armed forces. When losses in the fighting in Italy and France began to outrun replacements, Ralston insisted that the home forces be sent into battle to mitigate the casualties among the troops already overseas. King responded by replacing him with McNaughton, figuring the popular general could stimulate more at home to volunteer. He couldn't, and didn't. The result was that the thousands of English- and French-speaking troops who chose to stay in Canada were deeply resented by the general service soldiers, who nicknamed them Zombies.

"Jack Dacey was in town," a Canadian liaison scientist in Washington noted in his diary. "Told me the CW crowd in Ottawa drank 90 gals. of beer at the recent lab party which ended in a fist fight between the Zombies and the general service personnel."[26] Of the military personnel at Suffield, Sutton also remembered: "These were all active service people – no Zombies. If they'd brought a Zombie into Suffield, he'd have been shot. Nobody in Suffield would tolerate . . . You could be the lowest life . . . you could be a sex offender and working there but you would not be a Zombie. They wouldn't let him in the gate."[27]

Because French Canadians were generally and unfairly blamed for the situation, a deep division was driven between French and English Canada, a wound that after over forty years is not yet fully healed.

McNaughton as defence minister was the right man to look to ways of preserving Canada's chemical and biological warfare establishments after the war. It would be a pity to lose Suffield. Overtures were made to Britain on the possibility of continuing to share the facility after Germany and Japan surrendered. The Americans were encouraged to participate in cold weather tests of war gases at the station and in field trials with their own biological warfare weapons, notably the .22 and .30 calibre poison bullets they had developed. The British were invited to do jungle trials with mustard gas of their own at the U.S. proving ground off Panama. Allied co-operation in experiments got closer as the war wound down.

The poison bullets are worth explanation, for they were another deep, dark secret of the war. They were an American development and it was early discovered that organic toxins could not be used because they were so dangerous to handle. The answer was to hollow out the tips of the bullets and charge them with TL1217, a synthetic poison derived from meta-diethylaminophenol, a common chemical used in the dye industry. Sheep given flesh wounds in the hind legs at close range died within a half hour, but at 200 yards the velocity of the bullets was so slow that they failed to deform on impact and release the poison. The weapon was thus something of a failure. Poisoned shotgun pellets were also tried. All the field trials were done at Suffield in 1944 and 1945.

By the end of 1944 the Allies – including Australia – had developed areas of speciality. Porton, with its limited space, concentrated on small-scale quasi-theoretical experiments, like how a gas was dispersed in the atmosphere or how it moved through long or short grass. The Americans at Dugway and Edgewood did the same kind of thing on the large scale, studying the movement of war gases through wooded terrain and built-up areas, constructing dummy houses and fortifications to test penetration. Australia, India and Canada did the human experiments under simulated combat conditions, the Australians becoming expert in the casualty effect of mustard gas in jungles, and against tropical islands and beaches. Suffield dealt in the really grand experiments, when a really big cloud of gas was desired and elaborate shoots laid on, with whole platoons of soldiers used to measure the casualty effects.[28]

There was considerable duplication as the scientists of each country sought to test the findings of the others. By the spring of 1945 the pace of experiments was brisk. Suffield churned through the whole gamut of poison gases: phosgene, hydrogen cyanide, cyanogen chloride and the plethora of different mustard gases loaded into British and American mines, shells and bombs that now ranged up to 4,000 pounds. As much experimental information as possible was gathered while the spending was easy.[29]

With the surrender of Germany in May, the United States could afford to be generous with its stocks of poisonous substances, sending Suffield 10 tons of cyanogen chloride and 1,000 pounds of cadmium compound in mid-May.[30] The latter reflected the successful outcome of the cadmium poison gas experiments begun by George Wright at Toronto back in 1940. The cadmium was incorporated in a special incendiary bomb designated the M50-TA2 ordered by the U.S. Air Force. It looked, burned and smelled just like a normal incendiary except that it was designed to kill the enemy's firefighters. Tests in the Suffield bursting chamber showed its toxic smoke caused instant fibrosis of the lungs, killing one goat in two minutes and four goats in five.[31]

Professor Murray remained touchy in his relations with the British. In February he received a note from staff at Camp Detrick wondering why he hadn't contacted them about a Suffield field trial with brucellosis which Stamp had planned and for which Detrick was to supply "vaccine and skin-testing equipment." Brucellosis, otherwise known as undulant fever, is a highly infective, incapacitating agent with influenza-like symptoms. It can persist in the environment for weeks and can cause permanent bone and liver damage. Murray sent back a sharp note saying that he would bring the request before the C1 Committee but that this was the first he had heard of it.[32]

For the next few months, however, Murray had far more important things to worry about than keeping rein on the British. On November 14, 1944, a puzzling assemblage of paper and wicker had been found floating in the water off Hawaii. On being examined, it appeared to be some kind of balloon of Japanese origin. The following January complete balloons were sighted floating over the coasts of British Columbia and Washington

State. The desperate Japanese, encircled in their island homeland, had introduced a brand-new weapon of war. In Canada it
caused a minor panic.

In an ingenious use of available materials, the Japanese had
made the balloons out of rice paper and wicker and fitted them
with automatic devices to release ballast as they floated across
the Pacific on the eastward moving trade winds. They carried
several small incendiary bombs in the hope that on landing in
North America they would set fire to forests. Otto Maass and
Professor Murray, however, presumed a much more sinister purpose. On hearing the first reports of the balloons over Canada,
Maass immediately raised the alarm with Canada's Minister of
Defence and Chiefs of Staff. The balloons, the Director of Chemical Warfare said, were perfect vehicles to carry biological warfare
agents.[33]

"BW Not All over," Murray scribbled in his notes on February
3. "Alert Hale on Balloons. Maximum production." Colonel
M.W. Hale was an officer at Grosse Ile which for the past year had
got away from its original purpose – protection against rinderpest. Now Murray ordered an all-out effort to produce rinderpest
vaccine. If it were to turn out that the balloons carried the much-
feared animal disease, Murray intended to be able to contain the
damage.[34]

The Americans reacted cautiously. Under the authority of the
U.S. Secretary of War, all responsible civil and military authorities on the west coast were alerted to the danger of biological
agents. They were ordered to watch for outbreaks of any unusual
diseases, although they were not to be told this warning had
anything to do with the balloons. In the meantime, every balloon
that landed was to be examined by representatives of the Surgeon
General's Office, the Department of Agriculture or the Chemical
Warfare Service. The Canadians did likewise.[35]

It made so much sense for the balloons to be carrying biological agents that for a time it was hard to believe they were not. The
discovery that some payloads contained sand or water was very
suspicious. The remains of balloons were gingerly taken up,
immediately frozen, and rushed to the nearest lab for analysis.
The sand turned out to be sand and the water, sea water. It was
ballast.

The best lab in Canada for chemical analysis was Professor
Beamish's at Toronto and one of the balloons, suitably frozen,

was sent there for examination. It was carrying plain sea water but Professor Beamish's assistant, Dr. J. Ellwood Currah, remembered the incident well, chiefly for what he learned of American prewar ingenuity: "Before the war whenever an American ship dropped anchor off the coast of Japan, they took samples of the sea bottom. They kept a whole library of these suitably indexed, so they were able to precisely identify where in Japan the balloons were coming from by the ballast."[36]

Of the thousands of balloons released, few made it across the ocean. By the beginning of March, only 90 had been sighted or recovered on the continent against an estimated 15,000 released. They caused little damage but the Japanese authorities were reported to be boasting to their people about an awesome new weapon and the fear persisted that they still might be used to carry germs. Mindful of implicit Allied policy that a bacterial attack would be met by retaliation in kind, Professor Murray, certainly with the approval of Maass and presumably the Canadian Chiefs of Staff, did not confine himself to defensive measures. He had his own all-Canadian weapon prepared.

Waiting on the runway at Ottawa's Uplands Airport was a bomber. It contained several tons of finely ground peat. Dr. King, then in charge of gas mask assembly at the Chemical Warfare Labs, remembered:

> They were very worried about the Japanese toward the end of the war. And they called for volunteers . . . and I was supposed to be the OC [officer commanding] of this volunteer outfit and they had a plane at standby at Uplands Airport. And it was on standby 24 hours a day for us in case anything happened.
>
> When you volunteered you had to offer to do anything. It was to help bury the dead, etc., but you had to offer to do anything. So all the volunteers had to have this bubonic plague treatment and it was wicked. They'd just inoculate you and let you go. I never had anything quite like it. You could feel it circulating through the system until it hit the heart. It was like – like molten iron or something. It was so hot. Boom! It hit you.[37]

If retaliation was ordered, explained Dr. King, the plan was to infect the peat and then fly the bomber in a series of hops – Vancouver, Hawaii – to Japan. There it would disperse its deadly cargo. Five years after Banting's original sawdust experiment on Balsam Lake in Ontario's cottage country, the weapon he had only imagined had become reality.

Ironically, a very different weapon was rushing to completion that was destined to eclipse the efforts of all those involved in chemical and biological warfare. By the spring of 1945, the U.S. Manhattan Project was well on its way to assembling the first atomic bombs. After a tremendous outlay of money and talent, the Americans had solved all the problems of controlled nuclear fission and the production of uranium 235 and plutonium, the two atomic explosives which would enable a single bomb to blow a city apart.

It was an incredible accomplishment. Successful nuclear reactors had to be built as well as huge installations at Oak Ridge and Los Alamos to extract the explosive elements from irradiated uranium fuel rods and to fabricate the bombs. Whole towns were built to house thousands of workers and military personnel. Problems of design, safety and technique all had to be overcome where there was no previous experience to draw upon. The scientific achievement alone was immense and almost exclusively American. It was, after all, a weapon that would change the world.[38]

Thanks to Churchill and the Quebec Conference, there was a place in all this for Canada, although it took a while. Despite Roosevelt's promise to exchange information, the security-conscious military and scientific authorities on the Manhattan Project dragged their heels. It was not until April 1944 that the terms of interchange were finally agreed upon. While they were still restrictive, they were sufficiently generous for the scientists in Montreal to get seriously started on a practical program of nuclear research, directed toward building a power reactor rather than a bomb. The Americans had decided to keep the weapon technology to themselves.

The Montreal nuclear project was almost entirely Canadian. The refugee scientists were established in the newly built University of Montreal building and Canadians were added until they accounted for at least half the team. The scientists were led by the distinguished British physicist, J.D. Cockcroft, but the project was administered and financed – except for the salaries of the British – entirely through the National Research Council under the direction of C.J. Mackenzie's deputy, E.W.R. Steacie.

Work rapidly went ahead on plans to build a reactor at a bush site up the Ottawa River, later to be known as Chalk River. It was all made possible by the freeing up of information from the United States. Though they did much original work, including the entire design of the heavy water reactor, the Montreal group could not match the scope of American research.[39]

When the scientists from Canada went down to the United States to collect on the information exchange, they found the Americans paranoid about security. Harry Thode was a young Canadian chemist on the Montreal team and well remembers a wartime visit to the University of Chicago to have talks with a Professor Dempster:

> An army captain met me at the hotel and took me to the University and sat with me and Dempster and he had this document from Washington saying what we could talk about. Come lunch time, Dempster said, "How would you like to go over to the Quadrangle Club for lunch?" And I looked at this army captain and the army captain said, "Well, I've been here all morning. I think you two people know what you can and can't talk about. Do you mind if I be excused?" We didn't want to be too excited about it. We said, "Well, no, no. . . . "[40]

The conversation between Thode and Dempster became much more animated once the army captain left. The Americans, however, were not fooling around. When Dempster left his office for a few moments, Thode went into the hall to get a pop from a Coke machine and encountered another scientist he had known before the war. They had a brief chat about his work. As Thode was leaving the campus, he was stopped by security personnel at the gate and asked whom he had seen. He recited the names and they checked them off a list. When he mentioned the scientist at the Coke machine, he was closely grilled as to what they had talked about. The scientist's name was not on the list and Thode learned later the man was hauled up on the carpet for having spoken to him.

In a sense, the stringent American security precautions were hopeless. Scientists with shared interests would inevitably find ways to talk with one another. Trust was a better safeguard than military police. Unfortunately, the Americans had been right to be afraid of a security leak in the Montreal group. Churchill's indiscretion at the Quebec Conference with the communist scientist J.D. Bernal eventually came home to roost. As well as Cockcroft, Britain gave security clearance to two others over to help on the Canadian nuclear research program, Alan Nunn May and Bruno Pontecorvo. Both had prewar communist connections; both were spies for Russia.

The Montreal work was not entirely innocent of military application. The nuclear reactor planned for Chalk River was expected to have an exceptionally high output of plutonium. The Americans supplied a small sample to the Montreal lab for research purposes, and it was given to the French chemist, Jules Guéron. Nunn May, who by this time had made several visits to the United States on information exchanges, took a close personal interest in Guéron's work. As Thode remembered:

> They were close friends. And Nunn May was in his lab. And he knew where everything was. He was having Guéron explain what he was doing and where the plutonium was. Alan Nunn May was in his lab and the next day, Guéron couldn't find his plutonium. It was radioactive. He had (geiger) counters. He could easily detect it. It was gone. Finally he went into Steacie's office and said, "I'm the worst chemist in the world. You should fire me." He'd lost the plutonium.[41]

In the summer of 1945 as atomic research was gearing up, chemical and biological warfare work was gearing down. The U.S. Chemical Warfare Service hadn't quite given up hope. A plan was put forward to poison Japan's rice crop by salting the country's rice paddies with ammonium thiocyanate. Roosevelt had died suddenly in early April, so the biggest American obstacle to a first strike with chemical or biological agents had been removed. Perhaps the new president, Harry S. Truman, would be more receptive? The idea didn't get that far. Military planners rejected it on the grounds that the effects of destroying the rice crop would not be felt for a year, and then the United States would have the problem of feeding the starving Japanese after the surrender.[42]

The Canadians had not pulled back entirely either. On June 18 Suffield began trials with Compound "W" loaded into Type F bombs, obtaining promising results against goats, rabbits and guinea pigs staked out in a 50-yard arc. Early indications were that the toxic cloud was about fourteen times more lethal than the equivalent in phosgene and the Type F bomb gave a particle dispersal almost twice as effective as that from the bombs previously tried. The Suffield authorities recommended more trials and more research.[43]

Compound W deserves description. W is the code letter for ricin, the toxic agent in the familiar castor bean plant. A fast-growing, large ornamental with lush foliage, it used to be a favourite background planting in gardens. In wartime, the oil pressed from its beans made an excellent substitute for petroleum-based lubricants in aircraft engines and industry. The toxin was first identified and separated just at the close of the First World War.

It was Porton that first examined ricin as a possible war agent and did live-animal trials with it in 30-pound and 250-pound bombs as early as 1942, probably at Gruinard along with the first anthrax experiments. Results were disappointing, the scientists under J.H. Gaddum (of the Medical Research Council) concluding that it was no more lethal than phosgene, although it had a blinding effect equal to mustard. At about the same time samples were sent to Davies at Suffield, and to the Americans. The latter soon discovered that the toxicity of ricin could be considerably increased by refinements in processing.[44]

Ricin became mainly a joint U.S.-Suffield project from 1943 onward. Alsoph Corwin of Johns Hopkins University did the primary research under contract to the U.S. National Defense Research Council and developed a pilot plant for ricin production at the Procter & Gamble factory in Cincinnati. By mid-1943 the soap company was able to produce the toxin in 200-pound lots for shipment to Suffield.[45] There the various methods of dispersal were tested, and appropriate munitions developed. By the end of 1943 it was perceived to be as deadly as botulinus toxin and a lot cheaper and easier to produce. It was thought that this may also have occurred to the Japanese.

Ricin is often cited as the poison used in 1978 to kill an exiled Bulgarian who was shot by a tiny pellet from an umbrella as he walked up the steps at Waterloo Bridge in London. A similar attack was made at about the same time on a Bulgarian exile in Paris who survived.[46] During the Second World War, however, the scientists envisaged a much grander role for it. Loaded into bombs, it looked to be almost as effective at botulinus toxin.

On July 21, 1945, Professor Murray handed in his resignation. It appears to have been the result of a final altercation with Davies. Early in June Murray had complained to the chief superintendent that Suffield's "bursting chamber" was unsafe. This was a sealed structure used for static trials of chemical and bacterial weapons. It was completely enclosed and entered by an air lock to contain dangerous agents, and to keep them from escaping into the atmosphere. It enabled the scientists to assess weapons under closely controlled conditions.

Americans from Camp Detrick had visited Suffield and had expressed concern about the chamber. It appears to have been modelled after a "cloud chamber" at Camp Detrick, except that it had the singular disadvantage that it had to be physically entered to collect the exposed samples and dead animals. Murray considered this dangerous, and insisted the chamber was not safe for use with "hot agents." It was again a Canada-Britain confrontation. Murray vowed to take the matter up with Lord Stamp himself.[47]

The file is silent about whether Professor Murray's concerns were warranted or not, or whether they were addressed. A little over a month later, he quit the C1 Committee, naming Reed as his successor.[48] At the same meeting – and it may have had something to do with Murray quitting – the committee approved the last big experiment to be done at Suffield's Area E before the end of the war. It had been proposed by Suffield's biological warfare staff. It is worth quoting at length.

Trial E.15

Title and Purpose
1. Transmission to exposed human food of HL by flies released from cluster projectile, 500-lb, Mod 3-5.

Time of Trials
2. From 25 June – mid August at 7-10 day intervals. . . .

Site
4. A layout in Section 18, Range 6, Twp. 17 (ie. just east of the N-S Bingville Rd. at the northeast corner of area C.5). . . .

Sampling
6. (a) In each tent one or more sterile samples of human food

will be exposed for a period of one hour at intervals following release of the bomb. Specimen samples will be assayed in the laboratory for HL content.

(b) Samples of flies will be taken at intervals to determine the presence of HL.

The Bomb

7. (a) Two or three Suffield Mk. 5 bombs will be dropped per trial.

(b) Release will be made from 5,000. 10,000 and 20,000 feet, bomb to burst 1,000 feet above the terrain.

Charging

Depending upon the quantity of pupae received from Belleville, each bomb will contain 100,000 to 200,000 flies.

Procedure

. . . (b) Fish to be used as the standard food material for contamination studies, with such other materials as ground rice porridge, fruit, etc. added if deemed desirable.

Additional trials

Depending on the persistence of flies in the area, and their contamination by HL, in later trials HL LP may be put down in the grid area.

Safety

Standard rules of safety for handling an organism of this type will be observed.

Sampling

Assessment of bait samples (canned salmon) will be carried out by following the procedure developed at HI by Mjr. Gorelick and Capt. R. W. Reed.

Dr. A. J. Wood
i/c trials

The documents do not indicate what organism HL is. In his note to Suffield indicating that the C1 Committee had approved the experiment, Professor Murray added, "There is one comment. No mention is made of how flies are fed and infected."[49]

Two weeks later the first U-235 atomic bomb exploded over Hiroshima.

Two days later the first plutonium bomb devastated Nagasaki.

C·H·A·P·T·E·R

T·E·N

Journey of Fear

The sun glinted off the wings of the airplane, a Dakota with U.S. markings, as it swung through the sky over Hiroshima. The scientists and soldiers within squeezed to the windows to peer at the grey smear. After a circuit, the plane headed off to the next city, and more ruins, and then to the next, and the next. . . .

"Only a real specialist in bomb damage could tell Hiroshima and Nagasaki from the others," recalled Dr. O.M. Solandt, the only Canadian aboard the airplane. "They all looked the same from the air. They were destroyed."

Solandt had been working at Cambridge when war broke out and had been drawn into the British Army's Operational Research Group to specialize on the physiological problems associated with guns and tanks. He showed such talent that in 1942 he was made deputy director and director in 1944. After Germany's surrender, as he waited to take up another assignment, the atomic bombs were dropped on Japan. Solandt was asked by the British War Office to be part of a British mission to Japan to study the damage. As he flew over the flattened cities, he found little to choose between those destroyed by conventional bombing, and those destroyed by the A-bombs.

"The big raid effort was in March, 1945, on Yokohama and partly on Tokyo, and it undoubtedly killed more people than either of the bombs. It was much more horrible from the point of view of the people on the ground because they were burnt to death. There was very little HE [high explosive]. They just dropped enough HE to provide kindling and then set the whole thing on fire."

Solandt and a young mathematician named Jacob Bronowski, later to become famous as a philosopher of science, teamed up to do an analysis of the casualties caused by the atomic bombs. They toured the hospitals, talked to victims, their relatives and all they could find who had first-hand experience of the explosions. They spent two weeks at each city, and produced the first-ever report on the death and injury effects of an atomic explosion, complete with map showing ground zero and zones of injury. What most surprised them as they conducted their study was the attitude of the Japanese.

> Throughout this we never encountered the faintest trace of hostility. Not a bit. Anyone who spoke English would come up and speak to us. We never had to look for these people. They were anxious to tell us what they had seen and experienced. And the general attitude – we got to the point where we'd ask them, "Well, what do you think of the Americans?"

> Once they realized we were Canadians and not quite Americans, they all said, "Well, look, we thought we could beat them and they beat us. We don't feel badly that they beat us. It was a good fair fight and we started it. But they beat us. And we've got to learn from them how to do it." And, boy, have they done it.[1]

While Solandt was walking the ashes of Hiroshima, a related event of truly historic moment was occurring back in Canada. A young clerk at the Soviet embassy in Ottawa had the safe in the cipher room open and was picking and choosing from the files of secret memos, carefully folding his choices and stuffing them in the pockets of his jacket. Under orders to return to Russia, Igor Gouzenko had decided to defy his chiefs and defect to Canada. He would guarantee his welcome by offering the Canadian authorities a treasure more precious than gold – detailed evidence of Russian espionage in both Canada and the United States.

What happened next is a well-told story, although perhaps only in Canada. Clutching his stolen documents, on September 6, 1945, Gouzenko sought asylum at Canada's Department of Justice in Ottawa. To his surprise and dismay, he was greeted by a kind of righteous horror. No, the minister wouldn't see someone who had purloined the private papers of Canada's wartime ally. Gouzenko pointed out that he would be shot if he returned to the embassy. No, the minister wouldn't see him. Gouzenko suggested he might just as well kill himself. The answer was still no. Meanwhile, someone had the wit to notify the Department of External Affairs where the under-secretary, Norman Robertson, had been intimately involved in Canada's intelligence-gathering during the war. He immediately saw the implications of what Gouzenko was saying. While the young Russian sweated in the Justice Ministry's waiting room, Robertson rushed over to see the prime minister.

The last thing in the world Mackenzie King wanted was a confrontation with the Russians. He had just led Canada through six years of war and he was tired. He was 70. He did not want to hear it when Robertson tried to explain that Gouzenko's documents might be overwhelmingly important to Canada and the United States. The two men met again in the afternoon and Robertson insisted that the documents might be so important that they should be seen at any cost. He told King that Gouzenko had left the Ministry of Justice saying he was going home to commit suicide. That evening the prime minister recorded in his diary:

> I suggested that a Secret Service man in plain clothes watch the premises. If suicide took place let the city police take charge and this man follow in and secure what there was in the way of documents. . . . Robertson at one stage expressed the situation as that of the possibility of our being party to a suicide on the one hand, if we did not get the papers and protect the man, and murder on the other if we allowed him to fall into the hands of the Embassy which would send him back to Russia where he would be executed. There was this aspect to consider, but it was clear that we could not save the individual situation by any course we could take, but we might involve the countries in an open breech. . . .[2]

Poor Gouzenko. He certainly would have been a dead pigeon had events followed the course that Mackenzie King prescribed. Fortunately, the Russians themselves took the initiative. Instead of committing suicide, Gouzenko sought refuge in the flat of a next-door neighbour. That night a four-man delegation from the

Russian embassy arrived, pounded on Gouzenko's door, burst it open, and ransacked the apartment. This was a little too much for the watching police and they intervened, asking the Russians what they thought they were doing. Just looking for their missing comrade and some papers, they said.

After over forty years considerable mystery still surrounds the events of that night. What is known is that after the Russians had left, Gouzenko was discovered in the next-door flat and taken for questioning by the Royal Canadian Mounted Police, Canada's federal police force responsible for security and intelligence. By coincidence William Stephenson, the head of the British secret service in North America, happened to be visiting from New York and took charge of the situation. Gouzenko was sequestered and began to tell his story and present his documents.

The next day Mackenzie King had no choice. Robertson told him that Gouzenko's documents showed without doubt that the Russians had been running an elaborate spy ring in both Canada and the United States aimed at the secrets of the atomic bomb. It was all there, in writing. King told him to let the British and Americans know what had happened, but cautiously. Then he went home and worried.

C.J. Mackenzie, as head of the NRC and in overall charge of Canada's atomic research program, heard about the Gouzenko defection almost immediately. He had been in Chalk River to witness the start-up of the ZEEP nuclear reactor – the first nuclear reactor outside the United States – and when he returned to Ottawa the following evening, he received a call from Robertson:

> Well, then, the ZEEP goes critical and that night we drove down [to Ottawa]. This is a very interesting thing. I don't know whether this is published but it will be published some day. We got home about 7 o'clock and I got a phone message from Norman Robertson. He said, "I would like a word with you."
>
> I said, "Well, I have just got in from Chalk River and I am just having dinner. Is it important?"
>
> And he said, "I think it is rather important. You better come over."
>
> So I went over and he gave me a cocktail and he told me about this Gouzenko business. And, of course, this was very top secret then. They weren't spilling this at all. And then he

told me about the number of people at the NRC that were involved and about Alan Nunn May. And we had just left Nunn May up at Chalk River.[3]

Nunn May was one of those identified as a spy in Gouzenko's stolen memos. One of the few actual Englishmen in the hodge-podge of refugee scientists who had come over from Britain for the Montreal Lab nuclear project, he had been an intimate of the research for over a year. He had regularly visited the United States to see the work going on there. Mackenzie was thunder-struck. Worse, Robertson pledged him to secrecy. The Canadian government had not yet decided how to handle the situation. Mackenzie was ordered to keep his counsel.

The president of the NRC went through agonies. With the war over, Britain was recalling her scientists to England to set up her own nuclear program. Nunn May was one of those slated to go. Mackenzie had the excruciating task of attending his going-away party, knowing not only that he had been passing secrets to Russia, but he had actually stolen a sample of plutonium from the Montreal lab. Gouzenko's documents revealed it had been sent to Moscow via the embassy's diplomatic bag.

"He was to have a farewell party at which Cockcroft had to give him a vote of thanks for his services. And the thing we had to do was not let anybody know. . . . The expert spy gets more out of you when you don't talk than when you do talk – for your reactions – and it is awfully difficult to be the same person after you find out he is a traitor."[4]

Arrests did not immediately follow the Gouzenko revela-tions. May was allowed to return to Britain where he was to be watched for further spying. Gouzenko was taken into hiding for extensive debriefings and both the American and British secret services sent representatives to help. Tight secrecy was pulled around the whole situation and, for the time being, both Canadi-ans and Russians in Ottawa pretended nothing had happened. It was to be nearly six months before significant action was taken on Gouzenko's disclosures.

Meantime, Canada's chemical and biological warfare estab-lishments were trying to figure out their futures as best they could. They were temporarily secure. In what must have been one of his last official acts as Canada's Minister of Defence, on August 21, 1945, General McNaughton initialled an army memo proposing that most of the chemical and bacteriological warfare establishments be retained at half strength on the expectation that the British would want to resume their 50-50 involvement at Suffield. Grosse Ile was to be phased out the following February. That same day Mackenzie King accepted McNaughton's resignation.[5]

It is fitting that McNaughton should be the one whose scribbled initials ensured the postwar survival of Canada's chemical and biological warfare programs. It was he who had really started it all in 1937 by sending Flood to Britain to study chemical warfare technology. He also had been the one who had encouraged Banting's interest in bacterial warfare. While in Britain as head of the Canadian Army there he had constantly pressed the National Research Council, the Chiefs of Staff and the Cabinet War Committee to expand Canada's commitment to chemical and biological warfare research. It was his perception of the German threat, as the senior Canadian military officer in Europe, that provided the impetus and justification for the Chemical Warfare Labs, Suffield, Reed's BW labs at Kingston and the anthrax factory at Grosse Ile.[6]

McNaughton is something of a tragic figure. Having been denied the opportunity of leading in battle the army he created, he went from being one of Canada's most popular figures to one of the most maligned after becoming Minister of Defence. As he promised Mackenzie King, he campaigned for volunteers to finish the war in Europe and carry the fight to Japan. He nearly drowned in the tidal wave of hostility that surged back. Canadians felt that Canada's volunteer soldiers had done their bit in Europe and it was unfair to ask them to risk their lives again when there were thousands of trained conscripts who had chosen to stay in Canada. Most Canadians felt they should be forced to fight and they expressed that view in the June 1945 general election by rejecting McNaughton resoundingly. It was a sad end for a man who thought he was going to make history.

Viewed on its own, the document McNaughton signed preserving Suffield and the rest of the chemical and biological warfare establishments might be seen as a kind of last, noble gesture from a visionary scientist/soldier. What actually occurred is quite different. McNaughton submitted his resignation on August 6 and while the prime minister considered whether to accept it, Otto Maass, the Director of Chemical Warfare, had the postwar proposal drawn up and sent up to McNaughton's desk under the signature of the army's Master General of the Ordinance. Don Dewar, then Maass's principal aide, tells happened:

"Maass had been pushing to try and (keep) these things going – like Suffield and places like that – and I know I prepared a lot of memos. McNaughton was in at this time (as Defence Minister) and so a lot of the submissions went up to him. He put AGL on them and, I'm afraid, with Maass's approval, we went around saying McNaughton had approved them. All he'd done is just initial that he'd read the memo."[7]

That this had been a deliberate plan on the part of Maass is highly likely. With just such a trick he had got the former Defence Minister, Colonel Ralston, to approve expanding the work at Grosse Ile to include mass-producing anthrax. By manipulating financial paperwork he had illegally built a second lab for Professor Reed at Kingston. He was aware that McNaughton, as a former serving officer, would have followed the standard army practice of initialling all pieces of paper that came to his attention. It would have been a temptation too great to resist.

Maass's little subterfuge may have helped to buy time, but it did little to define the postwar role of chemical and biological warfare research. At a meeting on September 10 of the Chemical Warfare Inter-Service Board, Suffield's chief of research, Dr. H.M. Barrett, made a formal presentation regarding the future of the station. Suffield was valuable, he said, because it was the only facility in the Commonwealth capable of carrying out "full scale trials with long-range artillery, high altitude bombing or large scale experiments with CW and BW agents."

Barrett further said that research on mustard gas, phosgene and cyanogen chloride was no longer required but more could be done on botulinus toxin and "W." The "Haworth compounds" merited further research because they had already showed promise in Suffield tests. Useful work could also be done on agricultural pests because the technology for dispersing poison gases was similar to "efficient methods of dispersing insecticides on a large scale." Since early spring, in anticipation of the war's end, Suffield had been running experiments on the control of grasshoppers and spraying for spruce budworm.[8]

Most important of all, Barrett recommended using Suffield to test the war gases developed by the Germans. These were the huge stocks of nerve gases that both the Russians and the Allies had been shocked to discover when their armies overran Germany. As it happens, the Americans were so little impressed with tabun – possibly because of their own research on nerve gases – that they ordered much of this gas destroyed while shipping home considerable quantities of its more lethal relative, sarin.[9]

In other business, the meeting decided to mothball the Cornwall mustard gas plants while saving the chemical weapon charging machines as "essential equipment." Maass pointed out that the 2,800 tons of American-made Levinstein mustard at Cornwall should be disposed of, especially as it was notoriously unstable and tended not to keep well for long periods. The remaining 100 tons of high-quality IIT mustard could be sent to Suffield for bulk storage. The committee agreed on all these proposals.[10]

Most research that fall, however, was put on hold. As a kind of make-work project, in October Maass asked Suffield to design and test a combination smoke and tear gas grenade for the RCMP. Experiments continued on the aerial spraying of the new insecticide, DDT, which was made in a pilot plant at the Chemical Warfare Labs in Ottawa.[11] Specialists from Suffield in the dispersal of poison gas and BW agents also visited Chalk River to advise on what was to be expected in size and behaviour from a cloud of radioactivity in the event of a nuclear accident.

At the end of October, Maass received a severe jolt from an unexpected quarter. The Americans proposed to issue a public statement describing U.S. bacteriological research during the war. George Merck, the Secretary of War's consultant on biological warfare, had prepared a lengthy summary describing the type of research at Camp Detrick, the original recommendations of the WBC Committee, the role of the U.S. Chemical Warfare Service, and the fact that some thousand different poisons had been tested as possible war agents along with a wide variety of deadly germs. Because U.S. research had proved it to be a potent weapon, he concluded with the pious hope that biological warfare would never be used. There were only passing references to co-operation with Canada and Britain.[12]

Maass was furious. He deluged General Porter, the chief of the Chemical Warfare Service, with letters of protest. The Americans were taking all the credit and leaving the Canadians with nothing. What about Sir Frederick Banting and Professor Murray? What about Grosse Ile? What about the rinderpest project that had been a Canadian idea in the first place and had resulted in a successful vaccine against a devastating cattle disease? Dewar personally shuttled back and forth to the United States with Maass's angry letters.[13] It was to no avail. The Americans were going to go with the Merck Report. The Canadians and British could say what they liked.

Maass then sought to do a full report on Canada's bacteriological warfare program, or to at least publicize the successful development of the rinderpest vaccine. To his amazement and frustration, he was blocked by no less a person than Mackenzie King. He was ordered to describe Canada's BW effort only in general terms – no mention of Grosse Ile, Suffield, or Reed's germ warfare lab in Kingston. He was to be allowed to mention Banting's original interest and the fact that the program had been under Maass's direction. No more.

Britain, Canada and the United States were to make simultaneous public disclosures on January 3, 1946. Dewar wrote up a vague and low-key press release. The British did the same. Maass continued to protest vigorously, threatening to "spill the beans" on his own initiative. Dire warnings were passed down through channels to Maass's army boss, Brigadier G.P. Morrison. Dewar vividly remembered when the reports were to be released:

"Brigadier Morrison phoned me up and said that I was responsible for Maass's actions and I said, 'How could I be? I'm a junior officer.'

"He said,'I know that, man. For God's sake, help me out. I've got the flu and the Prime Minister has been on my back all evening by phone. He says Maass has to be shut up. He figures he'll stir up trouble with the Americans.'"

Dewar, with two other chemical warfare officers, arranged for a card game the next day in Maass's office. Although it was patently obvious what was happening, Maass acquiesced when the three men trooped in and sat down. They decided to play bridge. The cards were dealt and Maass opened. "One no trump." Dewar's partner stared at Maass. "Two no trump." Dewar's partner had four aces and three kings. Maass's crazy bid set the tone for the whole evening.

"I just couldn't figure out what the sam heck was going on," Dewar recalled. "But Maass knew darn well why we were there and various phone calls came in and he'd say (in a mincing voice), 'I'm sorry, I can't talk. I'm not allowed to say anything.' He'd say maybe you can phone so-and-so – the under-secretary of state or something. We played until 2 o'clock in the morning."[14]

Maass remained silent. Stories on the press release appeared in the next day's papers. They were suitably innocuous. The *Toronto Daily Star*'s story made it to page one, but below the fold. It said basically that Canada had been doing biological research throughout the war at "a number of research establishments across the country under the direction of a committee of highly qualified scientists." It did not say where it was done, what was done, or by whom. There was no mention of Professor Murray or of Dr. Reed. The only names in the story were those of Maass and Banting.[15]

It was Mackenzie King who clamped the lid of secrecy on Canada's biological warfare research, and there are strong indications why. Throughout the fall and into the early winter the prime minister had fretted about the Gouzenko revelations. Page after page of his diary reflect his concern about the consequences. It was not the espionage that troubled him – "most countries have their secret spies" – it was the fact that Gouzenko's information seemed to indicate that Russia was deliberately preparing for another war, this time with its former allies.

"At the Russian agency [embassy] the man said there was the freest talk among themselves about the next war," King wrote on September 7 and then, a few days later: "One of the most serious of all the documents found revealed that they had been asking their men in the secret service here to give them a report of the strength of the American army and forces. The extent of demobilization; where they are and where located today, to give also strength as regards other of the Defence services."[16]

The prime minister was shaken by the prospect of another war. He began to see Russian malevolence in all the incidents of labour tension that inevitably followed a return to peace. This was especially ironic because years ago he had made his reputation as an expert labour negotiator and always had had sympathy for the plight of the working man. Now, he agonized, there were Canadians who were willing to destroy their own country.

The only explanation is the ideological one, which causes one to think deeply, namely, that large numbers of men and women have their hand out against society as it is constructed today, whereby there are certain leisure classes too largely controlling the government and industry, and a readiness to go to any lengths in gaining for working men and women the fullest opportunities possible. The aim is all right but the terrible part is that with the Russians, use is made of that great human – one might even say Christian – desire for equality and freedom, to gain an imperial control, a world control. . . .

As I dictate this note, I think of the Russian Embassy being only a few doors away and of there being there a centre of intrigue. During the period of war, while Canada has been helping Russia and doing all we can to foment Canada-Russian Friendship, there has been one branch of the Russian service that has been spying on all matters relating to location of American troops, atomic bombs, processes, etc.[17]

King was over-reacting. Embassy small talk about war does not necessarily reflect a nation's foreign policy, nor does the secret assessment of the military strength of rivals mean a commitment to do battle. The truth of Russian intentions will never be known until Russian historians have a free hand to probe their own country's past. What is important to the events which followed is that King felt betrayed – and he believed Russia intended war, and soon.

In October King went to Washington to personally brief President Truman. Then he went to London and did the same thing with the new British prime minister, Clement Attlee. Both leaders were relatively guarded in their reactions but not so their close advisers. The leaves on the trees of Pennsylvania Avenue were turning a golden brown as Dean Acheson, then U.S. Assistant Secretary of State, drove King from the White House. He observed that a break with Russia would likely mean open conflict and it would be fought over North America "with Canada as the battleground." In Britain a month later, King echoed Acheson's remark to the British prime minister. "I told Attlee I was deeply concerned about Canada's position in the event of any trouble arising between Russia and other countries. That I believed it would be the battleground; that they were near neighbors of ours and to reach America, would come across Canadian territory."[18]

How far King's fear of Russia shaped attitudes in Britain and the United States is difficult to calculate. One thing is certain.

Most of those whom King saw shared his opinion that the Russians were certain to develop the atomic bomb, espionage or no. The basic science was already known. The real problem was how to avoid a war which would mean "total destruction" while reasonably containing Russian ambitions. After outlining his fears to Britain's Secretary of State for Dominion Affairs, on October 8 King noted in his diary: "Lord Addison said . . . that he really felt that the present situation was quite as bad, if not worse, than the situation which the world was faced with before Hitler declared war. That Russia's policy seems to be one of power politics, pure and simple."[19]

King recorded many similar views in his many talks with American and British officials. In this age of liberalization in Russia, King's diary should be required reading for those Soviet citizens wishing to understand the postwar alienation of the West which divided the world into two armed camps for decades. No one could seriously suggest that King was an imperialist, a warmonger, or even a serious champion of capitalism. He was just a lonely old bachelor who had dedicated his life to his country and now saw it threatened with armed conflict on its own territory. The Gouzenko disclosures had frightened him and his fear spread in ever-widening circles to the United States and Britain, both already frustrated by Russian intransigence at the postwar conference tables.

Undoubtedly, however, it was the fact that King conveyed his concerns to Churchill that most influenced events to come. Having lost the British general election that spring, Churchill was now out of power, but when he heard King was in London, he invited him over to his new home at Hyde Park Gate for a chat. It was a bit of a set-up, King suspected, for at lunch vodka was served along with wine and port, which gave Mrs. Churchill the opportunity of telling the waiter to throw it out and replace it with brandy. Presently, over "delicious" dishes of snipe and caviar, Churchill introduced the subject of Russia, complaining it was "grabbing" the countries of Eastern Europe.

After listening to a lengthy harangue on how Britain and the United States weren't standing up to Russia, King finally mentioned "in strict confidence" the Gouzenko affair. Churchill snapped like a trout at this new information. He was not surprised, he said, because communists would use any means to get their ends. He agreed with King that neither the British nor the

Americans could stand up to Russia alone, and urged a continued alliance between the United States and Britain. "It must not be written," he told King, "it must be understood. But if you can get them to preserve the Joint [Combined] Chiefs of Staff arrangement and have plans made to keep the two together you will be doing the greatest service that can be done the world."[20]

As the Canadian prime minister was leaving, Churchill mentioned that he had recently received an invitation to give a lecture on conditions in Europe at a small U.S. college in Fulton, Missouri. He was thinking of accepting it; it might also give him opportunity to talk privately with Truman.[21]

King, of course, had no business telling Churchill about Gouzenko, for it was a secret matter between governments and Churchill was no longer in power. King asked that he not disclose that he had been told, with the result that historians have generally failed to connect Churchill's famous 1946 anti-communist "Iron Curtain" speech with Canada and the Gouzenko affair. But the speech was still six months into the future as the two men shook hands and Churchill saw the Canadian prime minister off with a "God bless."

King's mournful journey of alarm ended in Washington with the opening on November 10 of a three-nation summit conference on the international control of atomic energy. After several days of discussion, Truman, Attlee and King made a joint declaration that said they would share with other nations the fundamental scientific knowledge essential for the development of atomic energy for peaceful purposes. They certainly also privately held discussions on the Gouzenko affair and how best to handle Russia, but for once King's diary is silent. The pages from November 9 to December 31 are missing, the only significant gap in a record that extends from before the First World War to his death. In the light of his concerns about Russian espionage, it would have been fascinating to know whether King mentioned meeting one particular member of the British delegation. His name was Donald Maclean, he was a British embassy employee, and he was spying for Russia.

The pages missing from King's diary are a serious, and mysterious, loss to the historic record. Not only would they have disclosed the exchange of views the three leaders must have had on Russian espionage, they would have revealed whether King had urged the "unwritten" alliance that Churchill suggested. They may also have showed what short-term measures the three proposed to take to counter Russian aggression should it occur in the near future. Truman would have been acutely conscious that he did not yet have an arsenal of atomic bombs, or even one for that matter. What if the Russians struck before the Americans had enough to make a difference? There can be no doubt the three leaders had such discussions but the substance of them is unknown because the Canadian archival record is curiously fragmented during this crucial period.

That fall and winter King kept the Gouzenko affair secret except for an inner circle of cabinet ministers which included Supply Minister C.D. Howe, who had contributed enormously to the development of Canada's atomic energy program, and C.J. Mackenzie. Howe and Mackenzie teamed up with the Chief of the General Staff, General Charles Foulkes, and at a meeting in early December pushed through a plan that would amalgamate all defence research under one umbrella organization, led by a director general who would sit as a Chief of Staff. This, in effect, would make a fourth arm of the military with separate financing and organization. Canada's chemical and biological warfare establishments would be retained, but they would be in a separate division of the armed forces on a par with the Army, Navy and Air Force.

It is in the context of these events that the prime minister intervened when Maass threatened to go public over the failure of the Merck Report to acknowledge Canada's contribution to biological warfare. Both before and after muzzling Maass, King repeatedly mentioned in his diary that he feared Russia would attack over the Arctic and the prairies. Canada did not have the bomb, but it was a world leader in bacteriological warfare and very knowledgeable in chemical warfare. King must have thought that this was something the Russians did not need to know about yet.

Also in December, General Foulkes formally recommended to the Minister of Defence that Canada go along with American proposals for close collaboration in military matters. That was followed a few weeks later by a detailed memo which proposed that Canada and the United States fully integrate their military establishments by regularly exchanging officers and pooling their efforts in intelligence gathering and weapons research. The U.S.-Canada joint defence plan of 1941 was also to be updated.[22]

Dates are the bane of a child studying history, but instructive to the historian. On February 4, 1946, the Gouzenko defection was leaked to the press. On February 15, amid blaring newspaper headlines, the suspects were rounded up. Seven days later Maass was seeking approval for the shipment of 2,000 Type F biological bombs from the United States which he deemed "essential for dealing with BW."[23]

More dates: On February 28 Churchill phoned Mackenzie King from the United States and asked whether they could meet in the next week to discuss a speech he was planning to give about Russia along lines King would "approve of." King begged off because of the "espionage matter" but they discussed the speech several times over the next few days by telephone and finally King sent his ambassador in the United States, Lester Pearson, to review it in detail. After a few minor changes suggested by Pearson, the Canadian prime minister assured Churchill he should go ahead with it.[24]

On March 5 Churchill delivered the "Iron Curtain" address at Fulton, Missouri, in which he drew a picture of Russia swallowing Eastern Europe and threatening world peace. He called upon the United States, Canada and Britain to unite against the menace. Stalin called it "a declaration of war."

On March 19 Maass requested permission to inoculate field staff at Suffield against Rocky Mountain spotted fever "in continuation of the program carried out during 1944 and 1945."[25]

On March 25 Reed wrote to Maass that the C1 Committee recommended that in view of the present political situation Grosse Ile should be maintained "in such a condition that it could be reoccupied and put into operation for its present or for a similar purpose at short notice."[26]

On March 28 Reed reported to Maass that the C1 Committee had decided against any release of information on Canada's biological warfare activities because of "the political state of the world."[27]

Finally, on April 4 Reed sent Maass an updated list of the current status of all biological warfare projects done in Canada during and since the war. There were thirty-six, of which nine were considered completed, twenty were still active, six inactive and one cancelled. The list consists of project code names only, but the scattered mention of these codes in other documents enables the identification of some of them. MS-33, for example, was the making of the toxoid against botulinus toxin (completed); MS-8 was the development of a munition to disperse fly baits (inactive); MS-10 referred to open-air field trials with anthrax in bombs and on peat (completed) and MS-36 to the development of bombs filled with Compound W.[28]

Documents in the same file also identify those projects that were done jointly with Britain or the United States. MS-1 to MS-5, for instance, were attributed to Britain and were the development of poison darts to be dispersed by cluster bomb. At Grosse Ile and Kingston the list shows there were nine projects that had been undertaken in co-operation with Britain, two with the United States, and one involving both allies. The two with the United States alone are easily identified. MS-33 was the already-noted production of botulinus toxoid which had been done in co-operation with Camp Detrick; MS-22 must therefore be the production of rinderpest vaccine at Grosse Ile which had been exclusively a U.S.-Canada undertaking. That leaves MS-12, identified in the files as the production of anthrax at Grosse Ile. Reed's list confirms it to have been a joint Canada–U.S.–U.K. project. Moreover, it also shows that as of April 4, 1946, it was still "active."[29]

The rapid disintegration of German and Japanese resistance in late 1944 had made it obvious that massive bombing with anthrax would be unnecessary. Consequently in early 1945, after a payout of $21 million for the plant at Terre Haute, the Americans suspended plans to produce anthrax on a large scale. The fact that Reed's list shows that MS-12 was still active means that the anthrax at Grosse Ile must still have been available. It also supports other documents which indicate that the anthrax factory resumed operation in late 1944 or early 1945.[30] Maass's request for 2,000 Type F biological bombs now becomes significant. He obviously had plenty of bacterial agent with which to fill them. They also could be loaded with botulinus toxin or Compound W. They were shipped from Camp Detrick in November.[31]

There was a resumption of activity in chemical warfare at this time as well. In April Maass was given details on how to do static trials with the new 8,000-pound chemical bomb the British were planning to manufacture.[32] In July he obtained approval for Suffield to do a whole spectrum of trials with captured German nerve gas on behalf of the U.S. Chemical Warfare Service. The gas – tabun, code-named GA – was to be used in the full range of existing chemical munitions and tested by static explosion, thermal generator, bombing run and artillery shoot, using live animals throughout. The tests were to extend into the winter to observe the low-temperature – that is, winter or Arctic – killing efficiency and other characteristics of the new gas.[33]

Even though in February it had disposed of 2,800 tons of its mustard gas stocks in the Atlantic, Canada still had an impressive arsenal of gas weapons with which to counter a sudden attack. As there is no record in the chemical warfare files up to 1948 to the contrary, the tens of thousands of chemical munitions in storage at the end of the war must still have existed. In addition, Suffield reported 621 tons of high-quality mustard gas and 75 tons of phosgene in bulk storage. Later 30 tons of nerve gas were ordered from the United States.[34]

Gas, nevertheless, in any confrontation with Russia could have nothing more than tactical value. Even the nerve gases could not be delivered in sufficient quantities over the vast distances of Russia and Siberia to act as a strategic deterrent. Atomic bombs were still in short supply, and were exclusively a U.S. weapon. For Canada, that left bacteriological warfare.

As in the case of the wartime chemical munitions, there is no record in the available documents that Canada destroyed its stocks of anthrax spores. On August 24, 1944, Grosse Ile reported producing its seventy-sixth batch of 1,280 trays of anthrax. If every batch had consisted of that many trays, the total would have been 97,280 trays.[35] Even subtracting whatever amount was delivered to the British – and it would not have been much – that means the amount on hand was substantial. If production did indeed resume in 1945, it would be that much more again. It was undoubtedly stored at Suffield which had the facilities to load it into bombs.

Botulinus toxin, however, had clearly become the most attractive weapon. When the Russians invaded Germany from the east, they overran the principal nerve gas facilities and seized both scientific personnel and 12,000 tons of gas. They became as knowledgeable as the Allies about this new chemical weapon, and somewhat better prepared. But Allied investigators examining captured chemical and biological warfare installations appear to have found no evidence that the Germans had been working on botulinus toxin. It was not a secret that the Allies had shared with Russia either. At 136 million lethal doses to a gram, its killing power far exceeded the nerve gases and only

Canada, the United States and Britain had a defensive inoculation. It would be a nasty surprise for the Russians if it were used against them.

Well before there was any announced new arrangement on defence with the United States – while Mackenzie King still had Churchill's "Iron Curtain" speech ringing in his ears – the commanding officer at Camp Detrick agreed to send a quantity of botulinus toxin to Suffield. It was in liquid form awaiting final processing. The shipment was to go by rail via Kingston so that Professor Reed could add what he had.

On July 16, 1946, a Canadian Pacific Railway train threaded its way out of Kingston, headed to Toronto, Sudbury, Fort William and points west. Buried in ice in one of the boxcars there were three 600-pound and five 200-pound drums labelled "CW stores." They contained a total of 2,800 pounds of botulinus toxin. More than a ton.[36]

If Russia suddenly attacked, Canada had a reply. One ton of botulinus toxin, suitably delivered and dispersed, was enough to kill the population of Russia ten times over and still have some to spare.

As kingpin of Canada's chemical and biological warfare program, however, Maass's days were numbered. The plan to organize defence research as a separate department under the Ministry of Defence had been moving forward steadily. The job of heading it up had been offered to O.M. Solandt, who had finished with the British War Office after his reports on Hiroshima and Nagasaki. The new Director General of Defence Research had arrived in Ottawa in February and, though initially without either organization or staff, set about designing the new department he was to command.

Solandt made it clear right from the start that the job of the new Defence Research Board was to be military research, period. "I had a great set-to with staff who were all NRC people who came to me in a body and said, 'We're not going to do any more applied research now that the war's over.' And I said, 'Well, find yourself another job because DRB is going to be an applied research organization. We're working for the Armed Forces.' And they said, 'Well, we're not.' So I said, 'You don't work for DRB.'"

Solandt resolved the dispute by getting the Chemical Warfare Lab scientists to agree to stay on for about a year while the army sorted out its postwar organization. Then intelligence came in about the German nerve gases, with actual samples soon following. "I sort of sniggered to myself when I heard this and didn't say anything for a while. I paid a formal visit to the chemical lab after six or eight months and there wasn't a person who wasn't working on respirators. The respirators they had were no good against nerve gases."[37]

One of those who plunged into nerve gas research with enthusiasm was Dr. Tom King, who had headed up gas mask research and assembly during the war. He soon found out how dangerous it was. One day a tiny drop escaped unnoticed. As he and a partner left the NRC building to go for a coffee, they noticed the day had gone strangely dim.

> I said to him, "Gosh, the sun has disappeared," and stared directly at the sun. You know, without blinking. It was just a smear. So he looked up and said, "That's right! Let me see your eyes." I looked at his eyes and you couldn't see his pupils, so small they'd contracted.
>
> So we went right into the nursing counsellor and she jabbed us with atropine, it was, and got the eyes back and they stayed and stayed dilated for about two weeks. She gave him a shot for his lungs. He was turning bluish.
>
> Anyway, he survived and I survived but over that period (of six months) every week, once or twice a week, they'd take blood samples and compare them to blood that hadn't been exposed and see how our cholinesterase levels were doing.[38]

It had been a narrow escape. A slightly larger dose would have caused the muscles of the heart and lungs to seize up and they would have died. Thereafter it was routine procedure for people in the lab to carry on their person a small syringe of atropine sulphate which they could jab into themselves in an emergency. King did not appear to have suffered any permanent damage.[39]

Throughout the remainder of 1946, though it soon became obvious that imminent attack from Russia was unlikely, there were extensive discussions between American and Canadian planners on the joint defence of North America. Mackenzie King considered it impossible to refuse the Americans should they want to build military bases in the Canadian Arctic, and wondered how to give in to them and still retain Canadian sovereignty. He was convinced that if the prairie provinces knew of the Russian threat as he saw it, they would invite the United

States in to protect them and Canada would fall apart. He insisted that the defence planners deal not only with the Americans, but include the British, finally appointing himself chairman of the defence committee to see that all was handled correctly.

In November King had the Chiefs of Staff meet in secret session with cabinet to outline the Russian threat and how vulnerable Canada was. Much of the information being presented was from U.S. and British intelligence sources and "was of such a strictly confidential character" that King felt he could not record it in his diary. He found it interesting, however, to observe how surprised his ministers were to find out that the "world situation is infinitely more dangerous than we have yet believed it to be. It would almost seem we are headed into . . . open conflict between East and West with Communism versus Capitalism or Atheism versus Christianity. The war will be in the nature of a religious war as well as a class struggle and may result in a sort of Armageddon."[40]

In the next few days King discussed with his ministers how to reorganize Canada's armed forces on a wartime footing in a peacetime context. This meant doing away with things like aircraft carriers and concentrating the reduced effort and manpower in the key area – northern Canada and the Arctic. He also proposed that the defence portfolio again be brought under one minister. Then he added in his diary a curious footnote. "As I said to the Cabinet, we had not, to any extent, discussed the bearing of atomic weapons and bacteriological warfare on the whole business of re-organization of the Defence forces, simply because we were not competent to do so."[41] Whatever King's thoughts were on how Canada would conduct the next war, he was not about to share them openly with his ministers.

Ultimately, King produced a compromise that was typical of his entire career as a politician. The following February he announced to Parliament that Canada had informally entered into an arrangement with the United States to collaborate for "peacetime security purposes." He stressed this was not a treaty or a formal agreement of any kind. Then he went on to say that it meant that Canada and the United States would seek common standards of armament, exchange key military personnel, exchange observers "in connection with exercises and tests of material of common interest" and mutually allow passage of each country's armed forces through the air space and territorial waters of the other, as well as access to military facilities and air bases. But, he insisted, "no treaty, executive agreement or contractual obligation has been entered into."[42]

A few months later, on June 20, Suffield hosted the biggest ever Canada-U.S. conference on chemical and biological warfare. Its theme was "The Dissemination of CW and BW agents" and invitations went out across the United States and Canada. Transport was laid on to fly the delegates to Suffield, including General Alden H. Waitt, the new chief of the U.S. Chemical Warfare Service, as keynote speaker with a retinue of top specialists from Camp Detrick and Edgewood Arsenal. E.G.D. Murray, chairman of the new BW Research Panel, sat at table with his old teammates, G.B. Reed and Charles Mitchell. Flood was there and so was Otto Maass and E.Ll. Davies. The assembled scientists gave or heard papers on the production of BW agents and defences against them, while the new director of the Defence Research Board, Dr. Solandt, told of a new era of co-operation between the United States, Canada and Britain, beginning with joints tests with nerve gases and regular tripartite committee meetings to co-ordinate and share research.

A dinner was held that evening to honour Davies and Maass. The former was retiring as chief superintendent of Suffield, presumably because Britain had decided not to continue sharing the cost of operating the station. Maass was bowing out as Director of Chemical Warfare and Smoke because the position was soon to disappear with reorganization under the Defence Research Board. There were speeches, toasts, laughter and much applause.[43]

There was cause for celebration among the old hands, even though two of the key leaders were stepping down. They had built in Canada an impressive chemical and biological warfare establishment, and for the foreseeable future it was there to stay. Not even Britain could boast as fine a facility as Suffield, and the anthrax factory on Grosse Ile was unique. Canada also had pioneered in insect vector techniques and while none of this had been tested by war, it had been available if needed. Better yet, it was still needed. The unstable international situation, the threat of war with Russia, meant that Canada had to remain ready to defend herself – and perhaps retaliate, if need be.

It would be unfair to suggest that any of the men at that dinner wanted to see the weapons they had helped make ever used. They had been created out of the fear and out of fear they would remain. It is a safe guess that they all felt that the threat of retaliation had made Hitler hesitate. Perhaps the same would apply to the Russians.

In May 1948 the *Yorkshire Post*'s Ottawa correspondent went on a press junket to the new Canadian Forces winter warfare station at Churchill, Manitoba. There he met and talked with Canada's new Defence Minister, Brooke Claxton, and attributed the following to him in a story he filed back to Britain:

> ## Lethal Germs in Warfare
> ## Devastating Deadliness Claim
>
> Such advances have been made by Canadian research scientists in Bacteriological and Chemical Warfare that it is believed that the Dominion now leads the rest of the world, not even excluding the United States, which has been concentrating on the atomic bomb.
>
> In a secret base near Suffield, Alberta, scientists have been working since the war ended on the production of lethal germs, and this research has resulted in the production of such deadly bacteria that enough to kill the bulk of the world's population can be stored in a large bottle.[44]

The *Yorkshire Post*'s London editor, Ralph Loveless, deserves to go down in history for what he did with that story. Choosing not to believe his own reporter, he sent a copy of the dispatch to the office of the High Commissioner at Canada House saying that he would be "much obliged" if "you can confirm or amplify the information."

Needless to say, a message flashed across the Atlantic asking Ottawa if it wanted the story killed. Yes! A few weeks later a Canadian official in London was able to report: "I had a talk with the editor of the *Yorkshire Post* . . . and you will be glad to know that he agrees with your view that it would be most unfortunate to publish the story."

It was all just too fantastic for words.

C·H·A·P·T·E·R

E·L·E·V·E·N

Costly Secrets

On March 24, 1970, Canada's ambassador to the United Nations Conference of the Committee on Disarmament, veteran diplomat George Ignatieff, told delegates that "Canada never has had and does not now possess any biological weapons (or toxins). . ." The statement was widely reported in the national and, presumably, in the international press. It was repeated in essentially the same form the following year before the First (Disarmament) Committee of the United Nations General Assembly.

It was not true.

This, then, is the real negative consequence of the secrecy that has surrounded Canada's chemical and biological warfare program. It has made Canada a liar in the councils of the nations.

Speaking from a prepared text on behalf of the Government of Canada, Ignatieff went on to say that Canada supported efforts to reduce or eliminate the possibility of chemical or biological warfare and that it "does not possess any chemical weapons and does not intend to develop, produce, acquire, stockpile or use such weapons at any time in the future unless these weapons should be used against the military forces or the civil population of Canada or its allies."[1] This was later refined to read: "Canada does not possess any chemical weapons other than the devices used for crowd and riot-control purposes. . . ."[2] This also was false.

The declaration had the right ring for the temper of the times. Newpaper headlines of the late 1960s had breathlessly advertised reports of the U.S. Army use of chemical weapons in Vietnam, in Yemen by Egypt, of nerve gas experiments gone awry and of massive protests and alarm in the international community. The following are a few samples, in large type, from the *Toronto Daily Star*:

> 5,000 U.S. scientists
> condemn use of gas

> Canadian doctor charges U.S.
> with using gas on Viet children

> 5,500 sheep die, U.S.
> nerve gas tests blamed

> U.S. has enough nerve gas
> to kill 100 million people[3]

In the late 1960s the war in Vietnam was reaching its climax. So, too, was the peace movement, student sit-ins at universities and the general condemnation of the so-called military-industrial complex.

These protests were mostly directed against the United States and mainly involved its own citizens, but young people worldwide imitated and echoed them. It led the United States to halt the use of chemicals in Vietnam, and to undertake to destroy stockpiles of biological warfare weapons. The 1970 disarmament conference also was a product of the revulsion against the war in Vietnam and, according to Ignatieff, many delegates felt the American use of chemical agents had given rise to the opportunity of achieving a total ban on them.

"I told the government that what Sweden, Mexico and Britain wanted was the total prohibition of chemical and biological weapons instead of no first use," Ignatieff said in a 1989 interview. "I felt we had to improve upon the 1925 Protocol. But the most they would agree to was that I was to read out that statement about chemical and biological weapons. What it did was preserve the reservation of retaliation. I was totally at odds with the government on that. That's why I left the service."

Ignatieff said that the statement was prepared by the then Defence Minister, Donald S. Macdonald, with the assistance of the Department of National Defence. "I never knew that we had been involved in bacteriological agents and toxins. I knew we had done some chemical warfare research but those were statements I was made to make. I was a mere spokesman for the government."[4]

Ignatieff's conflict with Ottawa was invisible to outsiders and the missed opportunity of supporting a total ban on chemical warfare was overlooked. But the government was nearly caught out on its disclaimer about stockpiles of chemical agents. In 1971 the *Toronto Daily Star* sought to verify Canada's professed innocence by sending a reporter to Suffield. Having been told by a Defence spokesman that Suffield was "as clean as new-fallen snow," he was welcomed in a spirit of great candidness and bonhomie, shown a beaker full of nerve gas, and assured that all work was of a defensive nature.

Though he dutifully reported what he was told, the reporter did his job and asked pointed questions. Most of these – especially those about germs – were deflected, but he got his reward when he learned that Suffield had 637 tons of mustard gas in bulk storage left over from the Second World War. "It has no military value," Suffield's director of research told him, "and it's perfectly safe where it is. I think the safest thing is to leave it there forever."[5]

Six hundred and thirty-seven tons of mustard gas is a chemical stockpile in any lexicon. It could have burned people as effectively in 1971 as 1941. It would have been just as useful in the jungles of Vietnam as it would have been against the Japanese-held islands in the Second World War. It also could have been used in retaliation during the Korean War had the Canadian contingent been attacked by gas. Its existence was in bald contradiction to the government's statement about chemical weapons, but the *Star* failed to recognize this or exploit it. Someone in Ottawa must have breathed a great sigh of relief.

The following year reporters were again invited to Suffield to do stories on how the station was trying to develop an incinerator to destroy the mustard gas. They were told it had sat around so long due more to "federal government carelessness than any kind of long-range military strategy." There are no followup articles to indicate that the gas was actually disposed of.[6]

Considering the secrecy that has cloaked Canada's chemical and biological warfare program, the Star reporter did extremely well to discover the existence of the mustard gas. Pity he did not know about the 30 tons of nerve gas that were stockpiled after the war, or the half-ton of powdered cadmium or 200 tons of phosgene. And what about the thousands of already filled chemical bombs and shells, not to mention the empty munitions and the chemical weapon charging machines of "no military value"? The nerve gas at least was still in existence, for destruction of an additional 18 tons of poison gas, including nerve gas, was not undertaken until January 1989.[7]

The reporter certainly also asked about the biological weapons and toxins Canada declared it never had, but he was less lucky there. Unaccounted for in 1972 – as in 1989 – was an undetermined but substantial quantity of anthrax spores, 2,800 pounds of botulinus toxin, 200 pounds of castor bean toxin, and 2,000 Type F biological bombs. Each of these bombs was designed to take 146 grams of toxin in a liquid carrier so there was enough botulinus toxin alone to fill that number twice over. Moreover, Suffield had developed its own 4-pound light case biological bomb by the end of the war and also had the much larger M78 HE/CW/BW bomb. Although the reporter was told that Canada had no stockpiles of chemical and biological agents, and no delivery system, it certainly once had.[8]

Moreover, after the war Suffield continued to breed house flies in an extension of the insect vector program. It had been first among the Allies to develop munitions to disperse infected insect bait and then infected insects or their pupae – a program which the Americans expanded grandly.[9] Another all-Canadian biological warfare novelty was the tons of refined peat which were to serve as carrier for pathogenic organisms suitable for spreading epidemic diseases. There's nothing of a defensive nature to this weapon. It undoubtedly went into postwar storage at Suffield as well.

Canada's defence ministers seem to have had a lot of trouble with their historical perspectives on the country's role in chemical and biological warfare. As late as 1983 Defence Minister Gilles Lamontagne stood up in the Commons and told his fellow MPs that Suffield had done joint chemical and biological testing with the United States from the 1940s to the 1960s only for defensive, not offensive, purposes.[10] This statement also seems widely at odds with the available documentary record.

The files of the Defence Research Board continue the story of chemical and biological research after 1947, but this book ends there because by the time research for it reached that date, no sensitive files were released without first being thoroughly laundered. However, one early foray into the DRB records yielded some of the following:

1. After the war Canada entered into a tripartite agreement with Britain and the United States on chemical and biological warfare whereby the Allies would share information and research assignments on both offensive and defensive weapons. It is unknown how long this secret understanding remained in force, but certainly through the 1950s and likely into the 1960s. Perhaps even to today.[11]

2. At the Sixth Tripartite Meeting on CW and BW Canada undertook the specific assignment of trying to find cheaper ways of making the nerve gas, sarin. It also promised to continue to search for new war gases and to do trials with nerve-gas bombs larger than 10 pounds.[12]

3. Following earlier bursting chamber tests, Suffield ran field trials with 25-pound shells filled with sarin in late 1951 and 1952. This was during the height of the Korean War to which Canada had contributed over 20,000 men.[13]

4. DRB scientists expressed interest in helping the Americans extract a new toxin from shellfish infected with red tide poisoning; scientists under contract at the University of Western Ontario "as part of the continuing requirement to find new CW agents" developed a new fluorine compound with a toxicity approaching those "in the G (nerve gas) range." The University of Saskatchewan undertook preparation of radioactive nerve gas.[15]

5. According to Dr. Solandt, after the war Suffield continued to field test both chemical and biological weapons for the United States when specific experiments were perceived by the Americans to be too "politically dangerous" to do in their own country. These included the use of Canadian military personnel as human volunteers. Similar tests were done for Britain.[15]

All this was done in the late 1940s and early 1950s and should surprise no one. Mackenzie King forged military ties with the United States that were inherited by his successors as the red scare built up with the Berlin crisis, the Korean War, McCarthyism and all the rest of it. In the political context of the day, preparing for germ and gas warfare probably seemed to make sound military sense. What's wrong is that in 1970 Canada denied this past, and in 1983 a defence minister still voiced ignorance of it. Equally strange is that successive governments seem to have failed to recognize the inherent contradiction in having a policy of retaliation on chemical and biological warfare while claiming a program that is only "defensive."

Perhaps the politicians have always simply deferred to the greater experience of their military advisers. Historians haven't exactly been clamouring to probe Canada's activities in military research, but the Department of National Defence must know its own history. It keeps records just like any other government department and even has a historical branch, the Directorate of History, to manage and retrieve them. If the considerable arsenal of biological weapons Suffield once had were indeed destroyed, as required by the 1972 Biological Weapons Convention that Canada signed, documentary proof must exist for the reassurance of Canadians.

In response to questions in Parliament, in 1988 Canada's Minister of National Defence ordered a review of the country's chemical and biological warfare research and training establishments. The report by William Barton, *Research, Development and Training in Chemical and Biological Defence*, was presented on December 31 and found "not a scintilla of evidence" that Canada is engaged in any research with offensive overtones, reiterating the myth that the wartime biological research at Queen's University and the postwar work at Suffield was only defensive in character. Barton apparently drew his conclusions from interviews and tours of the defence research establishments. Not a single internal document, past or current, is cited in his report. That is like an auditor giving a public company a clean bill of health without reviewing the company accounts.

Considering the scramble to withhold files as the research for this book progressed, it seems that the Department of Defence bureaucracy undertook to decide for itself what the people of Canada, and possibly even the government, should know. And it is not a question of national security, the only defined justification under the Access to Information Act for withholding purely domestic documents. Most of those requested had nothing to do with potentially still-secret technology; they dealt almost exclusively with decisions made over thirty years ago, and sometimes over fifty. And if the Russians have not known for a long time that Canada has been a major player in chemical and biological warfare developments, then their intelligence-gathering techniques are nothing to be feared.

The problem seems to be a reluctance to admit to Canadians that Canada has been both pioneer and innovator in germ and chemical warfare. The attitude does sad injustice to Banting, Murray, Davies, Maass and many other wartime and postwar scientists. No matter what one thinks of the nature of their research, the fact remains that they were all motivatated by the highest ideals of patriotism – they believed they were helping to prevent national catastrophe. They had personal flaws, to be sure, and engaged in petty rivalries and made mistakes, but all believed in the rightness of their actions and had the courage to persist with them. They deserve their place in history.

"You have to understand," said Ira Baldwin, "in 1943 we thought there was a good chance we could lose the war. The Japanese and the Germans still appeared to be winning. No one I asked to join our program [BW research at Camp Detrick] ever refused."[16]

Baldwin recalled walking the beach at the Horn Island proving grounds off Mississippi and seeing bales of rubber and oil washed up from the ships sunk by German submarines in the Gulf of Mexico. Murray, Reed and Maass undoubtedly heard the CBC's Earl Cameron intoning the fall of Hong Kong, or describing the rain of bombs on London. Men were dying, and as far as the wartime scientists were concerned, their job was to prepare their countries for the worst war possible – one of gas and germs. To a degree, their fears were vindicated, for although Germany was found not to have been preparing for biological warfare, the Japanese had done extensive research.[17]

When the war ended without chemical or bacterial agents being used, it briefly looked as though the research would be wound down and the weapons destroyed. Discussion in both the United States and Canada turned on how to maintain Suffield and Camp Detrick on a minimum basis and find peacetime applications for the facilities. The Canadians were even prompt to dispose of their main stockpile of mustard gas.[18] Then came the Gouzenko affair.

If ever a country made a major error of foreign policy, it was the Soviet Union with its decision to obtain by espionage what it could have developed in a few more years by the efforts of its own scientists. With the setting up of the United Nations and the dropping of the atomic bombs, none of the senior scientists and politicians in the United States seriously believed the nuclear secrets could be kept for long. There was actually much debate on how they could be shared with Russia.

In late 1945, despite truculent behaviour at the postwar conference tables, the Soviet Union was still a respected ally. Churchill was a notorious communist-hater, but he was out of power and Attlee in. Truman was a new man and all other Allied leaders, including Canada, did not really count. By giving Russia the benefit of the doubt, the United States and Britain had allowed Stalin to seize control of most of Eastern Europe. In a few more months he might have accomplished much more. By raising the spectre of war with Russia with Truman, Attlee and Churchill, Mackenzie King brought Russian ambitions to an abrupt halt. The United States began counter-measures that included massive aid to Europe under the Marshall Plan.

It is hard to believe – as Mackenzie King obviously did – that Russia really intended another war immediately after Germany's defeat. Its domestic economy was in tatters. But the Gouzenko disclosures certainly revealed Russian attitudes and actions that were distinctly unfriendly. After being caught badly unprepared when war broke out with Germany in 1939, the Allied political and military leaders were not going to make the same mistake twice. In a speech he gave in 1947, McNaughton probably spoke for most of those in postwar positions of power, including in Russia:

> I think that in the period between World War I and World War II, both in Canada and in the United States, we learned the very bitter lesson that unilateral disarmament is a delusion and a very expensive delusion that brought us near disaster and that cost us very dear in the lives of our young people. Just such a delusion would be the surrender of any of the weapons of great power, with which I include those based on atomic energy.
>
> The best protection for the countries of North America, as well as the world, would be an effective organization of secu-

rity under the United Nations but, until this can be brought about, the continued production and further improvement of *all* our weapons and the maintenance of our industrial efficiency, are vital to the prevention of aggression.[19]

Thus began the postwar arms race and the deep freeze between the Communist Bloc and the West. There was absolutely no way that each side would now evince the least trust in the other, and even reasonable positions by either at the United Nations were doomed to be perceived as springing from the worst possible motives. In that kind of international climate, and remembering that all in power in science, politics and the military had vivid memories of the folly of weakness in the face of Nazi Germany, it inevitably followed that chemical and biological warfare research received new impetus parallel to the advances in nuclear weapon technology.

Mackenzie King's most enduring legacy is the close link that was forged between the military establishments of Canada and the United States. The main instruments of co-operation were the tripartite agreements covering atomic energy, chemical and biological warfare, and intelligence sharing – plus the Permanent Joint Board on Defence. The agreements also involved Britain but the PJBD was strictly between the United States and Canada. Set up in 1940 following Mackenzie King's meeting with Roosevelt at Ogdensburg, during the war the joint board busied itself with defence plans which were never needed. In the new era of military co-operation with the United States it assumed much more importance.

After 1945 the Permanent Joint Board on Defence met regularly to discuss plans for North American defence in view of the communist peril. It soon became rather uncomfortable for the Canadian partners. By 1947, despite Mackenzie King's lingering fears to the contrary, a Russian attack across the Arctic was mainly theoretical. Nevertheless, the Canadian representatives were disconcerted to realize that their U.S. counterparts were talking not about "if" Russia attacked, but "when."[20] The United States also began unilateral aerial mapping of the Canadian Arctic which caused a flutter of memos and the request that they at least include a token Canadian on these surveys.

Sovereignty is a touchy issue, as is giving the military aircraft and ships of a foreign power access to one's own military bases on demand. The sharing of military research and joint testing of weapons is also fraught with the peril of public outcry. Canada's answer has been to establish a tradition of secret military agreements with the United States that, thanks to the Access to Information law, need never be disclosed. As late as January 1986 Defence Minister Erik Nielsen refused to reveal even the titles of eight such U.S.-Canada agreements which the Americans had refused a parliamentary committee visiting Washington. Neilsen said to do so would endanger the security of Canada and its allies. A few weeks later CTV News revealed that a total of forty-four defence documents were being withheld from Parliament, including a recently expired 1980 accord with Britain and the United States on chemical and biological warfare.[21]

Ignatieff became heated when asked about Canada's secret military agreements. "It's the civilians, not the military, who will suffer in the next war. If we use mass destruction weapons it will be death on a massive scale. But we are not told what's being done."[22]

Perhaps the majority of Canadians do not really care. Surely the real disappointment is the fact that the situation has enabled Suffield to keep its secrets all these years. In the 1950s and 1960s it was the Americans who were the bad guys of the arms race, doggedly building up massive stocks of atomic, chemical and biological weapons. Canada was a nation of peacekeepers. It would have caused an awful ruckus considering the student militancy of the 1960s had it been known that Canada had been a major player in the chemical and biological warfare arms race. And probably still was.

Nations must have their secrets. No one would disagree that there has to be confidentiality in security, intelligence, foreign affairs and defence. But surely there has to be a time limit. Secrecy is anathema to democracy, which requires that government be accountable to the people. If either elected or non-elected leaders can make decisions without anyone ever knowing about them, that principle is thwarted. It invites irresponsible, even criminal, actions if people can be sure that their deeds will never be scrutinized in their lifetimes. No free society can afford to give that kind of unqualified opportunity to anyone.

The only way around the problem is for governments and bureaucracies to keep careful records so that every decision made by those in power can someday by reviewed and judged by those subject to that power. That is the very reason that government departments keep central records, collecting all memos and correspondence for deposit in archives. It is not primarily for the convenience of biographers and historians. It is to keep government honest.

Unfortunately, Canada's Access to Information law defeats this principle. Under the avowed aim of giving citizens rights of access to government documents, both current and historic, it gives only the right to *request* documents, a right which people have always had. It does not give them the right to get them. It even systemizes secrecy. It allows government departments legally to withhold information indefinitely – forever – for specific defined reasons that cannot be challenged because the person seeking the document cannot see its contents and has no way of determining whether the withhold decision is appropriate or not.

There is, ultimately, recourse to the courts. How many ordinary citizens have the money or expertise – or the time – to take that route? Anyway, the best mechanism of secrecy is delay. The act provides that "access" people at the archives first review the files requested, but they lack specialized knowledge. Consequently, when in doubt they withhold access pending consultation with the department concerned. Many files sought for this book were kept back at this first stage even though it turned out that they were available elsewhere, had been previously declassified, or had been read by other scholars before being deposited in the National Archives.[23]

One of the most effective ways of keeping historians from probing awkward corners of the past is to do what has been done in Canada, the United States and Britain: give the national archives of the country responsibility for looking after records that have not been declassified. Since the archives staff has first to consult the department concerned before anything can be released, an extra layer of decision-making is automatically imposed on the retrieval of sensitive material. Add to that chronic understaffing and lack of expertise by access staff, and government agencies such as Canada's Department of National Defence can prolong secrecy without having to take responsibility for it. A similar situation exists in the United States.

Had this book had to rely solely on the Defence files and had they been reviewed as effectively as the act provides, it could not have been written.

The scientists themselves were not unwilling to have their actions examined. E.G.D. Murray regularly wrote memos to file and saved numerous personal notes. His son, also a distinguished bacteriologist, gathered this material after his father's death and deposited it in the National Archives knowing full well that it illustrated his father's weaknesses as well as strengths, and that it cast him as a pioneer in an area of military research which many regard with revulsion. So it was with Banting, J.B. Collip, Philip Greey and many other distinguished scientists, both dead and still living. Even Charles Best, Banting's co-discoverer of insulin, became an adviser to the Defence Research Board on biological warfare after the war. It is a poor scientist, indeed, who is afraid to have his work judged by others.

It is not likely, either, that Mackenzie King, or McNaughton, or General Foulkes would have required that their plans to counter perceived Russian aggression remain forever hidden. These men were their nation's policy-makers, and all were highly motivated. They were doing nothing of which they were ashamed, and when the necessity of secrecy no longer remained, would have wanted the story of their decisions told.

In an interview with the author, Dr. Solandt was outraged to learn that some of the files dealing with the early days of the Defence Research Board could not be obtained. "That's terrible," he said. "The files are being reviewed by people who don't know what's in them."[24] Solandt had reason for concern. As the first director of the Defence Research Board and a Chief of Staff during the Cold War he naturally was anxious that his actions and those of his colleagues be examined so that it could be judged whether they conducted themselves responsibly. This can never be demonstrated while key files are restricted.

For people such as Solandt it is not simply a matter of disclosing what they know. All the scientists interviewed for this book had taken oaths of secrecy which they still took seriously. They rarely volunteered information they had received as top secret until it could be demonstrated that the key facts were available in the public record. They were not the kind of men to break the faith that had been put in them.[25]

Longstanding secrecy surrounding chemical and biological warfare activities is not a Canadian monopoly. Most of the relevant wartime files in Britain are still closed and historians there have been almost completely blocked in their efforts to obtain details of Porton's activities, giving rise to many myths and misconceptions. At a guess, this sensitivity may involve fear about disclosing that after 1942 Porton arranged to have all its human experiments with mustard gas done in Canada, Australia and India rather than use U.K. troops. It also successfully pressed the Canadians to do large-scale aircraft trials with persistent bacterial agents like anthrax and brucellosis even though it had had its own anthrax disaster at Gruinard. If these trials went ahead as planned, then a large tract of windblown land at Suffield may still be contaminated to this day.

Secrecy tends to be more a cultural thing in Britain than in Canada or the United States. It has a long tradition of a society divided between those ruled and those who rule and in a kind of vestigial acknowledgment of this past there sometimes appears reluctance to disclose information that reflects badly on those who were in power. This seems the only conceivable reason for withholding the wartime minutes of the chemical and bacteriological warfare committees for fifty years. It fits with the sort of gentlemanly revulsion to even considering bacteriological warfare that characterized the attitudes of many of the people in Whitehall in the first year of the war.

Another Public Record Office file still closed in Britain is entitled "Employment of Chemical Warfare in the War against Japan" (May-December, 1944). Canadian archives and Stanley Lovell's memoirs indicate what this contains. Porton did elaborate studies on how to attack Japan as well as Germany with poison gas, and British authorities conspired with the U.S. Chemical Warfare Service to get it secretly used in a first strike against Iwo Jima. Perhaps the British public would also consider this ungentlemanly. By withholding the file, one never takes the risk of finding out.[26]

The Americans seem to be more forthcoming. While many of the wartime files in the United States still remain classified, the deliberations of the Joint Chiefs of Staff have been released. These records undoubtedly tell much of the story of how the U.S. military leadership pressed for the first use of gas against the Japanese. Roosevelt's absolute refusal to agree to the plan surely reflects great credit on him. It took courage in the tradition of Abraham Lincoln deliberately to sacrifice American lives rather than be first to unleash an odious form of warfare. Had Roosevelt lived to the end of the war, it is doubtful the atomic bombs would have been dropped on Hiroshima or Nagasaki.[27]

On the matter of biological warfare, the wartime files of the Surgeon General's Office are open, but those of the U.S. Chemical Warfare Service have been obviously culled. This is awkward for historians because the Chemical Warfare Service had a much more central role in the biological warfare program. It may, however, be nothing more than that these documents were separated years ago and simply have not come up for routine declassification. In the United States this process is often initiated by archives staff but there are many competing collections.

On the other hand, the United States has hardly had a tradition of openness with respect to aging secret files. As one U.S. archivist put it, "It depends on who's in the White House." Apparently under President Jimmy Carter declassification of out-of-date secret documents was easily accomplished; under President Ronald Reagan it became much more difficult. Canada has had the same experience. A National Archives person said that Prime Minister Pierre Trudeau suggested government departments try to release all confidential files more than thirty years old as a matter of principle. Unfortunately, this was a suggestion rather than a decree and the Access to Information Act brought down while he was still in office formally disposed of the idea.

The U.S. attitude to secrecy is certainly also linked to the sense of awesome responsibility it acquired as the first nation to develop the atomic bomb. The disclosures of Russian spying after the war just made matters worse. The Merck Report describing the U.S. wartime biological warfare program was deliberately withdrawn from circulation immediately after the Gouzenko story broke and even General McNaughton on the Permanent Joint Board on Defence had difficulty obtaining a copy.[28]

Gouzenko had warned of spies in the U.S. atomic bomb project as well as in Canada and, sure enough, in 1950 Klaus Fuchs was revealed to have been passing to Russia the most intimate secrets since 1943. Like Nunn May and Pontecorvo, he had been cleared by Britain despite being a known prewar communist. Then, in 1952, Donald Maclean, the British secretary to the Combined Policy Committee on Atomic Energy, defected to the

Soviet Union. He, too, had been spying on the United States from the British embassy since 1944 and also had prewar communist connections. The failure of British counter-intelligence – or even simple security screening, for that matter – was monumental.

Fuchs was lucky he was arrested on returning to Britain, for the Americans reacted to Russian spying by executing Julius and Ethel Rosenberg in 1953 in the midst of a comprehensive communist witchhunt and inquisition led by Senator Joseph McCarthy. Hundreds of innocent and respected Americans were pilloried and civil rights thrown to the wind by McCarthy's Senate kangaroo court. Not surprisingly, secrecy became a paranoia and the effect has lingered.

Whatever the background, prolonged secrecy (to state the obvious) works against the rights of a free society. It enables governments and bureaucracies to hide mistakes, dishonesty and similar embarrassments. It hides people like Oliver North, a key figure in the Iran-Contra scandal in the United States. One can sympathize with the discomfort of External Affairs when confronted by publication of the fact that Canada represented itself falsely at the United Nations Committee on Disarmament. But Canadians are entitled to know about such things, preferably not too long after the fact. How else can they get a chance to express their disapproval?

The same goes for the Americans and the British. The West has a tendency to claim moral superiority over other nations because its press has long had the right to criticize. What about the right to know? Secrets when necessary, yes, but not secrets indefinitely – not secrecy with no rules. Democracies should be careful about throwing stones at other countries when their own yards are not tidy. The vote becomes meaningless without accountability.

Perhaps the most insidious principle of secrecy that operates in all three countries is the requirement that documents received in confidence from other governments not be released without prior approval. With countries as closely allied as Canada, the United States and Britain, that means that the paperwork pertaining to any weapon exchange, or mutual research or defence planning, can remain forever secret if one party or the other forbids release. Theoretically, and perhaps with some probability, that enables the United States to store prohibited weapons in Canada, at Suffield, and then claim with some truth that it has no such weapons stockpiled. Canada, in turn, can also claim it doesn't have the weapons because the United States owns them. Nixon set out to destroy all biological warfare weapons in 1972. Did that include whatever the United States might have had at Suffield?

The above scenario may seem a little improbable, but it is precisely the kind of double-speak Britain has engaged in for years. Britain's official position, stated in 1980, is that "the United Kingdom has never possessed and has not acquired microbial or other biological agents or toxins in quantities which could be employed for weapon purposes."[29] This is only sort of true, for the anthrax produced at Grosse Ile was manufactured at Britain's request specifically for Britain's use in 30-pound and 4-pound bombs. How much was actually made still isn't known, but it was a substantial quantity and likely was the source of germ·agent for Britain's biological warfare tests in the Caribbean after the war.[30]

Perhaps Canada has adopted Britain's logic for claiming, as it still does today, that it never had any biological weapons or toxins. Britain never had the anthrax because it was made in Canada; Canada never had the anthrax because it was made for Britain. The same probably applies to all that botulinus toxin; perhaps it has never officially existed in Canada because it belonged to someone else. The only way to eliminate this kind of nonsense among nations is by saving all documents, and having a policy of timely disclosure.

Apart from all else, one of the greatest benefits to such a policy would be the trust it would cultivate among nations. No country comfortably tolerates being confronted with its own lies or half-truths, unless they are very old. The promise that all statements by a government be verifiable within a reasonable time limit would be as striking an advance in openness in the West, as an independent press is in the East. A thirty-year rule for disclosure would give citizens and foreign countries a lot more confidence in the honesty of governments. It would be a principle that also sits well in a democracy.

The saddest price of all to obsessive secrecy is in the way it prevents us from knowing how we came to be where we are. The link between the Gouzenko affair and the sudden U.S. hostility to Soviet postwar ambitions in Europe has not been generally known. It is doubtful whether even the current Russian leadership is aware of it. West and East have tended to assume the Cold War sprang from the supposed natural and mutual antipathy between capitalism and communism, a cliché interpretation of history if ever there was one. Ideological rhetoric aside, in the late 1940s the Russians most certainly regarded Eastern Europe as a military buffer zone in the same way the United States has regarded Canada. To them Churchill's Iron Curtain accusation must have seemed unfair and hypocritical given the natural desire to ensure strategic security after the blood-letting and devastation caused by the German invasion. The rights of smaller nations were certainly trampled upon, but a Russian could reasonably argue that Britain and the United States would have done likewise in like circumstances. Clearly Mackenzie King believed the United States was capable of doing so. On May 9, 1946, he expressed this fear to the cabinet:

> I said I believed the long range policy of the Americans was to absorb Canada. They would seek to get this hemisphere as completely one as possible. They are already one way or another building up military strength in the North of Canada. It was inevitable that for their own protection, they would have to do that. We should not shut our eyes to the fact that this was going on consciously as part of American policy. It might be inevitable for us to have to submit to it – being so few in numbers and no longer able to look to British power for protection.[31]

There was tremendous public sympathy for the ideals of communism in the West before and during the war. Russian friendship societies abounded and, at least in Canada, were endorsed by government. Stalin's gratuitous spying, and the fact he was caught at it, changed wary friendship into suspicion, anger and fear. The East-West confrontation was likely to happen anyway, but the catalyst when it did was a tired and lonely old man shambling through his last years in office and wishing for tranquillity after six years of war. It is not the first time that the course of history has been shaped by a leader when he was frail, vulnerable and fallible. In a nuclear age, it is something to remember.

Science, unfortunately, is always double-edged. Penicillin had enormous significance in biological warfare research. The rinderpest vaccine became a boon to Third World countries. Mustard gas ultimately became the basis for chemicals used in the treatment of cancer. Conversely, the genetic research now being undertaken even in private labs poses dangers far greater than all the deadly organisms developed in the Second World War combined. Mutants similar to the AIDS virus can now be deliberately, or accidentally, created. Counter-measures are harder to come by.

The parallel with atomic energy is precise. It can bring death as it did at Hiroshima and Nagasaki, yet saves lives in the treatment of disease. It produces power in a world choking on fossil fuel pollution and yet threatens with the hazards of waste disposal and runaway nuclear reactors.

The biggest illusion of all is that science can somehow be disarmed and everything will be right with the world. That will never be until nations achieve confidence in themselves and trust in one another. The key to that sometimes lies as much in the past as in the future.

The "bomb" that everyone wants to ban is not just a physical thing. It's something in all of us.

EPILOGUE

After the first edition of *Deadly Allies* appeared, the Department of National Defence undertook a systematic review of all its records pertaining to chemical and biological warfare. In informal meetings with the author, officials admitted that the microfilms he discovered contained a great number of documents that were not otherwise known to exist. The revelation in these documents that there had been safety problems involving anthrax at Grosse Ile led directly to the decision to probe the island for the deadly bacteria. There has also been an attempt to try to find out what became of the stockpiles of anthrax, botulinus toxin and ricin mentioned in Chapter 11.

There is no reason to doubt the Defence Department's sincerity in its attempt to address the issues raised by the book. The problem is that even the microfilm record is not complete; many key documents still appear to have been "lost." If it were otherwise, it should have been easy to find the paperwork associated with the decontamination of Grosse Ile (which appears to have been done) and the disposition or disposal of the various BW agents stockpiled at Suffield. It is not in the interests of the Defence Department to do other than promptly acknowledge such evidence when found.

The same applies to the question of open-air field trials with anthrax at Suffield. Because of the long life of the bacteria in its spore state, the latent contamination could still be a potential hazard. But so far the Defence Department has not been able to come up with a document that says the trials were cancelled. As the experiment was extremely important, cancellation would have been discussed by the C1 Committee and a formal order issued. No such documents have been found.

This raises the question of whether the existing BW record is fragmentary by accident or design. On the microfilm there are copies of telegrams from Suffield to Britain regarding BW from which messages have been torn off. One can only speculate when this was done, by whom, and why. In light of this obvious tampering, and bearing in mind that the anthrax field trials were instigated by Britain and the Gruinard catastrophe became a public scandal after the war, one can ill afford to conclude that the field trials at Suffield did not occur simply because no descriptive records of them can be found.

These are dark thoughts. They are much more disturbing than the actual work on chemical and biological warfare. The lesson, surely, is that Canada must keep complete and permanent records of its secret activities, even when these involve allies – and keep them securely.

There is a well-known saying to the effect that people who do not know their own past are doomed to repeat it. Perhaps it would be more appropriate to say that people who lose track of their past are liable to become its victims.

As of this writing, the Defence Department is pressing ahead with plans for the final destruction of chemical agents stored at Suffield. The most delicate aspect of this task is not the technology involved, but the problem of convincing the public that the disposal can be done safely. There are no easy answers here.

Perhaps most encouraging of all is the decision this year to set up an independent review committee of senior civilian scientists to spot check the Defence Department's current program on chemical and biological warfare. How effective this committee will be remains to be seen, but it could be a giant step toward convincing Canadians that our military preparations in this area are indeed defensive, and consistent with the declared policy of government.

ACKNOWLEDGMENTS

I am indebted first of all to the wartime scientists I interviewed who trusted me to tell their stories. I promised a history not a polemic, to report the facts as found – no matter what they were – as dispassionately as I could. That satisfied them and they spoke to me freely. I hope they see that I have tried to live up to my promise. My father, T.H. Bryden, also has contributed to this book. He joined Dr. H.G. Thode's lab at McMaster University during the war as an instrument maker in charge of the nuclear research shop where he built much of the experimental equipment of the scientists during and after the war. As I was growing up, he talked often about his work and the men he dealt with. I learned from him that scientists are just like the rest of us, with the same hopes and fears, the same strengths and weaknesses.

Dr. D.C. Mortimer, archivist at the National Research Council, and his charming assistant, Ann Roos, gave me invaluable assistance. Dr. Mortimer's suggestions directly led to interviews with Dr. Murray Sutton and Dr. Fred Lossing whose vivid recollections enhance this history immeasurably. I am thankful also to Dr. Mortimer's predecessors who assembled the NRC records in such exemplary fashion. I hope they will be rewarded by greater attention to Canada's scientific past, for I have told only one of the many fascinating stories that exist in the NRC archives.

Marian Hebb, a Toronto lawyer, took time from an impossibly busy schedule to give me vital encouragement and help. Diane Mew, the editor assigned by McClelland and Stewart, with four deft suggestions transformed the disconnected ramblings of a journalist into a book. I've never rewritten so much, so fast, so successfully in my twenty years in newspapers. (I'll be ready for her next time, though.)

Finally, there is my enduring family – my wife Cathy, and three children, Andrew, Katie and Deirdre. I've been there in body but not in spirit for many months. The grass grows long, the cars need repair, the proposed porch is a pile of lumber weathering in neat heaps. I'll get to it all . . . someday.

SOURCES

The most important Second World War documents on chemical and biological warfare in Canada are in the National Archives of Canada (NAC) in two main collections. The first is (record group) RG77 of the National Research Council (NRC) which excellently covers major developments between 1937 and 1941 plus the Chemical Warfare Inter-Service Board to the end of the war. The second, and even more important, collection consists of National Defence microfilms in RG24, C1, with the file designation 4354. Valuable additional insights are to be found in RG61, the records of the Allied War Supplies Corporation, and RG24 F, the Defence Research Board. The personal papers of C.D. Howe, A.G.L. McNaughton and E.G.D. Murray in the manuscript group (MG) were also helpful. In addition, the Directorate of History (DHist), the historical division of the Department of National Defence, has important files although they are randomly organized. Some of the documents withheld by the National Archives can be freely obtained there. Banting's diary and other important personal papers are at the Thomas Fisher Rare Book Library at University of Toronto (TFL). There is an additional important Banting collection at the NRC.

Documents cited from foreign sources are mainly those from Britain's Public Record Office (PRO) and from the U.S. National Archives and Research Administration (NARA). The most important record groups of the latter are those of the Surgeon General, RG112, 295A, and those of the Chemical Warfare Service, RG175. So that the reader can recognize the foreign sources at a glance, I have inserted U.S. or U.K. in parentheses whenever they are cited.

Important secondary sources have been few, mainly because not many books on the subject of chemical and biological warfare attempt historical documentation. There are a few notable exceptions. L.F. Haber's *The Poisonous Cloud* (Oxford, 1986) is a masterfully researched history of chemical warfare from its beginnings in the First World War to the early 1930s. I am indebted also to Robert Harris and Jeremy Paxman, *A Higher Form of Killing* (New York, 1982) for their examination of documents which reveal Churchill's desire to use anthrax and poison gas on Germany. These apparently were first discovered in 1973 by British historian Roger Parkinson. Michael Bliss, *Banting: A Biography* (Toronto, 1984) gave a splendid lead by uncovering the papers pertaining to Banting and biological warfare at the National Research Council. Shortly after he consulted them they were transferred to the National Archives and deposited in RG77. F.H. Hinsley, *British Intelligence in the Second World War*, III (London, 1988) also has been helpful. Those wishing up-to-date and authoritative information on the characteristics and toxicity of the most important chemical and biological agents should consult the Government of Canada publication, *Handbook for the Investigation of Allegations of the Use of Chemical and Biological Weapons* (Ottawa, 1985). Prepared for the United Nations by the University of Saskatchewan in co-operation with the Department of External Affairs and with the assistance of the Department of National Defence, it is excellent.

NOTES

CHAPTER ONE

1. Directorate of Chemical Warfare and Smoke reports and correspondence of Nov. 21,1945; Jan. 23, 1946; March 1, 1946; in NAC, RG24, C1, 4354-24-5-1 and 4354-24-5-2.
2. For this and subsequent eye-witness descriptions, see Dr. Donald Dewar, taped interview with author (1988), tape VI, side A.
3. Report of Tom King and Don Dewar, Mar. 1, 1946; Report re. scuttling of Hulk LST 209 by B.P. Young, Feb. 21, 1947, in NAC RG24, C1, 4354-25-5-1.
4. This seems the only conceivable explanation for withholding the file, Chemical Warfare – 1922 to 1939, in NAC, RG24, C1, 4354(1).
5. For an excellent and authoritative description of chemical warfare research in Britain and the United States based on documentary sources, see L.F. Haber, *The Poisonous Cloud* (Oxford, 1986).
6. *Toronto Star Weekly*, Aug. 1, 1936.
7. Ibid., June 27, 1936.
8. *Toronto Daily Star*, Sept. 5, 1936.
9. *Canada in the Great World War*, vol. III (London, 1919), p. 71. This was a typical popular history of the war and the quoted passage is an echo of what Conan Doyle wrote in his *The British Campaign in Flanders and France, 1915* (London, New York and Toronto, 1917), p. 49. Doyle, the creator of Sherlock Holmes, and fellow mystery writer John Buchan, in *Nelson's History of the War*, vol. VIII (London and New York, 1915), p. 17, appear to have supplied the essential components for most later descriptions of the attack.
10. J.E. Coates, "The Haber Memorial Lecture," *Memorial lectures delivered before The Chemical Society, 1933-42*, vol. IV (London, 1951), p. 143. The Nobel committee turned Haber down for the prize in 1918 on the grounds that his discovery had prolonged the

war, but the members changed their minds the following year. Haber, *The Poisonous Cloud*, p. 392, fn. 87.

11. General Max Hoffmann, *Der Krieg der versaumten Gelegenheiten* (München, 1923), p. 173, cited by Coates, "Haber," p. 145.

12. John Swettenham, *McNaughton*, I: *1887-1937* (Toronto, 1968), pp. 270-315.

13. J.T. Henderson taped interview (1975), in NAC.

14. E.A. Flood taped interview (1976) in NRC. Also at NAC.

15. Ibid.

16. *The Mackenzie King Diaries, 1923-1949*, University of Toronto microfiche at U. of T. and in NAC, MG26, J13. Cited by Brian Nolan, *King's War* (Toronto, 1988) p. 15.

17. C.J. Mackenzie, Introduction to Mel Thistle, ed., *The Mackenzie-McNaughton Wartime Letters* (Toronto, 1975), p. 3.

18. Most of the detail in the preceding paragraph is from Flood taped interview (1976).

19. Sept. 17, 1937; NAC, RG77, 87-88/104, box 69, 36-5-0-4.

20. The earliest *Toronto Daily Star* article on bacterial warfare appeared Mar. 27, 1935, and consists of an interview with a German scientist who predicted anthrax bombs would be used in the next war.

21. Ibid., Sept. 18, 1937.

22. F.G. Banting Papers, Thomas Fisher Rare Book Library, University of Toronto, MS. Corr 76/ box 20. Haldane was a long-time associate member of Britain's Chemical Warfare Committee which gave scientific direction to Porton.

23. Ibid., McNaughton to Banting, Dec. 8, 1937, with enclosure.

24. When Banting heard from Best that the department head J.J.R. Macleod was refusing publicly to correct a distinguished physiologist's letter in *The Times* which erroneously gave Macleod chief credit for the discovery and relegated him to status of collaborator, he marched into Macleod's office with a *Toronto Daily Star* reporter and demanded that the record be set straight. Michael Bliss, *The Discovery of Insulin* (Toronto, 1982), pp. 194-95. It's a good thing he did. As Macleod must have known very well, *The Times* was enormously influential and, had the letter gone unchallenged, his primacy in the discovery of insulin would have been unshakeable.

25. Without Banting the discovery would not have occurred where it did, when it did. All other arguments of priority and proportion of credit are purely academic. Years later, Collip said this himself, apportioning Banting 80 per cent of the credit for the discovery. C.J. Mackenzie transcript of taped interview (1967), NRC, p. 6.

26. Michael Bliss, *Banting: A Biography* (Toronto, 1982), p. 213. There are numerous references in Banting's diary to his attitude to ideas and creativity. The diary is at the Thomas Fisher Rare Book Library (TFL), University of Toronto.

27. The delay allowed time for essential war materials to be delivered from the United States to Canada for eventual delivery to Britain.

As a neutral, the United States would not have been able to ship to a belligerent. J.W. Pickersgill, ed., *The Mackenzie King Record*, I (Toronto, 1960), p. 31. Hereafter referred to as WLMK.

28. Swettenham, *McNaughton*, II, p. 6.
29. Ibid. McNaughton claimed that he suggested the arrangement and perhaps he did, but King accepted the idea with alacrity. It was the perfect political solution to the problem of appointing a Conservative.
30. Undated notes in CJM war diary, NRC, and NAC, RG77, 87-88/104, box 69, 36-5-0-3.
31. Dewar taped interview (1988).
32. E.A. Flood, "Otto Maass 1890-1961," *Biographical Memoirs of Fellows of the Royal Society*, IX (London, 1963), p. 185. Dewar taped interview (1988).
33. Coates, "Haber," p. 143.
34. Dr. Tom King taped interview with author (1988), tape III, side A.
35. Mellanby to Banting, Sept. 26, 1939. F.G. Banting Collection, vol. 7, NRC.
36. CJM taped interview (transcript), pp. 7-8.
37. C.J. Mackenzie to H.J. Cody requesting leave for Banting. CJM diary, miscellaneous papers.
38. F.G. Banting, war diary, University of Toronto (hereafter FGB diary). Also cited in Bliss, *Banting*, p. 259.
39. Flood wasn't impressed with everything he saw at Porton in 1937. "When I went there I think McNaughton thought it would take me a long time to learn how to test respirators. But when I saw the rather amateurish way it was done at Porton, I came to the conclusion two days would be sufficient. . . . I spent most of the time on all sorts of things associated with the manufacture of weapons. . . . " Flood taped interview, tape II, side A.
40. A wide variety of documents cited in later chapters are the source of this statement. Canadian records list available British chemical weapons in great detail for all stages of the war. The only innovation Porton appears to have been working on by 1940 was the concept of spraying mustard gas from bulk tanks in aircraft. See also Haber, *The Poisonous Cloud*, pp. 115-16, 313. British authors Robert Harris and Jeremy Paxman, *A Higher Form of Killing* (New York, 1982), p. 42, suggest that Porton scientists were working on a "new arsenic code-name 'DM'" but this was simply diphenylaminechloroarsine – Adamsite. They also cite work on DA, which was diphenylchloroarsine. Both were First World War gases.
41. Reports from Israel Rabinowitch, Dec. 30, 1939 to Jan. 6, 1940, in NAC, RG77, 87-88/104, box 69, 32-1-12. In 1922 there were 51 scientists, 57 technicians and 300 others. Haber, *The Poisonous Cloud*, p. 313.
42. The December 1939 reports and recommendations of Rabinowitch go into great detail about Porton. They are in NAC, RG77, 87-88/104, box 69, 32-1-12.

43. Notes of Dec. 7, 1939, visit to Porton by Banting in FGB Collection, 7, NRC.

44. NAC, RG77, 87-88/104, box 69, 32-1-12(1).

45. Ibid.

46. Ibid.

47. O.M. Solandt taped interview with author (1988), tape I, side A. Solandt was at Cambridge at the time and heard a number of adverse comments about Banting's visit.

CHAPTER TWO

1. FGB diary, Dec. 22, 1939. Descriptions of Banting's activities are taken from his diary unless otherwise noted.

2. C.J. Mackenzie taped interview, 1967 (transcript), p. 100.

3. Ibid.

4. FGB diary, Dec. 24, 1939.

5. Ibid., Dec. 27, 1939.

6. *Memorandum on the Present Situation Regarding Bacterial Warfare*, Copy 2 for the National Research Council. He also sent a copy to the Department of National Defence; NAC, RG77, 87-88/104, box 69, 36-5-0-3. It should be noted that mass bombing of civilian centres with conventional weapons during the Second World War and the Korean and Vietnam wars proved to be far less effective than expected. Japan's collapse was much more due to the total destruction of its mercantile fleet, mainly by U.S. submarines.

7. Bliss, *Banting: A Biography*, p. 262. The original document could not be located in the relevant file in NAC, RG77.

8. Banting's 11-page hand-written copy of "Some Notes on Defense against Bacteriological Warfare" prepared by the Medical Research Council, Oct. 24, 1939, is in RG77, 87-88/104, box 69, 36-5-0-6.

9. Because most documents pertaining to biological warfare are still secret in Britain, there is much confusion among British historians about the early activities of Hankey and the Microbiological Warfare Committee and the Bacteriological Warfare Committee. A useful description of the actions of the new committee can be found in *Defensive Measures against Possible Bacteriological Warfare - Summary of Actions Taken*, Dec. 10, 1941; NAC, RG77, 87-88/104, box 69, 36-5-0-6.

10. FGB diary, Nov. 3, 1940 and CJM taped interview (transcript), p. 62.

11. Mackenzie to McNaughton, Jan. 18; March 1, July 25, 1940. Thistle, ed., *The Mackenzie-McNaughton Wartime Letters*.

12. The idea had been to see whether ice would be useful in treating a mustard burn. It wasn't. Banting kept notes on the progress of the burn from May 3 to June 8, 1940; TFL, FGB Collection, box 20.

13. FGB diary, May 19, 1940.

14. For the foregoing, see ibid., May-June.

15. James S. Duncan, *Not a One-Way Street* (Toronto, 1971), p. 121.

16. CJM taped interview (transcript), pp. 30-31 and 46. Mackenzie is a little hazy sometimes and confuses the visit by Hill with the visit by the Tizard mission.

17. *Memorandum on Scientific and Technical War Development Work of the National Research Council* by C.J. Mackenzie, July 6, 1940, at NRC and list of proposed projects from J.D. Cockcroft, Aug. 2, 1940; CJM diary, miscellaneous papers, file 1.

18. War Technical and Scientific Development Committee, Minutes of first meeting, Sept. 6, 1940, at NRC.

19. Mackenzie to Beatty, July 23, 1940; CJM diary, miscellaneous papers.

20. C.J. Mackenzie, *Memorandum on Scientific and Technical War Development Work of the National Research Council*, July 6, 1940, at NAC. In the event, the committee voted $25,000.

21. Mackenzie's description of the meeting with Ralston is in the minutes of a meeting at the NRC, Nov. 13, 1941; NAC, RG77, 87-88/104, box 69, 36-5-0-5. Also see NAC, Cabinet War Committee minutes, July 9, 1940. One suspects that Ralston did not tell the committee that Banting was going to undertake actual experiments.

22. FGB diary for July 9-15, 1940. Also Banting notes for July 13-18; NAC, RG77, 87-88/104, box 69, 35-5-0-1. Banting was apparently keeping two diaries at this time, and these notes were copied by Philip Greey from the second.

23. FGB diary, July 18, 1940.

24. Banting's aviation medicine team was the only group doing significant high-altitude and pressure-suit work at this point in the war, the British giving the need for the work very low priority. Thus it was that the flying suit invented by Wilbur Franks became the original model for the pressure suits used by pilots when jet aircraft made their debut. It was one of Canada's most original and significant technological contributions of the war but although Banting provided the lab, the financing and the over-all direction of the program, he never made any attempt to claim a percentage of the credit. Frank had the original idea, and that was that.

25. FGB diary, Sept. 2, 1940.

26. Ibid., Sept. 4, 1940, and monograph by George Laurence at NRC.

27. FGB diary, Sept. 16-19, 1940.

28. Minutes of the WTSDC, Sept. 20, 1940, at NRC. Other projects included: $30,000 for chemical research at universitites; $7,000 for aircraft pressure cockpits; $15,000 for chemical warfare field trials; $25,000 for flight masks; $15,000 for de-icing experiments; $35,000 for proximity fuses; $15,000 for a microwave radio tube; and $2,000 to Professor Gray at Queen's University to study the phenomenon of fission in uranium.

29. NAC, RG77, 87-88/104, box 69, 36-5-0-20.

30. The North Sea idea is in CJM diary, miscellaneous papers, while the others are in NAC, 87-88/104, 36-5-0-3.

31. C.A. Mitchell to E.G.D. Murray, June 9, 1942; NAC, MG30, B91, vol. 17, 26.18.

32. Details of the experiment, undated, are in NAC, RG77, 87-88/104, box 69, 36-5-0-4 and in FGB diary, Oct. 9-10, 1940.

33. There is no evidence, either in his diary or from other sources, that Banting was an alcoholic as Maass was. He seems to have only resorted to alcohol when under extreme mental pressure, a practice not uncommon among people faced with heavy responsibility or conflicts. Otherwise, Banting appears to have been a moderate drinker by today's standards.

34. CJM taped interview (transcript), p. 47. (Note that there are at least two transcripts at the NRC and pagination is sometimes confusing.)

35. Ibid.

36. Ibid., and FGB diary, Oct. 28, 1940.

37. FGB notes, Nov. 19, 1940; NAC, RG77, 87-88/104, box 69, 36-5-0-3. Also FGB diary, Nov. 19.

38. Ibid., Nov. 20-26.

39. See correspondence in NAC, MG30, B91, vol. 17.

40. Government of Canada, Handbook for the Investigation of Allegations of the Use of Chemical or Biological Weapons (Ottawa, 1985), p. 118. Hare wrote a paper during the war on the spread of influenza in a military camp but it (No. 146, C.6016) is missing from the NRC collection of the records of the Royal Canadian Army Medical Corps.

41. FGB diary, Dec. 10, 1940.

42. Both memos were received Dec. 11, 1940; NAC, RG77, 87-88/104, box 69, 36-5-0-3.

43. Veldee to Defries, Dec. 23, 1940; Banting to Veldee, Dec. 30, 1940; NAC, RG77, 87-88/104, 36-5-0-1.

44. Banting was a cunning judge of character, for Duncan was not being very truthful. The following January he was named president of the company, "a goal toward which I had been working for over thirty years" (Duncan, Not a One-Way Street, p. 123). It appears from the tone of this book and other papers in the archives of Varity Corporation that he later realized he had missed his chance to make a historic contribution, and regretted it.

45. CJM taped interview (transcript), p. 11.

46. Ibid., p. 12.

47. Ibid., p. 13.

48. R.L. McIntosh taped interview with author (1989)

CHAPTER THREE

1. NAC, RG77, 83-84/106, box 6, 4-C9-25.

2. Memos, Mar. 18 to Apr. 24, 1941, in NAC, RG24, C1, 4354-12-1.

3. Dr. Jack Dacey taped interview with author (1988), tape II, side B. Dacey had been given the job of transporting the frogs from the Chemical Warfare Labs in Ottawa to Montreal for the first leg of their flight to Britain.

4. CJM diary, Oct. 31, Nov. 2, 1940. There are references also in FGB diary and Flood taped interview.

5. CJM diary, Nov. 4, 1940.

6. Ibid.

7. CJM diary (miscellaneous papers).
8. Harris and Paxman, *A Higher Form of Killing*, p. 111, from original documents.
9. Ibid., p. 112.
10. Maass to Davies, Aug. 19, 1941, in NAC, RG77, 83-84/106, box 6, 4-C9-19(1).
11. PC 2506 gave approval in principle to allow work to get started at Suffield and PC 1/6687 formally set up the CW organization. See "Narrative of the Directorate of Chemical Warfare and Smoke," (C.1945) in Directorate of History, Department of National Defence (D.Hist.), HQS 5393-3.
12. Report to the Advisory Committee of Industrial Chemists (1940), Wright Papers, University of Toronto. The field trial is described in NAC, RG77, 83-84/106, box 6, 4-C9-19.
13. Dr. J. Ellwood Currah, taped interview with author (1988). There are many stories about Wright, most of them not very favourable to his character, but he had one curious peccadillo. He always signed his name George F Wright without a period to the initial. Apparently, George was his only given name so he added the F because he felt it looked better. The F had no period because it didn't stand for anything.
14. Flood taped interview.
15. Suffield War Diary, NAC, RG24, vol. 17489.
16. Oct. 27, 1941, in NAC, RG77, 83-84/106, box 6, 4-C9-19(2).
17. Report by Maass, Nov. 7, 1941, in ibid.
18. Dr. R.L. McIntosh taped interview with author (1988). By this time British military intelligence had heard that the Germans had developed a "nerve" gas.
19. McIntosh taped interview.
20. DCW&S list of noteworthy accomplishments, June 22, 1944, in RG24, C1, 4354-29-13-3.
21. W.W. Goforth report on Z, Nov. 7, 1941, in NAC, RG24, C1, 4354-11-12.
22. Ibid.
23. McIntosh taped interview.
24. Dr. Fred Lossing taped interview with author (1989).
25. By order of PC 7549, Dec. 21, 1940. NAC, RG61, vol. 4, Project 18.
26. Ibid.
27. NAC, RG77, 85-86/178, box 10, 4-C9-41.
28. The preceding is from various items of correspondence in ibid., RG77, 83-84/178, box 10, 4-C9-41 plus CJM diary, June 20, 1942. Churchill issued his warning on May 10, 1942, and Roosevelt on June 6.
29. NAC, RG24, C1, 4354-24-5-1.
30. Memo, May 26, 1942; CCWISB minutes July 1, 1942 in NAC, RG77, 85-86/178, box 10, 4-C9-41. Also Suffield War Diary, Aug. 22, 1941, RG24, vol. 17489.
31. CJM diary, Mar. 28, 1942. For details of the experiment, see NAC,

RG24, C1, 4354-6-1 and NARA (U.S.), RG175, box 179, 350.05.32. CJM diary, June 20, 1942.

32. CJM diary, June 20, 1942.

33. E.A. Flood, "Otto Maass," *Biographical Memoirs*, p. 192.

34. Ibid., p. 194.

35. Dr. Richard Tomlinson taped interview with author (1988).

36. King taped interview for the container story; various memos on problems with the ointment are in NAC, RG24, C1, 4354-5-5 and 4354-12-1.

37. King taped interview. A photograph of the Mickey Mouse mask is to be found in a U.S. Chemical Warfare Service gas equipment manual, 1942, in NARA (U.S.), RG175, box 136, 321. It's quite amazing.

38. Various files; NAC, RG24, C1, reel 5001.

39. These were not Goering's exact words, but OSS scientific adviser Stanley Lovell's version of them. Nevertheless, they have a ring of truth. It is well known that after the Allied invasion of France the defending German armies received their supplies mainly by horse-drawn vehicles. Stanley Lovell, *Of Spies and Stratagems* (New York, 1964), pp. 85-86.

40. Minutes of meeting, July 31, 1942. NAC, RG77, 85-86/178, box 10, 4-C9-41.

41. Dewar taped interview.

42. Minutes of Extra-Mural Section Meeting, Feb. 5, 1943, in NAC, RG77, 85-86/178, box 10, 4-C9-41. Also Professor Ron Graham taped interview with author (1988).

43. J. Ellwood Currah taped interview with author (1988). Currah was Beamish's assistant and wrote his Ph.D. thesis during the war on work in the lab. It was never published because it was Top Secret.

44. Minutes of Extra-Mural Section Meeting, Feb. 5, 1943, and Dr. D.C. Mortimer taped interview with author (1988).

45. NRC, Banting Papers, file M-1000.

46. Lossing taped interview.

CHAPTER FOUR

1. CJM, taped interview (transcript), p. 15.

2. NRC, Minutes of the WTSDC, Feb. 25, 1941 at NRC. Mackenzie liked this line so much that he used it again in his eulogy to Banting in Toronto a year later.

3. CJM diary, May 9, 1941. Report of Dr. Donald Fraser on vacuum-drying of *s. typhi murium* on sawdust with later attempts at various times to restart the bacteria in broth. As the experiment ran for six months, it must have been started in late October or early November, 1940; NAC, RG77, 87-88/104, box 69, 35-5-0-4.

4. See the first report of the Porton Experiments Subcommittee on Bacteriological Warfare, BW(P)(41)1, Feb. 10, 1941; NAC, RG77, 87-88/104, box 69, 36-5-0-6. The state of American BW research is dealt with later in this chapter.

5. O.M. Solandt taped interview with author (1988).

6. Ronald Lewin, *The American Magic* (New York, 1983), pp. 54-60.

7. Quoted by E.B. Fred in letter to Frank Jewett, Feb. 1942; NAC, RG77, 87-88/104, box 69, 36-5-0-8.

8. CJM diary, Aug. 6, 1941.

9. Notes of a meeting held at NRC, Nov. 13, 1941; NAC, RG77, 87-88/104, box 69, 36-5-0-5. Present were: C.J. Mackenzie, J.B. Collip, E.G.D. Murray, G.B. Reed, O. Maass, E.A. Flood, Donald (?) Mitchell and Col. Rankin.

10. E.G.D. Murray notes to file, Nov. 26, 1941; NAC, RG77, 87-88/104, box 69,36-5-0-5 and personal notes in NAC, MG30, B91, vol. 29, 26.23.

11. "E.G.D. Murray, 1890-1964," *Journal of General Microbiology* 46 (1967), pp. 1-21.

12. Notes of a meeting at NRC, Nov. 27, 1941; NAC, RG77, 87-88/104, box 69, 36-5-0-5. The request to DND was made Dec. 24; ibid., 36-5-0-9.

13. Murray notes to file, Dec. 2, 1941; NAC, RG77, 87-88/104, box 69, 36-5-0-3.

14. Ibid., Dec. 3-6, 1941.

15. Ibid., Dec. 10-13, 1941. Greey soon relented and on Dec. 15 informed Murray he would serve as secretary on the new committee; NAC, MG30, B91, vol. 29, 26.22.

16. Ibid. See also Murray's rough notes of this meeting in NAC, MG30, B91, vol. 29, 26.18.

17. N.H. Grace to Maass, July 4, 1940; NAC, RG77, 87-88/104, box 69, 36-5-0-4.

18. Murray notes to file, Dec. 18, 1941; ibid., 36-5-0-5. The report itself from the U.S. National Institute of Health to the Surgeon General, Dec. 16, 1940, is in ibid., 36-5-0-7.

19. Ibid.

20. Mackenzie to McNaughton, Dec. 6, 1940, in Thistle, ed., *Mackenzie-McNaughton Wartime Letters*.

21. Banting received a letter from Mackenzie in Washington re. the Tizard mission; FGB diary, Sept. 25, 1940.

22. Minutes of meeting, Dec. 19, 1941; NAC, RG77, 87-88/104, box 69, 36-5-0-5.

23. Murray's quote is taken from a brief note on the meeting by Colonel James Simmons, Dec. 29, 1941, in NARA (U.S.), RG112, 295A, box 6. Otherwise, the desciption of the meeting is from Murray's ten pages of minutes; NAC, RG77; 87-88/104, box 69, 36-5-0-8.

24. Ibid. Hagan's written report to the WBC committee on animal diseases containing his warning about anthrax is in ibid., 36-5-0-8.

25. Fred to Jewitt, ibid., Dec. 27, 1941.

26. Ibid., Jan. 26, 1942.

27. Minutes of meeting, Jan. 28, 1942; ibid., 36-5-0-5.

28. NAC, MG30, B91, vols. 29, 26.11, 26.17, 26.22.

29. *Globe and Mail*, Feb. 3, 1942; and NAC, RG77, 87-88/104, box 69, 36-5-0-7. Simons was extensively investigated in the United States which has a large file on him in NARA (U.S.), RG112, 295A, box 12.
30. Murray's notes of meeting, Feb. 15, 1942; NAC, MG30, B91, vol. 29, 26.18.
31. Ibid. Also see excerpts from *Second Report of the Committee M.1000*, June 12, 1942, in NAC, RG77, 87-88/104, box 69, 36-5-0-9.
32. Mansfield-Clark to Murray with enclosure, Mar. 6, 1942; NAC, RG77, 87-88/104, box 69, 36-5-0-8.
33. Ibid., Ney to Murray, undated but apparently early March, 1942.
34. Ibid., Ney to Murray, April 7; Murray to Ney, April 9, 1942.
35. Minutes of meeting, June 12, 1942; NAC, RG77, 87-88/104, box 69, 36-5-0-5.
36. Stephen Roskill, *Hankey: Man of Secrets*, III (London, 1974). Through lack of primary sources on Hankey's involvement in bacteriological warfare, this author has made a number of errors which have tended to be repeated in subsequent books.
37. Full details of what Hankey did or did not do, plus the setting up of the Bacteriological Warfare Committee is in *Defensive Measures Against Possible Bacteriological Warfare: Summary of Action Taken*, Dec. 10, 1941; NAC, RG77, 87-88/104, box 69, 36-5-0-6. This document is still secret in Britain.
38. Feb. 8, 1940; PAC (U.K.), Cab. 65/5, cited in Roskill, *Hankey*, III, p. 432.
39. *Resumé of the Status of Chemical Warfare*, Oct. 9, 1940, prepared in Q & A form in a reply to questions supplied by the British Technical Mission to the Chief, U.S. Chemical Warfare Service; NARA (U.S.), RG175, box 143, 350.05.
40. The relevant Porton reports are: Aircraft spraying and possible BW application (Fildes), BW(P)(41)3, Feb. 24, 1941; Effect of air-borne anthrax on cattle (Fildes, Henderson, Woods, Gladstone), BW(P)(41)4, May 6, 1940; Air-borne anthrax on cattle, second report (Fildes, Henderson, Woods, Gladstone, Blout), BW(P)(41)10, July 12, 1941; Animal disease experiments (D.A.E Cabot), BW(P)(41)14; Infection of cattle with brucella militensis (Cabot), BW(P)(41)15, Nov. 22, 1941; and Attempts to infect cattle with rinderpest, BW(P)(41)1, Feb. 13, 1942. All these documents are still secret in Britain.
41. *Defensive Measures Against Possible Bacteriological Warfare . . .*, Dec. 10, 1941; NAC, RG77, 87-88/104, box 69, 36-5-0-6. A request for this document was refused by Canada's Department of External Affairs.
42. *Report on Visit of Lt. Colonel James H. Defandorf to United Kingdom*, Apr. 18, 1942; NARA (U.S.), RG112, 295A, box 6. Defandorf spent March 9-16 touring Porton and in particular the biological warfare section. This included much discussion with Fildes, who is probably the source of his seeing Hankey's directive. Defandorf called it "naive."

43. Ibid.

44. CJM diary, Feb. 23, 1942. Murray to Fred, May 30, 1940; NAC, RG77, 87-88/104, box 69, 36-5-0-8.

45. Letter to Murray, Aug. 13, 1942; NAC, MG30, B91, vol. 29, 26.30.

46. Harris and Paxman, *A Higher Form of Killing*, pp. 95-96, quote Stimson's memo at length which was obtained from the judgment of *Mabel Nevin et al.* v. *The United States of America*, May 20, 1981

47. Reed to Maass, Apr. 20, 1942; NAC, RG24, C1, 4354-33-17-1. Maass was still not officially administering the biological warfare program so it would be interesting to know whether this expenditure was officially authorized. Maass was notorious during the war for ignoring red tape when it came to projects he was interested in.

48. Minutes of meeting, June 11-12, 1942; NAC, RG77, 87-88/104, box 69, 36-5-0-5.

49. Ibid., 36-5-0-9.

50. Ibid. See also, memo by Defandorf, June 16, 1942, in ibid., 36-6-0-8.

51. Various letters in NAC, MG30, B91, vol. 29, 26.22, 26.31.

52. Ibid., 26.26, 26.18, 26.31.

CHAPTER FIVE

1. The recommendation to reorganize M-1000 under Maass is in Barton to Murray, May 29, 1942; NAC, RG77, 87-88/104, box 69, 36-5-0-3. "I think the anthrax idea is a good one. . . . " Mitchell to Murray, Aug. 15, 1942; NAC, MG30, B91, vol. 29, 26.31.

2. Murray notes to file, July 14-25, 1942; ibid., 26.26.

3. Dr. Murray Sutton, taped interview with author, 1988.

4. Report of visit by Mitchell, May 21, 1942; NAC, RG77, 87-88/104, box 69, 36-5-0-3.

5. Murray notes to file, Aug. 1942; NAC, MG30, B91, vol. 29, 26.26.

6. Maass to Murray, Aug. 21, 1942, ibid., 26.31. CJM diary, Aug. 21, 1942.

7. Harris and Paxman, *A Higher Form of Killing*, pp. 69-74.

8. George Merck, *Official Report on Biological Warfare*, Bulletin of the Atomic Scientists, Mar. 1946, pp. 16-18. Also Murray to Maass, Oct. 19, 1942; NAC, RG24, C1, 4354-33-17-1.

9. Ibid., Reed to Maass, Oct. 21, 1942.

10. Ibid., Murray to Maass, Oct. 19, 1942. Hoover was being very nosy. As a civilian agency, the FBI was called in to give security clearance to individuals for secret war work, but it was not to be privy to the military secrets themselves.

11. NAC, RG24, C1, 4354-33-13-3. The visit of Fildes was remembered by R.G.E. Murray and I.L. Baldwin. Davidson Pratt letters from Canada, Nov.-Dec., 1942, are in ibid., 4354-12-1.

12. Ibid., Murray to Maass, Dec. 12, 1942, 4354-33-13-3.

13. This convoluted arrangement and its rationale is described by Lt.-Col. Millard S. Peake, U.S. CWS, Aug. 22, 1942; NAC, RG24, C1, 4354-18-2.

14. Ibid. The agreement was added as a supplement to the Grosse Ile "contract," Feb. 1, 1943.

15. Ibid., Maass to MGO, Jan. 9; Note on document by Ralston, Jan. 13; Maass to Ralston, Jan. 18, 1942.

16. Ibid., 4354-33-13-3, Murray to Kelser, Jan. 29, 1943.

17. Ibid., Feb. 2, Feb. 6, Feb. 9, 1943.

18. Greey to C.H. Best, Dec. 9, 1942; NAC, RG77, 88-89/046, box 32, 4M-46(1). See also Robert D. Defries, *The First Forty Years* (Toronto, 1968), p.181.

19. Hare to Defries, in Connaught Archives, box 83-016-04-06. He claimed Greey was sloppy in his research procedures but just had to tell Defries all about it in confidence. It's quite a nasty letter that reflects very badly on Hare.

20. Most of the foregoing is from Lovell, *Of Spies and Stratagems*, pp. 152-60. This is the only previously published reference I could find indicating the wartime role Reed and Murray played in biological warfare planning. Lovell's recollection has not been confirmed in the wartime records of the U.S. Joint Chiefs of Staff but it certainly rings true.

21. NAC, RG24, C1, 4354-33-17-1.

22. Report of DMO, July 30, 1943; NAC, RG24, C1, 4354-33-14-12.

23. Murray to Demers; Murray to Maass, Aug. 6, 1943; ibid., 4354-33-17-1.

24. Ibid., Murray to Maass, Feb. 16, 1943, 4354-33-17-1. Murray to Reed, June 18, 1943, 4354-33-13-3.

25. Dr. Ira L. Baldwin, taped interview with author (1989), tape I, side A.

26. Ibid.

27. Interviews with eyewitnesses in Harris and Paxman, *A Higher Form of Killing*, p. 72.

28. Ibid. The information that 30-lb., and 4-lb. bombs were tested at this time is from Canadian documents.

29. The request on Sept. 27, 1943 for field trials is described in Murray to M.B. Chittick (CO Camp Detrick); NAC, RG24, C1, 4354-33-17-1. The shipment of the bomb charging machine is reported Sept. 15, 1943; ibid., 4354-33-13-3.

30. "They lost the island and I think they lost some personnel, too. Those are the things you will never know because they have people dying of pneumonia – it says 'cause of death pneumomia', or something like that. You will never be able to prove it one way or another." Dr. Murray Sutton taped interview with author, tape X, side A.

31. Murray to Cameron, Oct. 12; Murray to Maass, Oct. 12, 1943; NAC, RG24, C1, 4354-33-17.

32. Murray to Maass, July 23, 1943, refers to Davies's request for staff increase for BW field trials and comments, "Great Britain is looking for us to carry out trials on her behalf"; NAC, MG24, C1, 4354-33-17-1.

33. Murray to Maass (reciting past grievances), Dec. 13, 1944; Maass to Davies, Nov. 24, 1943; ibid., 4354-33-17.

34. Baldwin taped interview, tape I, side A.

35. U.S. Arms Requirement Branch to Canadian Procurement Division (Army) Aug. 2, 1943, regarding two trailer-mounted mobile autoclaves "required by Lord Stamp who is presently employed on a secret project at Suffield Experimental Station." D.Hist, 314.009(D323). This was quick off the mark considering that Camp Detrick had been operational only four months.

36. The specifications for the lab are in NAC, RG24, C1, 4354-26-8-1. It was completed in May 1944.

37. Notes on a conference in Washington, Dec. 29, 1943; ibid., 4354-33-13-5.

38. Ibid., Notes by Murray, Jan. 18, 1943.

39. Ibid.

40. Ibid., Murray to Maass requesting $30,000; Ralston to Howe same day requesting $25,000, Feb. 16, 1944.

41. The committee met several times during January and February, 1944. Key members were Merck (chairman), Baldwin and General Alden Waitt of the Chemical Warfare Service, who was at this time aggressively promoting the use of gas against Japan; NARA (U.S.), RG112, 295A, box 3, 13.

42. Maass to Porter, Apr. 14, 1944; NAC, RG24, C1, 4354-33-13-5. The reply from Porter on May 12 was equivocal.

43. Stuart to Lt.-Gen. J.C. Murchie (Defensor in Ottawa), May 19, 1944; NAC, MG27, III, B11, vol. 39.

44. Ibid., Murchie to Stuart, May 25, 1944.

45. Ibid., Stuart to Murchie, May 26, 1944.

46. Ibid., Report of a meeting with SHAEF, Stuart to Murchie, May 27, 1944. The deaths were likely caused by hepatitis (R.G.E. Murray).

47. F.H. Hinsley, *British Intelligence in the Second World War*, III(2) (London, 1988), p. 577.

48. F.W. Winterbotham, *The Ultra Secret* (New York, 1974), pp. 123-24.

49. Murchie to Stuart, May 29, 1944; MG27, III, B11 vol. 39, BW file. The Americans at the meeting included General N.T. Kirk, General G.F. Lull, Colonel J.E. Zanetti, Dr. I.L. Baldwin and Dr. N. Paul Hudson.

50. Ibid. See also, NAC, MG30, B91, vol, 17, 14.29.

51. CJM diary, Jan. 14-19, 1942. T.A. Stone to Ralston, Jan. 6, 1944; NAC, MG27, III, B11, vol. 53.

52. Dewar, Tomlinson taped interviews. Murray expressed his bitterness to Maass about this episode, Dec. 13, 1944, NAC, RG24, C1, 4354-33-17.

53. Murray to Davies, Apr. 18, 1944; ibid., 4354-33-17-1.

54. Ibid., Murray to Chittick, April 1944.

55. Ibid.

56. Camp Detrick's liaison officer at Porton, William Sarles, recalled witnessing the trials at Gruinard in 1943 on the *NBC Magazine*, NBC-TV, May 15, 1983. Cited by Leonard Cole, *Clouds of Secrecy* (Tatowa, N.J., 1988), p. 30.

57. April 16, 1944; NAC, RG24, C1, 4354-26-8-5.

58. Murray to Maass, Dec. 13, 1944; ibid., 4354-33-1. One of Murray's

complaints about the conduct of trials at Suffield refers to an experiment involving ducks.

59. The description and procurement of cluster bombs from Nov. 13, 1943, to July 18, 1944, is in NAC, RG24, C1, 4354-26-7-20.

60. Barton Bernstein, "The Birth of the U.S. Biological-Warfare Program," *Scientific American*, June, 1987, p. 118. From an original document but sources are not cited in this article.

61. Murray to Duthie, July 12, July 31, 1944; NAC, RG24, C1, 4354-33-13-3.

62. Ibid., Murray to Duthie, Aug. 14, 1944.

63. Ibid., Duthie to Murray, Aug. 18, 1944.

64. Ibid., Duthie to Murray, Aug. 24, 1944.

65. Murray to Zanetti, July 29, 1944; ibid., 4354-33-17. Zanetti to Duthie, Aug. 7, 1944; ibid, 4354-33-13-3. Production of anthrax to end Aug. 31 with complete shutdown of operation Sept. 30, Murray to Duthie, Aug, 19, 1944.

66. Ibid., Duthie to Murray, Aug. 24, 1944.

67. Baldwin taped interview, tape I, side B.

68. Authorization to proceed with anthrax field trials is in Murray to J.C. Patterson, Aug. 14, 1944; NAC, RG24, C1, 4354-33-13-3. A document in DND possession indicates that the trial, code-named MS-10, was postponed, but a 1946 list of BW experiments states that MS-10 was "completed." See Reed to Maass, April 4, 1946, ibid., 4354-33-13.

69. Ibid., Paget to Maass, 4354-33-11.

CHAPTER SIX

1. Pyke's biographical details are taken from David Lampe, *Pyke: The Unknown Genius* (London, 1959). This author lists no sources that can be checked, although he appears to have had access to Pyke's papers and interviewed Mountbatten at length. His later descriptions of Pyke's wartime activities are frequently in error when compared to existing documentary material.

2. Ibid. Lampe ignores mention of the political philosophies of Pyke and J.D. Bernal except for one reference to Pyke's Marxism on p. 198.

3. For excellent descriptions of communism at Cambridge during the 1930s, the reader should consult Andrew Boyle, *The Fourth Man* (New York, 1979) and John Costello, *Mask of Treachery* (New York, 1988).

4. The foregoing and following description of Montbatten's career in the Navy is taken from Philip Ziegler, *Mountbatten: A Biography* (New York, 1985), pp. 121-47.

5. Ibid.

6. Lampe, *Pyke*, p. 87.

7. Ibid., pp. 89-95.

8. This assessment of Cherwell's standing among other scientists is from Solandt taped interview, tape III, side A. Cherwell's obdurate personality and isolation is fully described by one of the scientists

most sympathetic to him in R.V. Jones, *My Secret War* (London, 1978), passim.

9. Solandt taped interview, tape IV, side B.

10. Ibid.

11. Solly Zuckerman, *From Apes to Warlords* (London, 1978), p. 103.

12. As a professor Bernal was making more than enough money to dress as he pleased. However, a non-conformist appearance in his Cambridge days complemented non-conformist ideas.

13. Solandt taped interview.

14. C.P. Stacey, Official History of the Canadian Army in the Second World War, *Six Years of War* (Ottawa, 1960), I: pp. 387 and 389.

15. Lovell, *Of Spies and Stratagems*, pp. 179-180. He apparently got the information from a colleague in the British SIS. *Six Years of War* is vague about the date set for the attack.

16. A.J.P. Taylor, *Beaverbrook: A Biography* (London, 1972), pp. 538 and 638.

17. F.H. Hinsley, *British Intelligence in the Second World War*, II (London, 1981), pp. 696-98. Hinsley had access to all the files of British military intelligence and says Combined Operations ignored this service entirely. This can only be viewed as incompetence, or negligence, or both.

18. Lampe, *Pyke*, pp. 115-20.

19. Ibid., pp. 127-37. The name Habbakuk was derived, but misspelled, from the reference to Habakkuk in Voltaire's *Candide*. Pyke's 232-page submission of Sept. 23, 1942, to Mountbatten is in PRO (U.K.), ADM 116/4818.

20. Zuckerman, *Apes to Warlords*, p. 159.

21. Mountbatten memo Dec. 5, 1942 in PRO (U.K.), PREM 3 216/6, cited by Ziegler, *Mountbatten*, p. 210.

22. Photograph of Churchill's memo in Lampe, *Pyke*, p. 120. Cited in full in Sexton, *Moneco*, p. 86.

23. Laidlaw, Jan. 1, 1943; NAC, RG25, vol. 2119, file AR1011/1. Also CJM interview (transcript), p. 76.

24. Mountbatten to Churchill, Jan. 8, 1943. NAC, RG25, vol. 2119, AR1011/1.

25. W.H. Cook, *My 50 Years with the NRC, 1924-1974*, NRC monograph, p. 138.

26. Laidlaw to Mackenzie, Jan. 14, 1943, enclosing " . . . detailed programme on Canadian research . . . drawn up by Professor Bernal." NAC, RG26, vol.2119, AR1011/1. Pyke was still in the United States at this time. Zuckerman, *Apes to Warlords*, p. 159.

27. Laidlaw to Mackenzie, Jan. 15, 1943; NAC, RG26, vol. 2119, AR1011/1.

28. Cook, *My 50 Years*, p. 139.

29. Lampe, *Pyke*, p. 115. From an interview with Goodeve.

30. Maurice Goldsmith, *Sage: A Life of J.D. Bernal* (London, 1980), p. 63.

31. Lampe, *Pyke*, p. 137.

32. Zuckerman, *Apes to Warlords*, p. 159.

33. Laidlaw to Mackenzie, Feb. 9, 1943. NAC, RG25, vol. 2119, AR1011/1.

34. Cook, *My 50 Years*, p. 140.

35. CJM taped interview (transcript), pp. 78-80.

36. Lampe, *Pyke*, p. 65. Mackenzie must have told this story widely because even Zuckerman had heard about Pyke wandering around in the Canadian winter in shoes without socks.

37. CJM taped interview (transcript), pp. 80-81.

38. Zuckerman, *Apes to Warlords*, p. 158.

39. Jack Sexton, *Moneco: The First 75 Years* (Montreal, 1982) p. 91.

40. Massey to Mountbatten, March 21, 1943; NAC, RG25, vol. 2119, AR1101/1.

41. CJM diary, May 1, 1943.

42. Ibid., May 6, 1943. Also CJM taped interview (transcript), p. 83.

43. Ibid., pp. 84-85.

44. Ibid., p. 85.

45. Ibid., pp 86-87.

46. CJM diary, June 10, 1943.

47. Ibid.

48. CJM taped interview (transcript), pp. 88-89.

49. CJM diary, June 10, 1943.

50. Richard Hewlett and Oscar Anderson, Jr. *A History of the United States Atomic Energy Commission*, I, *The New World, 1939/1946* (Pennsylvania, 1962), pp. 263-80. This book is recognized to be the authoritative history of the U.S. atomic energy program and was compiled mainly from archival sources.

51. J.W. Pickergill and D.F. Forster, eds., *The Mackenzie King Record*, II (Toronto, 1968), p. 543. Hereafter WLMK.

52. Boyle, *The Fourth Man*, p. 215, and Costello, *Mask of Treachery*, p. 393.

53. Goldsmith, *Sage*, p. 67.

54. PRO (U.K.), CAB 78/11.

55. Bernal appeared to be the "man in authority" and most frequent visitor to the Montreal Engineering Company as it worked on Habbakuk in June and July, 1943; Sexton, *Monenco*, pp. 90-91, from personal recollections and company documents. Bernal's biographer says that one of Bernal's "favourite stories" was the tale of how he persuaded Mountbatten to take him to the Quebec Conference; Goldsmith, *Sage*, p. 103.

56. Kennedy-Purvis to Massey, Aug. 31, 1943; NAC, RG25, vol. 2119, AR1011/1.

57. Zuckerman, *From Apes to Warlords*, p. 160.

58. Goldsmith, *Sage*, p. 103.

59. Costello, *Mask of Treachery*, pp. 353-54, 418-19.

60. Ibid., p. 431, and Winston Churchill, *The Second World War*, V: *Closing the Ring* (Cambridge, Mass., 1951), p. 705.

61. CJM taped interview (transcript), p. 90.

62. There are numerous versions of this incident. The account of the Chief of the Imperial General Staff, Alan Brooke, from his diary is most amusing. See Arthur Bryant, *The Turn of the Tide* (London, 1957), p. 584.

63. At first the British thought they had obtained agreement for a three-nation review of the Habbakuk project (see PRO (U.K.) PREM 3 216/6) but before the conference ended, the Americans had rejected this and said they would study it alone (see CJM, oral transcript, p. 91). In pykrete a Habbakuk would have cost $50 million, in concrete $30 million. The deliberations of the U.S. Committee, on which there was a Canadian representative, are in D.Hist., 87/78 and 181.009 (D1188).

64. Mountbatten claimed Bernal and Pyke were essential to the development of the Mulberry artificial harbour used at D-day (Goldsmith, *Sage*, p. 121) but there is no evidence from any other sources to support this statement.

65. Goldsmith, *Sage*, p. 122.

66. Having failed with the Americans and the Canadians, Mountbatten apparently tried to rope the Australians into the Habbakuk scheme. However, the Public Record Office files dealing with Habbakuk and Australia have been destroyed at the request of the British Admiralty. Perhaps the Australians, noted for being rather direct, informed the British in no uncertain terms that the whole thing was ludicrous.

CHAPTER SEVEN

1. Report of Lt.-Col. Stewart Alexander, Dec. 27, 1943, in NAC, RG24, C1, 4354-29-9-1. Reprinted in Glenn Infield, *Disaster at Bari* (New York, 1971), pp. 258-74.

2. Harris and Paxman, *Higher Form of Killing*, p. 122.

3. Dwight D. Eisenhower, *Crusade in Europe* (New York, 1984), p. 204.

4. PRO (U.K.), WO, 193/712 cited by Harris and Paxman, *Higher Form of Killing*, p. 122.

5. Ibid.

6. Infield, *Disaster at Bari*. The author reproduced several original documents, including a sketch on p. 257 on which the wind is marked from the SSW, the prevailing direction. This is corroborated by eyewitness accounts of the direction of drift of other ships on pp. 59 and 276. It would appear Infield assumed the wind was opposite, and therefore blowing over Bari, because the *John Harvey* was said to have been "drifting" away from the mole. More likely the captain had got under way and was trying to escape the flames. A photograph Infield used to show smoke over the city obviously is actually coming from a locomotive in the picture.

7. Descriptions of experiments at Tipnor (Porton Report 297), Lyme Bay (PR 585) and Saunton Sands (IR 347) in NAC, RG24, C1, 4354-29-9-1.

8. Ibid., June 16 and June 24, 1944.

9. FGB Collection, box 20, TFL.

10. Nov. 11, 1940 in NAC, RG77, 83-84/106, box 6, 4-C9-25.

11. Ibid., July 28, 1941.

12. Ibid., Sept. 3, 1941.

13. Porton Report 2377 dated Oct. 6, 1942. NAC, RG24, C1, 4354-6-1.

14. NAC, RG77, 85-86/178, box 10, 4-C9-41.

15. Flood taped interview.

16. Correspondence between Suffield and Maass, Maass and Pratt, June, 1942; NAC, RG24, C1, 4354-12-1.

17. DCW&S to U.S. CWS, Nov. 4, 1946, in NAC, RG24, C1, 4354-31-1.

18. Minutes of the Chemical Warfare Laboratories Advisory Committee, Aug. 28, 1942; NAC, RG77, 85-86/178, box 10, 4-C9-41.

19. Suffield to RCAMC, June 21, 1943; NAC, RG24, C1, 4354-26-10-1.

20. U.S. CWS to Suffield, May 8, 1943; ibid., 4354-31-1.

21. Aug. 8, 1942, in ibid., 4354-12-1 and a memo to the Chief, Medical Division, U.S. Chemical Warfare Service, Oct. 19, 1943; NARA (U.S.). RG175, box 138, 334.8. A Class II casualty was a man badly burned but still able to defend a static position.

22. ". . . over a thousand Canadian soldier volunteers were exposed to mustard gas in field trials at Suffield, and blistered." Proposed press release of late 1945 from DCW&S (possibly never approved) in NARA (U.S.), RG175, box 179, 350.05.

23. DCW&S to DGMS DND, Mar. 19, 1946, in NAC, RG24, C1, 4354-26-10.

24. Report of meeting between General McNaughton and selected chemical warfare and army personnel, Feb. 9, 1942; ibid., 4354-1-8, and report on a trip to England by J.R. Donald, June 29–Aug. 9, 1942, in NAC, MG27, III, B20, S-9-16.

25. Capt. Howard Skipper to U.S. Chemical Warfare Service, Dec. 27, 1943; Jan. 4, 1944, in NARA (U.S.), RG175, box 136, 319.19.

26. Description supplied to U.S. CWS of the Chemical Defence Research Establishment, Rawalpindi, India, Jan. 21, 1944, in NARA (U.S.), RG175, box 181, 470.6.

27. Report from the Chemical Defence Research Establishment, Karachi, India, Nov. 18, 1943; NARA (U.S.), RG175, box 154, 470.6.

28. Suffield Field Experiment 141 cited by General William F. Porter to the U.S. Joint Chiefs of Staff, Dec. 6, 1943, in NARA (U.S.), RG175, box 157, file 470.6.

29. General Brunskill to Maass, Mar. 6, 1944. NAC, RG77, 85-86/178, box 10, 4-C9-21.

30. Meeting of the Canadian CCWISB, Dec. 10, 1943. NAC, RG77, 85-86/178, box 10, 4-C9-21.

31. For FDR story, see Flood interview, tape II, side A. See descriptions of Bushnell field trials and complaints about using protected troops in report, Feb. 14, 1944, in D.Hist, 314.009(D323). See also, NAC, RG24, C1, 4354-20-18.

32. The exchanges of correspondence and details regarding volunteers all are in NAC, RG24, C1, 4354-26-10-1.

33. Report of A.E. Link, U.S. CWS, of visit to German CW experimental station at Raubkammer, May 13-14, 1945; NAC, RG24, C1, 4354-29-14-2.
34. DCW&S to U.S. CWS, Nov. 4, 1946, in NAC, RG24, C1, 4354-31-1.
35. E.A. Flood, "Otto Maass," Biographical Memoirs, p. 192.
36. Army Medical Corps experiment C. 6020, Nov. 17, 1943, at NRC.
37. J.G. Malloch diary, NRC.
38. Proposed press release, c.1945, in NARA (U.S.), RG175, box 179, 350.05
39. Flood taped interview.
40. Minutes of the U.S., U.K., Canada CW Advisory Committee Nov. 8, 1944, in NARA (U.S.), RG175, box 142, 334.8. Also an Oct. 12, 1944 report in NAC, RG24, C1, 4354-29-13-2.

CHAPTER EIGHT

1. CJM diary, Feb. 16, 1941.
2. Flood taped interview.
3. L.P. Brophy, D. Miles and R.C. Cochrane, United States Army in World War II, The Technical Services: The Chemical Warfare Services, II, "From Laboratory to Field" (Washington, 1959), f.6, p.50.
4. Government of Canada, Handbook for the Investigation of Allegations of the Use of Chemical or Biological Weapons (Ottawa, 1985) pp. 82, 90-92. This is one of the most up-to-date and handiest texts on the toxicity of the major chemical and biological warfare agents. It was prepared with the assistance of Canada's Department of National Defence which, as we have seen, has had considerable experience with the subject.
5. The Germans are estimated to have produced up to 30,000 tons of tabun by the end of the war. The other two gases had not reached the stage of full factory production. Stockholm International Peace Research Institute, The Problem of Chemical and Biological Warfare, vol. I (New York, 1971), pp. 71-73.
6. Resumé of the status of (U.S.) Chemical Warfare Prepared for the British Government, Oct. 9, 1940, in NARA (U.S.) RG175, box 143, 350.05.
7. All the facts in the preceding paragraph are contained in a July 31, 1943, report on fluorophosphate gases submitted to the Chief, U.S. Chemical Warfare Service. NARA (U.S.), RG175, box 157, 470.6. In 1939, at the suggestion of Maass, George Wright at the University of Toronto began work on an early version of PF-3, but this was phosphorous trifluoride which was much less toxic; NAC, RG77, 83-84/106, box 4, 17-96-7(1).
8. Harris and Paxman, A Higher Form of Killing, p. 66, from "Chemical Warfare Intelligence Sept. 30, 1939 to June 30, 1944" in PRO (U.K.), WO 193/723.
9. July 31, 1943, memorandum for Chief, Chemical Warfare Service; NARA (U.S.), RG175, box 157, 470.6.
10. Ibid.

11. Flood taped interview, tape I, side B.
12. Regarding PF-3, see memo to War Department from Office of the Chief, U.S. Chemical Warfare Service, Feb. 14, 1944; NAC, RG24, C1, 4354-31-2. Regarding Z, see report of the U.S. Subcommittee on Persistent and Non-Persistent Gases, Aug. 5, 1944; NARA (U.S.), RG175, box 142, 334.8.
13. Tomlinson taped interview.
14. Minutes of the first meeting of U.S.–Canada CW Advisory Committee, Sept. 24, 1943; NAC, RG77, 85-86/178, box 10, 4-C9-21.
15. Ibid.
16. Ibid., Summary and quotes for speech of Brigadier-General Alden H. Waitt, Jan. 13, 1944.
17. Ibid.
18. NAC, RG24, C1, 4354-26-7-14.
19. General William F. Porter to the Joint Chiefs of Staff, Dec. 6, 1943; NARA (U.S.) RG175, box 157, 470.6
20. Report of Major A.R. Gordon, RCAMC, undated, but apparently Jan., 1944; NAC, RG24, C1, 4354-29-17-2.
21. Dewar taped interview, tape VIII, side B.
22. For the record, the members of the committee were: Dr. W.D. Walters (U.S.), Dr. W.E. Winsche (U.S.), Mjr. D.J. Dewar (Cdn), Capt. G.W. Hang (Cdn) and Dr. B.A. Griffith (Cdn).
23. NAC, RG24, C1, 4354-31-4. D.Hist. has a more readable hard copy.
24. Dewar taped interview, tape VIII, side B. Porter may well have been surprised by this stand taken by junior officers, considering that Maass appeared to be much more pliant. "I consider General Porter one of my Chiefs," Maass told a senior officer of the Chemical Warfare Service on Aug. 15, 1944; NAC, RG24, C1, 4354-31-1.
25. Porton memorandum, Apr. 14, 1945; NAC, RG24, C1, 4354-31-4.
26. Lovell, Of Spies and Strategems, pp. 75-82.
27. D.Hist, 181.006 (D52).
28. Ibid., 181.009 (D2883). According to the report, 292 tons of HT mustard in 65-lb LC bombs would have been sufficient to drench central Hamburg and 877 tons would have done the same to Berlin. Compare that with the 3,000 tons of mustard Canada had in storage at Cornwall by this time.
29. PRO(U.K.), PREM 3/89 quoted at length in Harris and Paxman, Higher Form of Killing, p. 127.
30. Gen. Sir Hastings Ismay to Churchill, July 28, 1944; ibid., p. 133.
31. Ibid., p. 134.
32. The Canadian Chemical Warfare Inter-Service Board discussed this change at its meeting of Apr. 1, 1944, noting in the minutes that it had been proposed by the British Chiefs of Staff; NAC, RG77, 85-86/178, box 10, 4-C9-21.
33. SIPRI, The Problem of Chemical and Biological Warfare, I, p. 73.
34. For over a year previously, Paget had been the British liaison officer on the U.S. Chemical Warfare Committee which set policy for the

U.S. Chemical Warfare Service. Canada was not represented; NARA (U.S.), RG175, box 141.

35. Col. H. Paget to Otto Maass, Oct. 5, 1944; NAC, RG24, C1, 4354-33-11.

36. PRO (U.K.), PREM 3/65, cited by Harris and Paxman, *Higher Form of Killing*, p. 100.

37. The three services were represented on the original Chemical Warfare Committee set up in 1921. *Organization of the Experimental Station, Porton* (1921) in NARA (U.S.), RG175, box 137, 323.7. It seems safe to assume that the Canadian Chemical Warfare Inter-Service Board was modelled on the British committee and both would have had essentially the same powers and responsibilities over CW and BW. See also, Dewar taped interview, tape V, side A.

38. This is speculation and can only be confirmed by analysing the membership of the BWISSC and the previous relationship and control over biological warfare exercised by the Chemical Warfare Inter-Service Committee versus the Bacteriological Warfare Committee. Unfortunately, the minutes of these committees in the Public Record Office in Britain are still closed. Significantly, according to Harris and Paxman (*A Higher Form of Killing*, p. 133.), the Chiefs of Staff had also rejected using anthrax against Germany but, as 500,000 anthrax bombs were still on order from the United States in October, Churchill must still have been pressing the scheme.

39. Baldwin taped interview, tape II, side B. Baldwin was not out of the picture for long. He sat on the CW Advisory Committee for the rest of the war and then became chairman of the post-war BW committee.

40. The preceding two paragraphs were put togther from the following sources: An unpublished Chemical Corps monograph, "The History of the Chemical Warfare Service in World War II" (1947) by Rexmond Cochrane; an unpublished (and rejected) history of biological warfare (1946) prepared for the Surgeon General's Office, in NARA (U.S.), RG112, 295A, box 12, and information supplied by Dr. Baldwin during an interview with the author, tape II, side B. It should be noted that other than describing his clash with Ditto, Baldwin only once hinted that there had been wider problems with the military authorities.

41. Memo from General Alden Waitt, Feb. 10, 1944, in NARA (U.S.), RG112, 295A, box 3, 13.

42. Camp Detrick history, unpublished monograph at Fort Detrick, possibly 1968.

43. CW Technical Committee request for 4-lb. aerosol bomb for dispersion of chemical or organic agents, Dec. 12, 1944; NARA (U.S.), RG175, box 140.

CHAPTER NINE

1. Tomlinson taped interview.
2. Dr. Murray Sutton taped interview, tape II, side B.

3. See, for an early example, the CW weapons manifest for Suffield for May 26, 1943, which includes 16,500 25-lb. shells, 12,000 6-lb. shells, 2,000 mines and 36,000 4.2" mortar bombs all charged with mustard. Plants for filling shells and bombs with mustard and phosgene were built at Suffield that summer; NAC, RG24, C1, 4354-26-8-1.

4. Murray to J.C. Patterson, Aug. 14, 1944; ibid., 4354-33-13-3.

5. The lethal dose of botuninus toxin is 0.02 mg-min/m³ versus 100 mg-min/m³ for sarin, 400 mg-min/m³ for tabun and 3200 mg-min/m³ for phosgene. *Handbook for . . . Use of Chemical or Biological Weapons* (1985). Other authorities rate the lethality of the toxin up to 100 times higher. See Erhard Geissler, ed., *Biological and Toxin Weapons Today* (SIPRI, 1986), p. 41.

6. Murray to J.C. Patterson, July 31, 1944, setting Aug. 7 as date for X trials; NAC, RG24, C1, 4354-33-17-1. See also Aug. 14, 1944; ibid., 4354-33-13-3. The trials were with the 4-lb. toxin bomb the Canadians had developed the preceding December. This was simply a tin can fitted with a brass burster filled with low-temperature explosive and shaped for the use in a 500-lb. cluster bomb. Details of this weapon are in a report to the U.S. Chemical Warfare Service of a meeting at Suffield, Dec. 1, 1943; NARA (U.S.), RG175, box 136, 319.1.

7. Not even G.B. Reed was trusted. Sutton, with his special combat skills, was originally assigned to the Kingston labs secretly to keep an eye on Reed who was suspected of having prewar fascist leanings; Sutton taped interview.

8. Sutton taped interview, tape II, side A.

9. Murray to J.C. Patterson, July 31, 1944, in NAC, RG24, C1, 4354-33-17-1.

10. Sutton taped interview, tape II, side A.

11. Minutes of early meetings of the M-1000 Committee, Nov. 13, 1941 and Jan. 28, 1942; NAC, RG77, 87-88/104, box 69, 36-5-0-5. However, U. of T.'s *President's Report* for June 30, 1942, mentions that Dr. Helen Plummer was working on "factors concerned with the production of potent botulinus toxin and toxoid." Laboratory notebooks of the period which do survive in the institution's archives also contain recipes for growing the bacteria as well as references to the related organisms of gas gangrene. There is no mention of botulinus research in the Connaught's official history.

12. Sutton taped interview, tape I and II, side B.

13. Ibid. In a taped interview with the author, Dr. Ira Baldwin confirmed that insect vectors were not under study at Camp Detrick while he was scientific director.

14. Mention of 1944 and 1945 field trials with the tick-borne disease are in a memo from the Directorate of Chemical Warfare, May 19, 1946, in NAC, RG24, C1, 4354-26-10. Dr. Murray Sutton also remembered being vaccinated for it at Reed's lab in Kingston. The list of bacterial agents being worked on or proposed that General Waitt reported to the Joint New Weapons Subcommittee of the

U.S. Joint Chiefs of Staff, Feb. 10, 1944, does not include Rocky Mountain spotted fever; NARA (U.S.), RG112, 295A, box 3.

15. Murray to James Patterson, Dec. 12, 1944 and other references in NAC, RG24, C1, 4354-33-13-8.

16. The technique developed by Camp Detrick to separate and coat bacteria is still a military secret and a genuine one.

17. "Agents of direct infection with possible epidemic spread, e.g. the 'LP' group." This is from *An Appreciation of the Possibilities of Bacteriological Warfare* dated Dec. 1, 1944, in NAC, RG24, C1, 4354-33-1. However, all documents in this file have been withheld, including this one.

18. Aug. 19, 1944 in NAC, RG24, C1, 4354-33-11; Aug. and Sept. 7, 1944 in ibid., 4354-33-13-3; June 19, 1945 in ibid., 4354-33-13-8.

19. Murray to Maass, July 23, 1943. ; NAC, RG24, C1, 4354-33-17-1.

20. Suffield report to DCW&S, Nov. 24, 1944 and subsequent correspondence; NAC, RG24, C1, 4354-33-1-1.

21. The reports and correspondence on this peculiar weapon are all in ibid.

22. Unsigned and undated monograph on the history of Camp Detrick, p. 10, obtained from Fort Detrick. Also mentioned by Baldwin in taped interview with author.

23. Murray to Maass, Dec. 13, 1944; NAC, RG24, C1, 4354-33-17. The complaints about Capt. Brown are in ibid., 4354-33-13-8.

24. Ibid., 4354-33-18-2. It should be "alkalescens."

25. The U.S. Army biological warfare histories cited above all say this. However, no actual documents of the period have been found to confirm it.

26. Oct. 30, 1944, entry in J.G. Malloch's diary at NRC.

27. Sutton taped interview, tape III, side A.

28. This summary is taken from the descriptive bibliography to the report comparing the relative merits of HE and CW presented to the U.S.-Canada CW Advisory Committee on July 20, 1944; NAC, RG24, C1, 4354-31-4. There also are numerous references in other documents.

29. Undated summary of Suffield tests expected to be completed by the end of the war; NAC, RG24, C1, 4354-33-13. An M47A2 bomb charged with mustard and white phosphorus was also under trial.

30. U.S. Supply Control to DCW&S, May 11, 1945; NAC, RG24, C1, 4354-20-17.

31. The existence of this weapon appears not to have been previously recorded, having been overlooked by the SIPRI survey, *Incendiary Weapons* (1966). Reference to it was found in NAC, RG24, C1, 4354-12-1 and elsewhere.

32. Nov. 27, 1944; Feb. 15, 1945; Feb. 20, 1945, in ibid., 4354-33-18-2. All these documents refer to the germ agent by its code letters, US, which American documents identify as brucellosis. See memo of July 18, 1945; NARA (U.S.), RG175, box 2, 7.8.

33. 35th Meeting of the Canadian Chemical Warfare Inter-Service Board, March 1, 1945; NAC, RG77, 85-86/178, box 10, file 4-C9-41.

34. Pages from E.G.D. Murray's notebooks; NAC, MG30, B91, vol. 17, file 14.32.
35. Ibid. Details of the Canadian response are in the minutes of meetings held in the New Army Building, Ottawa, on Jan. 20, 1945, and Feb. 14, 1945, at which it was decided to increase the output of rinderpest vaccine and co-ordinate response to the threat to American actions. These documents are in RG24, C1, 4354-33-1 but have been withheld.
36. Currah taped interview plus reports to C1 Committee by James Craigie, Feb. 7, 1945, and Charles Mitchell, April 27, 1945; NAC, RG24, C1, 4354-33-20 (file missing). News of the concern belatedly leaked out, however, enabling the *Toronto Daily Star* on May 31, 1945, to indulge in some lurid headline writing: "Germs, Fire, Death dropped on British Columbia by Jap Balloons." On orders of the military authorities the *Star* removed the reference to BW in later editions; *Report of the Committee on Japanese Balloons*, June 2, 1944; D.Hist, 75/316.
37. King taped interview, tape II, side B.
38. The most authoritative description of the Manhattan Project is to be found in Richard Hewlett and Oscar Anderson, Jr., *A History of the United States Atomic Energy Commission*, I: *The New World, 1939/1946* (Pennsylvania University Press, 1962).
39. In a Nov. 3, 1945, Top Secret memo to brief the prime minister for the upcoming tripartite talks on atomic energy with Truman and Attlee, C.J. Mackenzie summarized the financing and administration of the Montreal Lab/Chalk River project which was expected to cost Canada $20 million by the end of fiscal 1945 while Britain's contribution had only been for the salaries of its scientists. He estimated the U.S. project at $2 billion; NAC, RG25, B3, vol. 2458, unnumbered file on atomic energy.
40. Dr. H.G. Thode taped interview with author, tape I, side A.
41. Ibid., tape I, side B.
42. Barton Bernstein, "The Birth of the U.S. Biological-Warfare Program," *Scientific American*, June, 1987, p. 120.
43. A full description of Suffield Field Experiment 310 (withheld in Canada) is provided by Major Robert Fox, CWS, June 29, 1945, in NARA (U.S.), RG175, box 150, 400.112.
44. The history of ricin development is fully described by R.J. DeGray, CWS Research Divison, June 6, 1945, in NARA (U.S.), RG175, box 157, 470.6.
45. The nature of W is identified by the phrase "the Cincinnati castor bean and W processing plant of Procter and Gamble" in a cipher dispatch of Apr. 28, 1943, from Ottawa to Washington in NAC, RG24, C1, 4354-31-1. Mention of the 200-lb. shipment to Suffield is in a memo of June 17, 1943, in ibid., 4354-24-5-2.
46. This use of ricin is much reported but the toxin would have been a very poor choice for this application by assassins. It would have

been difficult and dangerous to load in the pellets, and there are many more appropriate poisons. In the absence of documentary evidence to the contrary, it is improbable ricin was used on these occasions.

47. Murray to Chief Superintendent, Suffield, June 5, 1945; NAC, RG24, C1, 4354-33-17-1.
48. Ibid., Murray to Maass, letter of resignation, July 25, 1945.
49. Murray to Chief Superintendent, Suffield, with enclosure July 23, 1945; NAC, RG24, C1, 4354-33-13-8.

CHAPTER TEN

1. Solandt taped interview, tape IV, side B; tape V, side A. Bronowski forswore military research from then on.
2. *WLMK*, vol. III, pp. 7-9. The foregoing and subsequent description of events and are from King's diary. For eyewitness descriptions see John Sawatsky, *Gouzenko: The Untold Story* (Toronto, 1984).
3. CJM, taped interview (transcript), p. 61.
4. Ibid., p. 62.
5. J.H. MacQueen (MGO) to McNaughton, Aug. 11, and approved Aug. 21, 1945; NAC, RG77, 85-86/178, box 10, 4-C9-41.
6. Canada's CW/BW establishments ended the war with the following personnel: Suffield, 660; Chemical Warfare Labs, 139; Reed's labs, 40; Grosse Ile, 133; directorate of Chemical Warfare and Smoke, 42. Memo of Sept. 13, 1945; ibid.
7. Dewar taped interview, tape VIII, side B. The correct routing for official requests and recommendations from Maass to the Minister of Defence would have been through the office of the Master General of the Ordnance (MGO) to whom the Director of Chemical Warfare and Smoke reported.
8. Meeting of Sept. 10, 1945; NAC, RG77, 85-86/178, box 10, 4-C9-41.
9. Transcript of a telephone conversation between General Porter and U.S. Army authorities in Germany, autumn 1945; NARA (U.S.) RG175, box 143, 337.
10. Meeting of Sept. 10, 1945; NAC, RG77, 83-84/106, box 6, 4-C9-41.
11. NAC, RG24, C1, 4354-29-13-3.
12. *Official Report on Biological Warfare* by George Merck, reprinted in *Bulletin of the Atomic Scientists* (March, 1946), pp. 16-18.
13. Dewar taped interview, tape VIII, side B.
14. Ibid.
15. *Toronto Daily Star*, Jan. 4, 1946, p. 1.
16. *WLMK*, III, pp. 11, 17.
17. Ibid., p. 30.
18. Ibid., pp. 71-2.
19. Ibid., p. 49.
20. King's diary must be in error here. Churchill is almost certain to have said "Combined" Chiefs of Staff, for the remark doesn't make sense as it stands. The Joint Chiefs were the U.S. military leaders whereas the Combined Chiefs were the chiefs of staff of both the United States and Britain; Oct. 26, 1945, in *WLMK*, III, p. 87.

21. Ibid.

22. Foulkes memo of Dec. 4, 1945; Permanent Joint Board on Defence memo of Dec. 14, 1945, in NAC, MG30, E133, vol. 288, 1-8-1.

23. Maass to DMGO(C), Feb. 15, 1946; in NAC, RG24, C1, 4354-33-3.

24. King lamented in his diary at length that he didn't have the eloquence or strength of character to speak as finely as he felt Churchill did on this occasion, especially as they shared the same sentiments about Russia. See *WLMK*, III, pp. 180-83.

25. DCW&S to Director-General, Medical Services; NAC, RG24, C1, 4354-26-8-5.

26. Reed to Maass, ibid., 4354-33-17-1.

27. Ibid.

28. The foregoing and following is from Reed's report of Apr. 4, 1946; ibid., 4354-33-13.

29. File 4354-33-13-3 in RG24, C1, is headed MS-12 and contains most of the documents describing the setting up of the anthrax production unit at Grosse Ile and leading to field trials with anthrax bombs at Suffield.

30. Murray to Maass, Apr. 14, 1945. He informed Maass that the C1 Committee had decided that the "N Project" should continue separately under Dr. Reed. This is almost certainly a reference to the anthrax factory because the document is in a Grosse Ile file – 4354-33-17-1. The anthrax was also reported in storage as of Dec. 20, 1944; ibid., 4354-33-13-3.

31. Shipping order of Nov. 20, 1946, for 2,000 Type F bomb bodies to go from Camp Detrick to Suffield via the Pennsylvania RR; ibid., 4354-33-13-1. Suffield also had 4-lb. BW bombs of its own design as well as the M74 BW bomb.

32. U.K. Ministry of Supply to Maass, Apr. 17, 1946; ibid., 4354-29-17-2. The British Air Ministry, however, decided to retain a substantial "war reserve" of its 65-lb. and 500-lb. mustard gas bombs, and 500-lb. phosgene bombs. See U.K. CMHQ (Canadian Military Headquarters) memo of June 6, 1946, in ibid., 4354-30-1.

33. Memos of July 1, July 4, and Aug. 14, 1946; ibid., 4354-29-13-1 and 4354-31-1. Trials with tabun in various weapons continued to 1948, after which interest shifted to sarin – GB – which was similarly field tested at least into the mid-1950s. See NAC, RG24 (F), vol. 4151, 53-900-302-2.

34. Memo regarding toxic stores in bulk storage, Feb. 8, 1948, in NAC, RG 24, C1, 4354-24-5-1. DWC&S to Mjr. N.A. Klaehn at Edgewood Arsenal, Feb. 15, 1947, in ibid., 4354-31-2. Thirty tons of nerve gas seems rather a lot just for field trials.

35. Duthie to Murray, Aug. 24, 1944; ibid., 4354-33-13-3.

36. It should be mentioned that the original request from Suffield to DCW&S to receive the botulinus toxin from Detrick said that it was wanted for "field trials." Not only had Suffield been doing trials with it at least since 1944, the huge amount being shipped makes the statement hard to accept. It is likely a cover explanation. See

correspondence from Suffield, DCW&S and Detrick of June 12, June 21, June 25 and July 3, 1946, and G.B. Reed's report of July 16, 1946, with enclosed bill of lading. All in NAC, RG24, C1, 4354-26-5-1.

37. Solandt interview, tape II, side A.
38. King taped interview, tape II, side B.
39. Ibid.
40. Nov. 13, 1946, in *WLMK*, III, p. 367.
41. Nov. 15, 1946, in ibid., pp. 368-69.
42. Text of speech, Feb. 10, 1947, in NAC, RG25, vol. 2153, unnumbered file entitled Permanent Joint Board on Defence.
43. Agendas and planning memos for the Suffield meeting are in NAC, RG24 (F), vol. 4133, 4-901-43-2 and MG30, E133, vol. 288, 1-3-1-5.
44. Only these two paragraphs were quoted in the cable from the High Commissioner to External Affairs in Ottawa, although the messages makes clear that the statements were being attributed to Claxton. The May-June 1948 exchange of messages is in NAC, RG25, vol. 2120, AR1054/8.

CHAPTER ELEVEN

1. Policy statement of the Government of Canada of Mar. 24, 1970, reprinted in Robin Ranger, *The Canadian Contribution to the Control of Chemical and Biological Warfare*, Wellesley Paper, Canadian Institute for International Affairs, May 1976, p. 56. This author's favourable assessment of Canada's activities is marred by the reliance on secondary sources. Almost no original documents were cited.
2. Policy statement of Nov. 16, 1971, reprinted in William Barton, *Research, Development and Training in Chemical and Biological Defence within the Department of National Defence and the Canadian Forces* (Ottawa, 1989), p.8.
3. *Toronto Daily Star*, Feb. 16, 1967; Jan. 5, 1968; Mar. 22, 1968; May 3, 1969.
4. Telephone interview with George Ignatieff followed by taped interview (1989).
5. Full page story by Tom Hazlitt, *Toronto Daily Star*, June 3, 1971.
6. *Toronto Star*, June 25, 1973.
7. *The Spectator*, Jan. 26, 1989. Defence Minister Perrin Beatty described the destruction as being "speeded up" as though it had been in progress for some time. If that means it was begun in 1972, progress has been slow indeed. By coincidence the author's formal Freedom of Information Act requests for withheld chemical warfare records were submitted on Oct. 28, 1988. National Archives staff later said that the requests would probably have to be reviewed at the ministerial level.
8. Details on the toxin capacities of the two 4-lb. biological bombs are in a June 29, 1945, memo to the U.S. Chemical Warfare Service describing field trials at Suffield with Compound W, the castor

bean toxin. Suffield had also installed special equipment for air-drying toxin; NARA (U.S.), RG175, box 150, 400.112.

9. A photograph dated June 2, 1960, in the archives at Fort Detrick shows a machine for processing pupae.

10. *Toronto Star*, Mar. 2, 1983.

11. And undated summary of the results of the sixth Tripartite Meeting on CW and BW is in RG24 (F), vol. 4133, 4-901-43-2. Internal evidence places it between 1949 and 1953.

12. Ibid. Based on an interview with a Porton scientist, Harris and Paxman, in *A Higher Form of Killing*, p. 175, state that only the Americans were involved in offensive research and that the Canadian and British work was purely defensive. However, at the sixth Tripartite Meeting one of the assignments was "a continued search for new agents to the limit of the potential of each country."

13. NAC, RG24 (F), vol. 4151, 53-900-302-2.

14. List of DRB projects, 1949, in ibid., vol. 4133, 4-901-43-2. The mention of red tide toxin is in a letter from Glen Gay to E.G.D. Murray, Jan. 22, 1948; ibid., 4-935-43-1.

15. Solandt taped interview, tape IV, side A; tape V, side A.

16. Baldwin interview. It should be noted that some of the most prominent scientists of the day were involved in setting up bacterial warfare research. In Canada it included the three insulin pioneers, Banting and Collip during the war, and Charles Best after it. Best was chairman of the Defence Research Board's Bacteriological Warfare Review Committee in 1950 and was privy to the work that was also going on in Britain and the United States. See D.J. Goodspeed, *A History of the Defence Research Board of Canada* (Ottawa, 1958), p. 156.

17. It was discovered after the war that the Japanese had operated a large biological warfare research station in Manchuria where anthrax, plague and a host of other diseases were examined for their weapon potential. Field trials were conducted, some on prisoners of war, and a prototype anthrax bomb was developed.

18. The Americans were a little slower off the mark and with the deterioration of relations with Russia evidently decided to hang onto their wartime stock of poison gas. It was finally disposed of at sea in 1969 and was transported in 1,100 rail cars. Based on the number of rail cars needed to move the Canadian stocks, that would have amounted to roughly 16,500 tons; *Toronto Daily Star*, May 7, 1969.

19. McNaughton's grammar is peculiar. Speech to the Economic Club, Detroit, Mar. 24, 1947, in NAC, RG25, vol. 2153, unnumbered file entitled Permanent Joint Board on Defence (author's italics).

20. Cabinet secretariat response of Nov. 18, 1947, to a memo by U.S. Major-General Guy Henry on the Canada-U.S. security plan in McNaughton's personal papers, in NAC, MG30, E133, vol. 288, file 1-8-2. Unfortunately, file 1-1-8-14 containing the text of General Henry's memo is missing.

21. *Toronto Star*, Jan. 20, 1986. Neilsen's action would have been

acceptable in time of war, but it is hard to understand why Parliament should not know about Canada's military arrangements with its allies in times of peace.

22. Ignatieff interview.

23. The M-1000 files on bacteriological warfare were readily available to Michael Bliss for his *Banting: A Biography*. They were subsequently moved to the National Archives where the author had to wait months to receive them in bits and pieces as they went through the review process.

24. O.M. Solandt taped interview with author, tape I, side B.

25. "I'm not telling you anything that I know hasn't already been declassified," said 93-year-old Ira Baldwin during an interview with the author. "I've been out of touch so maybe I'm being overcautious. But it can't be helped."

26. A list of chemical and biological warfare files still withheld in Britain is in Andy Thomas, *SIPRI Chemical & Biological Warfare Studies* (London, 1985), pp. 121-25.

27. The reason usually cited for Truman's decision to use the atomic bomb is that the Americans feared they would sustain severe casualties in an invasion of the Japanese homeland. But Japan was completely defeated on the sea and in the air. They could have been starved into surrender, making invasion unnecessary.

28. NAC, MG30, E133, Vol. 288, file 1-6. See also Seymour Hersh *Chemical and Biological Warfare* (New York, 1968), p. 11.

29. Statement made at the Review Conference of the Convention on Biological and Toxin Weapons cited by Harris and Paxman, *A Higher Form of Killing*, p. 86. The authors say the assurance was repeated on Mar. 5 and 11.

30. These tests from 1948 to 1954 apparently involved infecting animals on rafts at sea with anthrax, tularemia and brucellosis; see Harris and Paxman, *A Higher Form of Killing*, p. 155. Solandt recalled that the British got into such trouble with one of these experiments that an expert from Suffield had to be sent down to help them out. Solandt taped interview.

31. *WLMK*, III p. 219.

SELECT
BIBLIOGRAPHY

Barton, William. *Research, Development and Training in Chemical and Biological Defence within the Department of Nation Defence and the Canadian Forces*. Ottawa: Queen's Printer, 1989.

Bernstein, Barton."The Birth of the U.S. Biological Warfare Program." *Scientific American*, June, 1987.

Bliss, Michael. *Banting: A Biography*. Toronto: McClelland and Stewart, 1984.

Boyle, Andrew. *The Fourth Man*. New York: Dial Press, 1979.

Brophy, L.P., D. Miles and R.C. Cochrane. *United States Army in World War II, The Technical Services: The Chemical Warfare Service*. II, "From Laboratory to Field." Washington, D.C.: U.S. Government Printing Office, 1959.

Costello, John. *Mask of Treachery*. New York: William Morrow and Co., 1988.

Defries, Robert D. *The First Forty Years, 1914-1955; Connaught Medical Research Laboratories*. Toronto: University of Toronto Press, 1968.

Eggleston, Wilfrid. *Scientists at War*. Toronto: Oxford University Press, 1950.

Goldsmith, Maurice. *Sage: A Life of J.D. Bernal*. London: Hutchinson, 1980.

Goodspeed, D.J. *A History of The Defence Research Board of Canada*. Ottawa: Queen's Printer, 1958.

Government of Canada. *Handbook for the Investigation of Allegations of the Use of Chemical or Biological Weapons*. Ottawa: Queen's Printer, 1985.

Granatstein, J.L. *Canada's War: The Politics of the Mackenzie King Government 1939-1945*. Toronto: Oxford University Press, 1975.

Haber, L.F. *The Poisonous Cloud*. Oxford: Clarendon, 1986.

Hare, Ronald. *The Birth of Penicillin*. London: George Allen and Unwin, 1970.

Harris, Robert and Jeremy Paxman. *A Higher Form of Killing*. New York: Hill and Wang, 1982.

Hewlett, Richard G. and Oscar E. Anderson, Jr. *A History of the United States Atomic Energy Commission – The New World 1939/1946*. The Pennsylvania State University Press, 1962.

Hinsley, F.H. *British Intelligence in the Second World War*, III, part 2. London: Queen's Printer, 1988.

Infield, Glenn B. *Disaster at Bari*. New York: Macmillan, 1971.

Jones, R.V. *Most Secret War*. London: Hamish Hamilton, 1978.

Lampe, David. *Pyke: The Unknown Genius*. London: Evans Brothers, 1959.

Lewin, Ronald. *The American Magic: Codes, Ciphers and the Defeat of Japan*. New York: Farrar Strauss Giroux, 1982.

Lovell, Stanley P. *Of Spies and Stratagems*. New York: Pocket Books Inc., 1964.

Pawle, Gerald. *The Secret War 1939-45*. London: The Companion Book Club, 1958.

Pickersgill, J.W. *The Mackenzie King Record, 1945/46* Vol. III. Toronto: University of Toronto Press, 1970.

Roskill, Stephen. *Hankey: Man of Secrets*. 3 vols. London: Collins, 1974.

Sawatsky, John. *Gouzenko: The Untold Story*. Toronto: Macmillan, 1984.

Stafford, David. *Camp X: Canada's School for Secret Agents 1941-45*. Toronto: Lester & Orpen Dennys, 1986.

Stockholm International Peace Research Institute. *Incendiary Weapons*. Cambridge, Mass.: MIT Press, 1975.

―――. *The Problem of Chemical and Biological Warfare*, I. New York: Humanities Press, 1971.

Swettenham, John. *McNaughton*. 3 vols. Toronto: The Ryerson Press, 1968.

Thomas, Andy, "Effects of Chemical Warfare: A selective review and bibliography of British state papers." *SIPRI Chemical & Biological Warfare Studies*, I. London: Stockholm International Peace Research Institute, 1985.

Thistle, Mel, ed. *The Mackenzie-McNaughton Wartime Letters*. Toronto: University of Toronto Press, 1975.

Ziegler, Philip. *Mountbatten*. New York: Alfred A. Knopf, 1985.

Zuckerman, Solly. *From Apes to Warlords*. London: Hamish Hamilton, 1978.

INDEX